DATE DUE

DEMCO 38-296

ALMOST AN ISLAND

ALMOST AN ISLAND

TRAVELS IN BAJA CALIFORNIA

Bruce Berger

THE UNIVERSITY OF ARIZONA PRESS

TUCSON

The University of Arizona Press
© 1998 Bruce Berger
First Printing

♾ This book is printed on acid-free, archival-quality paper.
Manufactured in the United States of America

03   02   01   00   99   98   6   5   4   3   2   1

Library of Congress Cataloging-in-Publication Data

Berger, Bruce
    Almost an island : travels in Baja California/ Bruce Berger.
        p.   cm.
    ISBN 0-8165-1901-3 (acid-free, archival-quality paper)
    ISBN 0-8165-1902-1 (pbk.: acid-free, archival-quality paper)
    1. Baja California (Mexico)—Description and travel.   2. La Paz (Baja
California Sur, Mexico)—Social life and customs.   3. Berger, Bruce—
Journeys—Mexico—Baja California.   I. Title.
    F1246. B44 1998   98-9012
    972'.24—ddc21   CIP

British Library Cataloguing-in-Publication Data
A catalogue record for this book is available from the British Library.

CONTENTS

PREFACE

Most books about Baja California in English dwell on natural marvels while ignoring the human inhabitants. Guidebooks, valid for a few seasons, endlessly succeed each other, as do books of photos with texts about camping trips. Packing the shelves are accounts, often self-published, of personal exploits by foot, by jeep and, in the case of mystery writer Erle Stanley Gardner, by trail bike and helicopter. The most readable introduction to the landscape, flora and fauna remains Joseph Wood Krutch's *The Forgotten Peninsula* (1961), a book that pleads for the land's preservation. Historian Harry Crosby has given us focused studies of aspects of the mid-peninsula, and Ann Zwinger has gracefully surveyed the botany of the cape. The perennial favorite is John Steinbeck's *Log from the Sea of Cortez* (1941), a narrative still treasured for its humor and thought—but the Steinbeck is really about marine biology and philosophy and seldom touches terra firma. Of all these writers in English, only Crosby, in his book on ranchers of the sierra, has looked at the way residents interact with their setting.

Books in Spanish on Baja California tend to be scientific or anecdotal. The monographs on biology and history are generally well done, were useful in composing this book, and were written by professors; the *anecdotarios* are character sketches, largely written for those who knew the characters personally, and are longer on sentimentality than perspective on the peninsula. Surprisingly, they too were mostly written by professors. A bright exception, loved and reread in Spanish as the Steinbeck is in English, is *El Otro Mexico* (1951) by Fernando Jordán. Jordán, a reporter drawn to Mexico's wildest corners, was born in Mexico City, reached Baja California in his twenties, fell in love with its landscape, and never left. Inspired by impassable roads, he absorbed all he could from the American border to the cape and tried to deliver the entire peninsula as literature rather than as guidebook. He was defeated by his very scope, for his short chapters are constantly forced to summarize and move on. Jordán was planning a companion book on the Gulf of California when, at the age of forty, in a room overlooking the Bay of La Paz, he took his own life.

Choosing among flaws, this book has avoided Jordán's sin of completeness. Like many who arrived before the paved highway, I traveled for the sheer adventure of it, wanting to see it all. When I became a partial resident, chance and my own eccentricities took over and I ceased being the general observer. Thus there are tales of a piano cult in a land where the arts barely exist. Of the peninsula's extraordinary fauna I have devoted a chapter to the Peninsular pronghorn, a creature with ordinary American cousins, because I became involved in a program to protect it. There is a season of comic hell behind a convent, the tourist madness of a total eclipse, the story of the inheritor of an oasis. Because a third of this book takes place in La Paz, it is surely the most urban book on the peninsula by a foreigner. Near the beginning I have tried to locate the reader in what is known of the land's history and near the end I have surveyed, quasi-politically, the peninsula's present, with a view toward its future. Despite the overviews, my approach is the opposite of Jordán's and I have not tried to account for it all. It is my hope that vivid tangents will ramify into a whole place, much as a landscape may be made out, complete with fragmented observer, through a splintered mirror.

Books about place are necessarily rooted in time, and this one extends from the late sixties to the late nineties. Three decades do not seem enough, and this is the first book I have not been anxious to finish. What will happen to the pronghorn? Will the new saltworks violate the lagoon? Will Héctor regain the privacy of his orchard? Closure is a luxury of fiction; reality merely perseveres, veering in odd directions, and if there is to be a book of place at all, there is no choice but to nip it off arbitrarily and declare it a document of its era. The only consolation is the possibility of more words and, unlike Fernando Jordán, I plan to stick around.

Meanwhile, I wish to thank those who have gotten me this far. Residents of the peninsula who have instructed me in the course of friendship include Tim and Nora Means, Mary and Mac Shroyer, María Eugenia Ortega, Consuelo Amador de Rivera, Quichu Isaïs, Alejandrina Hernández Real, Fernando Ruan Ayala, Marcos Rivera Amador, Iberê Gewehr, Bertine and Henk Nienhuis, Rubén Sandoval, Jeni Bergold, Antonio Rosales, Enrique Hambleton, Francisco and Ruth Merino, Aurora Breceda, Salvador García Pineda, Elma Vidaurri and the Savín family of San José de la Noria. For putting up with my volunteerism I am grateful to biologists Fernando

Heredia, Jorge Cancino, José Angel Sánchez, Victor Sánchez Sotomayor and other men who run with the pronghorn, along with pilots Bruce Gordon and Bill Taylor, of Project LightHawk, and especially Sandy Lanham, of Environmental Flying Service. San Ignacio wouldn't be my own oasis without Héctor Arce Espinoza and the Arce family, Hercilia Ceseña, Carlos Avila, Oscar Fischer, Abel Aguilar and the late Rebeca Carrillo. Fermín Reygadas and Lorella Castorena Davis, professors, respectively, of anthropology and sociology at the Autonomous University of Baja California Sur, La Paz, generously criticized the historical portions of this manuscript, and vulcanologist John McNerney has surveyed those on geology. Su Lum, of Aspen, Colorado, remains the literary critic I can't do without. I would like to mention a few unforgettable companions of the road: Katie Lee, Ed Brandelius, Joey van Leeuwen, Clifford Nickerson, Beth Goforth, Carlos Silva, Andrew Davidson, Joe Hutska, Walter Hill, Robert Fadal, Gail Laughlin, and Dennis Friedan, whose proposed title for this book, *Peninsula Envy,* was the most amusing reject.

To all of the above, I dedicate what follows.

ALMOST AN ISLAND

MAIN TRANSPENINSULAR HIGHWAY

1

L ooking back on a three-decade obsession with Baja California, I see that I have been caught by a cul-de-sac. Longer than Florida, longer than Italy, Baja California is an eight-hundred-mile dead end. To the west, the Pacific Ocean stretches a third of the globe's circumference before striking another continent. To the east lies the Gulf of California—more romantically known, particularly to the travel industry, as the Sea of Cortez. A finger of the Pacific, the gulf is a peninsula of water to complement the one of land. The very concept of that land teases the imagination, for it is a shaft of desert surrounded by the substance whose scarcity defines deserts—water—and that particular water mocks the desert by being salty, malign. Literally engulfed by the sea, Baja California is an island with one loose end.

Most visitors, in fact, use the peninsula as an enormous pier to get to the beaches, the coves, the surf: the endless brine. I approve of their taste, for they leave me the drought I prefer. Though I like a good swim, I find the beauty of marine life less companionable than that of the scorpion, and my idea of a good day at sea is to lie on a hot rock reading Conrad. What compels me is the landmass of Baja California, a continuation of that most prodigal of North American deserts, the Sonoran. Split from the main, it has spawned divergent species, some found nowhere else. Human culture is also an offshoot with odd adaptations. Best of all, the landscape doesn't blur into other landscapes. Sheared off by the sea, it is finite, framed. It holds out the hope that with sufficient perseverance one might exhaust it, internalize it, conjure it whole in one's mind—and if one appropriates a locale completely, hasn't one seized a proxy for life itself? That goal, to be sure, recedes like all mirages, for no land is so shriveled in space as a human lifespan is in time.

This urge to consume a peninsula started casually. I had spent three years in Spain, playing the piano in nightclubs, basking in a new language. I returned in 1967, settled in Aspen, Colorado, and renewed a longstanding friendship with Katie Lee, a folksinger a generation older than I. A few years before, Katie had introduced me to Glen Canyon, a portion of the Colorado River destroyed immediately afterward by the dam that created Lake Powell. Katie, embittered, was looking for a place that wouldn't break her heart. I had just bought a new jeep.

"Just what we'll need for Baja," said Katie.

"What's that?" I asked.

"That's what Americans are calling Lower California these days."

"Baja" to me was an off-road race for souped-up cars somewhere south of the border. Lower California, remembered from grade school geology, was a herniated finger sticking from the bunched hand of Mexico. So I would not remain wholly ignorant, Katie lent me a copy of *The Forgotten Peninsula* by Joseph Wood Krutch. Krutch's Baja California was a spine of volcanic mountains flanked by waterless plains, and three-quarters of its length was threaded only by a one-lane track through igneous rubble. I especially took to heart a passage that described roads "of the terrifying sort which consists of all but impossible grades strewn with boulder-sized rocks and clinging to the sheer wall of a canyon whose bottom lies hundreds of feet below. They are also, just to cap the climax, barely one car wide." On our way toward the peninsula in April 1968, we passed through Tucson, where Krutch lived, and Katie called him. It never occurred to me you could just look up an author in the phone book and fire questions, and I was shocked at Katie's temerity. Mr. Krutch took it in stride and replied genially that the roads were surely no worse than when his book was published, and might even be better. Take plenty of food and water and gas, he advised, and take it the way it comes.

We crossed the border at Yuma, intending to shortcut toward the peninsula over agricultural roads. I had never been in Mexico before, and even my years in Franco's Spain left me unprepared for the border region's hovels of cardboard and sheet metal, with cars like overturned insects in the yard. We stopped in small stores for counsel, and competing directions kept us lost. What was by some definitions the world's longest peninsula lay around the corner and we couldn't find it.

We reached a single-lane wooden bridge with a railroad track down the center, allowing cars and trains to pass in either direction. A man at each end directed traffic.

"What's this?" I asked Katie.

"The Colorado River."

Knowing Katie's sarcasm about the choked Colorado, I took her answer for black humor as we wobbled on railroad ties over a stagnant trickle eighteen inches wide, a fraction of the stream that passed my cabin in Aspen. At the far end a man asked for two pesos, roughly sixteen cents, and handed me a ticket that said Río Colorado.

"Now do you believe me?" came Katie's deadpan.

So this was the source of nutrients for the Gulf of California, reputed to have more species for its size than any other body of water in the world. Five dams on the main stream, dams on every tributary, diversions in seven American states and a last half-toxic canal in Mexico had turned the Colorado River Basin into a fantasia of bad plumbing and we crossed a delta like cracked ceramic. It was almost a relief that there were no genuine streams in Baja California, and we left the tragedy of trashed rivers in the rearview mirror.

Katie had been born in Tucson, I had first met the desert outside Phoenix at the age of eight, and what might seem a vegetal phantasmagoria to outsiders was normality to us. We briefly lost that habitat when we wandered through the agricultural zone, but as soon as we left pavement at San Felipe, a fishing town mopping up from a hurricane, we found ourselves on one lane over packed sand, the desert sprang up around us, and we were at home. The soaring fluted columns of the saguaro, the ocotillo's frozen whips, the cholla's barbed grenades, the organ-pipe's heroic candelabra were as reassuring to us as maples to a Vermonter. Yet all our familiar ghouls had subtly shifted form. The soaring cactus was not really the saguaro but its cousin, the *cardón*, the world's tallest, most massive succulent. Rather than emerging at full width from the ground like the saguaro, the *cardón* swells from a foot of exposed root, as if standing on tiptoe. Other changes—fewer needles, more open space between the fluting, the ruddiness of sunburnt khaki, limbs that branched near the base and ascended parallel to the trunk without the saguaro's hominid contortions—gave the *cardón* an air of regularity, even rectitude. The ocotillo, on the other hand, tends to be less symmetrical, with spindles that twist, gyrate, then explode near the top into a web of intricate branches like a frosted rim. Possessing no counterpart in deserts we had known was the elephant tree, similar in appearance to the unrelated baobab of Africa: a knot of bulbous turnips peeling like parchment and branching into rubbery twigs and leaflets of jade. Because it was spring, paloverdes misted with yellow bloom and elephant trees were hazy with first foliage.

Arroyos paled with the smoke tree—farther north a resident of the Mojave Desert rather than the Sonoran—whose ashen plumes perform photosynthesis without leaves. We looked up the Spanish for smoke tree: *palo triste*, the sad branches.

As we worked our way south the desert reinvented itself like a familiar piece of music that modulates into increasingly remote keys until we reached the domain of a plant we called by its irreverent American nickname, the boojum. It flourishes in a landscape of exfoliated granite, shack-sized boulders that have weathered into some of Baja California's richest soil. Its long naked trunk tapers as it rises and often splits near the top into branchlets like fringe, sometimes at heights of fifty feet. Fibrous, greenish white, it bristles with diamond patterns of stiletto-like needles that flare into delicate leaves. Sometimes the central shaft splits into wildly gesturing arms; sometimes it rises straight in columns that brandish spindly candelabras. Spastic yet full of tensile strength, spineless tuning forks, limp javelins, boojums sometimes become so top-heavy that they lean over in an arch, even rising again from the sand. Later we learned that the boojum's growth and weight are at cross-purposes for an upright plant, and when the water-storing tissue at the plant's core becomes too heavy for the encasing wooden cylinder, the boojum begins to list. The taller a boojum grows, the more top-heavy it becomes and the more it ultimately pitches toward the desert floor. Since all plants grow upward toward the light, when a boojum bends all the way to the ground, it rises again as if beginning a second arc. Sheathed with needles and occasional foliage like body hair, boojums in fields struck us like the exposed taproots of some more sensible plant that flourishes underground.

But boojums were only one element in this forest among boulders. Also in climax stands were *cardón*, ocotillo, creosote, agave, yucca and paloverde, each spurred to extravagance by the granitic soil. At the western edge of this plant complex, nightly visitations of Pacific fog nurtured parasites such as dodder and Spanish moss, which hung from the vegetation the way seaweed clings to collapsing pilings. The tableau became still more erratic when the last glow from the west turned the plants to warring silhouettes. Wood gathering was oddly like shell collecting and my arms quickly filled with unwieldy bouquets of cactus skeletons, dead roots and twisted branches. In later years we refrained from burning habitat for scorpions, but on our first visits we typically made two fires, a coal bed for warming canned chow mein and a pile of exotics for sport. Flames devoured the dry, porous wood, spurring us to heap on more. Once I propped a dead boojum in the middle.

It remained upright, smoked for a minute, then broke into a small flame at the tip like a ten-foot candle. I thought at the time that the boojum's Spanish name, *cirio,* or church candle, must have derived from some explorer who tried the same trick. Later seeing them in bloom, I decided they were more likely named for their creamy blossoms, a pale fire also at the tip.

While I kept a sharp eye on landscape, I kept an even keener one on the track whose terrors I had been led to expect by Mr. Krutch's prose. For two days beyond pavement we dawdled along the Gulf of California, savoring novel flora and aquamarine coves, then the road swerved inland and began to climb toward the three *cuestas,* or slopes, the author most dreaded. Hardly wider than the jeep, the track wobbled with loose basalt that clinked as we advanced. Crawling determinedly, we topped the first *cuesta* before we realized it. The next two, surely, were the deadly ones. We descended almost to sea level and stopped at a chunk of hollowed lava that cradled a portrait of the Virgin framed by slabs of broken windshield and Christmas tinsel. I lit the candles, left a Kennedy half dollar, and we tackled the second *cuesta.* The pitch was steeper, a cross stood by the edge, and over the brink lay two overturned trucks. These calamities seemed out of proportion to the drop-off and I wondered whether the trucks hadn't been pushed out of the way when they refused to continue. We were soon atop the last *cuesta,* where a sterner Virgin commanded a small grotto. We were almost disappointed that we hadn't been more seriously challenged and felt that if this was the worst the peninsula offered, we would muddle through on perseverance.

The hazards of driving in Baja California, we learned, most often involved mechanical failure. Vehicles did drive toward each other from opposite directions on single lanes, but they could see each other far ahead, speeds were too slow to do much damage and we seldom encountered more than one other vehicle a day. Even a seventy-mile straightaway between El Arco and San Ignacio, which from hilltops appeared to race toward the horizon in a pale shaft, required veering, probing and avoiding boulders, keeping us at twelve miles an hour and consuming a day. The most innocent-looking descents, on the other hand, might hide one lethal, pan-banging drop-off. Firm sand could go soft without warning, requiring us to shovel out and chink rocks under the wheel. Flat tires—from scraped rocks, cactus spines and causes unknown—were too common to leave separate memories. On the Pacific side, in the alluvial runoff from gulf-side ranges, extensive flats of fine powder were stirred up by our wheels, sealing us in private clouds that traveled with us and encased us like mosquito netting while we drove choking and blind. For immense distances the route ran like chalk through oxidized stonefields, or made a pale incursion on undulating headlands— softness that turned, on arrival, into dusty cobbles. When we did reach a hard, smooth area where we could let the car out, the track would fission into eight or eighteen variants, some seemingly bound elsewhere. Sometimes a thoughtful driver had left arrows on a paper plate stuck to a cactus, but usually we just took the road more traveled.

We did pack the great American icon of the period, the *Lower California Guidebook,* which we referred to by its authors, Gerhard and Gulick. The book attempted to account for the track and its branches in tenths of a mile, omitting those tenths, or those miles, where nothing happened. The contents had been updated every few years since 1956 and ours was the fourth edition. The book was a minor help rather than a spoiler of surprise, for it helped us distinguish the main track from its many variants, alerted us to side trips we might have missed, had little descriptive flesh, and was just inaccurate enough that it sometimes added rather than spoiled the unexpected. Best of all, it referred to the one-lane track, which actually vanished at high tide where a promontory shoved it into a bay, as the Main Transpeninsular Highway or, as we fondly called it, the MTH.

To the extent that the MTH was maintained at all, it was repaired by occasional traders in pickups who used it for a living rather than by adventurers like ourselves. Once we came upon a sign that said, in Spanish and English, "Volunteer road worker. If you appreciate improved quality of road, please leave a contribution." The volunteer turned out to be Mateo Pico, a man Krutch reported encountering farther south, camped under a car hood and surrounded by empty tequila bottles. We found, less scandalously, a fixed-up house whose owner was roused by our noise and who waited for us, grinning, and invited us in. Each of his two rooms—a living quarters and a kitchen—was a separate building, with swept dust in between. Fenced into the yard were chickens and goats and the living quarters were festooned with exotic birds in cages. Mateo introduced his wife and three daughters, and Katie asked if we could buy a meal. Katie watched the señora slap tortillas while I fetched some rum for myself and Mateo. I sipped while Mateo downed shots like oysters and told me that a young man from San Jose, California, had recently generated a rescue party by failing to kill himself when he leapt from a nearby cliff. It was our introduction to Baja California society and, full of fried eggs, beans, tortillas and gossip, we left on a much improved road.

Aware of the long stretches between merchandise, we stopped in the tiny stores of fishing villages and ranching crossroads that appeared every sixty or hundred miles. We could fill our water cans at the well of any ranch and on the first trip we learned which ranches had flavors to avoid. We carried extra gas in cans strapped to the outside of the jeep, and because the stores were often out of gas, we used it. The pumps often tapped clear gas bottles of what looked like cherry pop and at one store I asked how much water was in it.

"Oh, around 25 percent," said the attendant.

"Incidentally," I added, "where can we get some drinking water?"

He laughed. "You're safe drinking this."

I worried that my Spanish from Cádiz wouldn't work, but Baja Californians actually spoke slower and no more ungrammatically than Andalusians. Only quirks of vocabulary threw me off. I had never heard the Latin American word for green beans, *ejotes,* and when I asked for *una lata de judias verdes* I received a wild stare from the shopgirl, having asked, literally, for a can of green Jewesses.

Between settlements we scarcely encountered another vehicle a day, and whenever we did, we stopped and talked. The first of three parties in three days was a pickup of men cutting firewood. They appeared to have been dredged in black flour and I asked what wood they had. *Palo fierro,* one answered, ironwood. Because it was the oldest tree in the desert, the heaviest and densest, it burned with the hottest flame, nearly smokeless, and made the finest fuel. The trees were two thousand years old, boasted one man. No, they were younger than that, countered another. Insects ate the layer between the bark and the wood, reducing it to a fine black powder that coated the men with soot.

Next morning we pulled alongside a Wagoneer headed the opposite way, rolled down our windows, and met a soft-spoken traveler named Edward Taylor. With a far blue gaze and a faintly British inflection, he seemed suffused with calm horizons. Seeing that it was to be a long exchange, he and Katie and I got out, leaving our cars blocking the road. In two hours there was no one to obstruct. Conversation covered history and politics, then veered to the music of Francis Poulenc—the greatest composer of the twentieth century in Taylor's opinion. When I mentioned that we had enjoyed the boojum forest, Taylor replied, "There is no need to be condescending toward that remarkable species by calling it by a demeaning nickname, for there is nothing ugly nor ludicrous in the natural world. In Spanish the plants are called *cirios,* after the wax tapers lit in honor of the Virgin, but they are best referred to by their perfectly lovely Latin name, *Idria columnaris.*" Since Taylor's sermonette I have called them, by compromise, *cirios.* He spent a month each year in Baja California absorbing images for his woodcuts and sent all observed changes to Gerhard and Gulick.

The following day we came upon two men on horseback leading a string of heavily loaded burros. Their saddles were incised with floral designs, and we were fascinated that their chaps were built into the saddles themselves, covering their legs from seat to stirrup and allowing them to step out freely. They had ridden all the way from Miraflores, a town just short of the peninsula's tip that was renowned for its leatherwork. The packs were filled with leather goods they sold in towns hundreds of miles apart. It took them months to cover terrain that vendors in pickups covered in weeks or days.

Each of these encounters resonated afterward, and without fresh travelers to interrupt our thoughts, our imaginations played about the last people we had met. By the late sixties, in the wake of such books as *The Population Bomb,* the notion of humanity as a kind of algae bloom exhausting the earth had reached common consciousness. In these isolated meetings we could see the alternative. Like desert plants distanced by their need for nutrients, each person appeared briefly in the round, an eruption among rocks and plants, a tiny fuse—in the human case—of self-awareness. There were few enough of our kind that we found ourselves replaying them afterward, concerned for what happened to them next. Socially as well as economically, value accrued through scarcity. Beyond the logistics of the earth's carrying capacity lay the deeper, less generous limits on caring capacity.

We pressed southward, through further modulations of the Sonoran Desert until, past the Tropic of Cancer, our familiar desert plants merged with what officially passed for the subtropical. Taking a side road bordered by a strand of phone wire strung between peeled tree trunks so gnarled that communication seemed an act of jugglery, we came out at a crossroads where a store owner directed us to a track through a field leading to a palm grove, lagoon and beach.

Brambles stopped the car short of the sand. In a brackish lagoon reflecting the granitic mountains of the cape wandered a dozen horses grazing on submerged grass as if browsing on their images. Common and snowy egrets and great blue herons posed by them in the water, stalking, freezing, stabbing. A palm grove nearby was densely littered and I always entered it carefully to avoid stepping on the curled end of a palm stalk and sending the other end smack into my face. A palm log extended a bench. The surf receded to white noise through which a single woodpecker or flicker would tap insistently on the far side of a trunk. King snakes, yellow and black and five feet long, oozed noiselessly over palm litter that made my steps crackle like fire. Gazing through my binoculars until my neck ached, I watched hooded orioles pull fibers off the fan palms into threads, then weave them into baskets that seemed miraculous fruits of the tree. Sitting on the beach, I counted pelicans in strings of seven, nine, thirteen—always, inscrutably, odd numbers. Once at sundown several small boys from the little town came down the shore fishing without poles, coiling their lines like lassos and pulling in fish with nearly every throw. We tried to ask them about it but they were intent on their task, graceful against the nightfall, and vanished wordlessly. Their silence resembled our own hypnosis, a spell we counted on over the years, long after our first spring forays.

We returned from our first journey with a maelstrom of images. We had scrutinized a mountain range because something about it seemed wrong, then realized that it appeared shadowed under a clear sky because of dark, cloud-shaped intrusions. We had soaked in a spring of soda water in a travertine formation while hornets sunbathed on our skin. We had stopped at an onyx mine where a few families were still quarrying the stone for paperweights, ashtrays and chess sets whose look was now cheaply faked in plastic. Wading in a bay, we found ourselves surrounded by undulating three-foot pancakes that turned out to be copulating sting rays, and we shuffled in a slow panic to shore. But oddity is a point of view, as we realized one dawn when a vaquero rode up and asked if we had seen any stray cows. I was still getting up and pulled my parka out of its stuff bag. The vaquero, seeing the huge, billowing blue coat burst from the nylon pouch, stared wild-eyed, then trotted off without hearing my answer. From the standpoint of Baja California, we too were passing strange.

AIR AND FIRE

2

My favorite icon of Baja California is an aerial postcard that shows the peninsula crawling like a Rorschach lizard into the sea. Skinnier than the normal jumbo card, it runs the land parallel to the margin rather than trending north-northwest to south-southeast as it would on a map. The image itself is geographically sound, for it is based on a photograph taken from Gemini 5 and was either snapped in black-and-white or drained of color so that better ones could be supplied by the artist. Land tints vary from liverish green in the mountains to fawn-colored deserts to outcroppings of rust to jade cross-hatching at the Colorado River delta. The Pacific Ocean, the Gulf of California and the Salton Sea are a bright, flat, uniform blue. Contradicting the clarity is off-target printing that overlaps the colors, blurs the forms, defeats the eye. On sale when we first reached La Paz, its discrepancies are the very essence of its subject. Suitable for framing, particularly in meditation, it may well be the only tintype from outer space.

The sort of meditation that can frame such a card is what one arrives at from consulting the experts. As soon as I got home from that first trip, and continuing over the next twenty-five years, I plowed through what had been written, bought books as they came out, took the word of professionals over amateurs, and new professionals over their predecessors. But how was one to pit the firsthand journals of padres about the peninsula's inhabitants against, say, the later siftings of anthropologists? There was disagreement over basics. Fact laid over fact blurred the larger picture. I was spurred by a relish for paradox and the luxury of choosing data by plausibility. With no agreed-upon peninsula, I would assemble my own from available parts. I wasn't trying to create a Rorschach lizard—merely a land I could visit without finding that my knowledge had betrayed me.

When, for instance, did Baja California first become an identifiable place? One authority has said that the peninsula and the Gulf of California could probably be made out 100 million years ago, while another authority doesn't detect a breach to create the Gulf of California until 25 million years ago. It seems established, in any case, that around 100 million years ago, volcanic pressure pushed into warm shallow seas that were brewing limestones and shales. Instead of breaking the surface, the magma lifted the sediments thousands of feet in the air, cooling into granite beneath them. With the sediments long worn away, the granite stands revealed in the aborted volcanoes known as batholiths, which form the tall ranges at either extremity of the peninsula—the San Pedro Mártir and Sierra Juárez in the north and the Sierra de la Laguna of the cape. Between those high anchors, Baja California's central thousand kilometers are stretched like a hammock.

Mexico's long indifference to its peninsula is nicely represented by the fact that mainland Mexico rides the North American Plate while Baja California rides the Pacific Plate. About 25 million years ago, the peninsula began to rift northwest in relation to the mainland along the celebrated San Andreas Fault. The movement, slow at first, accelerated to three centimeters a year, so that about 5 million years ago the gap was breached by seawater. The Gulf of California is thus an extension of the San Andreas Fault.

The mountains of the cape moved more slowly than those in the north, stretching the crust between them and inviting magma from beneath. The crumbling, scrambled, hallucinatory ranges that compose Baja California's spine are volcanic breakthroughs, blowouts, spills of lava, settlements of volcanic ash, the earth's innards recomposed for inspection. The spectacular triple volcano of Las Tres Virgenes, midpeninsula, was active as recently as 1746 or 1790 (even historic events having no settled date). Along with vulcanism came a steady uplift along the peninsula's eastern flank, where volcanic escarpments rise starkly from the gulf to taper westward through alluvial deserts until they blur in Pacific fogs. The western edge of the peninsula is subsiding still, enlarging the great mangrove-encrusted lagoons that form the breeding waters for the grey whale.

While geology was shifting scenery, life held on. Forty to 30 million years ago, North America grew increasingly arid. Cacti, succulents and other water-hoarding plants that populate our current deserts are believed to have evolved from tropical species, some conjectural, that adjusted and flourished as they migrated north. Little moisture fell, and when a deluge struck the lava-topped mesas and plains of alluvium, what didn't pour off in flash floods continued straight down until it reached an impermeable layer—to emerge miles away in the rare permanent spring. In denser terrain, water ran into shallow lakes that shimmered for a season, sprang into meadows for a few seasons more, then swirled with granulated dust before they shimmered again. Aquifers underlie much of the peninsula, including the Magdalena Plain, southernmost of Baja California's deserts, where agriculture thrives on fossil water whose level continues to sink. But the peninsula's midregion has developed some of the planet's most improbable vegetation by forcing on it the need to grab what surface water it can. The existence of such species proves that there is enough soil and moisture to sustain adaptation, but Father Baegert, sourest of the Jesuit padres, remarked that of the four elements, Baja California was composed of only two: air and fire.

Did our own species reach Baja California by sea or pour in successive waves up the geological dead end when times were more hospitable, then adapt like the foliage to drought? The latter seems likelier, but proof is lacking either way. Because of the smashed bones of such animals as horses and camels, creatures long extinct, it is conjectured that the peninsula was occupied as early as 12,000 B.C. The oldest tangible evidence consists of great piles of clam shells and primitive arrows known as Clovis points that can be dated to around 9000 B.C. But while mainland Mexico, the Yucatán Peninsula and Peru were evolving complex, hierarchical, astronomy-oriented cultures, the wandering tribes of Baja California lacked the least fumblings of agriculture or the simplest storage devices of pottery or woven baskets.

Yet there is one spectacular anomaly: the greatest primitive murals in the Western Hemisphere. Scattered throughout Baja California, but concentrated in the Sierra San Francisco in the peninsula's center, overhangs of canyons are brilliant with scenes up to 150 feet long and 20 or 30 feet high, of deer, mountain sheep, pronghorn, snakes, birds, rabbits, even whales and manta rays, as well as humans male and female. The figures are stylized in red and black, occasionally ochre or white. Humans tend to be blocklike, sometimes with elaborate headdresses and arms outstretched. Image is heaped carelessly on top of image, yet the frequent division between colors by means of a line through the vertical axis that does not pertain to the subject's anatomy, emphasizing style over representation, adds a jarring aura of chic. A few animals are shown with their mouths open, as if panting and pursued, with bristling lines suggesting arrows launched from above. The position of some overhangs above water suggest that they may have been blinds from which to hunt the animals themselves, and that the paintings were acts of propitiation—though a cave miles from the nearest ocean would seem an odd place to propitiate whales and manta rays.

Whatever the motive, their execution required a knowledge of form and the compounding of mineral dyes, primarily iron oxides. Brushes made from the frayed ends of marsh reeds have been found, but the lack of any trace of scaffolding leaves one wondering how they were wielded so high, with such precision. Preliminary radiocarbon tests have dated some paintings between 3000 B.C. and A.D. 1600, with age differences of more than three thousand years in the images of a single cave. Some Indians interrogated by the first padres toward the end of the seventeenth century said the murals were created by a race of giants, but others had no thoughts about their origins or complained that the overhangs gave them claustrophobia.

What the first Europeans found in the way of locals was, in any case, less than an art colony. Scattered here and there, amounting to perhaps fifty thousand people throughout the peninsula, were small bands that subsisted entirely on hunting and gathering. They had no permanent homes and passed the cold under thatched hollows and heaps of foliage. Mountain groups hunted deer and bighorn; those by the shore subsisted on fish and mollusks. Tribes in the desert dined instead on crickets, ants, grasshoppers, snakes, mice, bats, spiders, worms—even the very lice from their hair and, during famines after the arrival of the padres, leather boots. They were so repelled by the notion of cannibalism, however, that they wouldn't eat badgers because of their humanlike footprints. Dependent on local water sources, isolated from each other, they kept moving, gradually developing languages and habits so peculiar to each group that they had little communication with each other. But for almost all tribes the grand event of the year was *pitahaya* season.

For two months every summer, unless untimely rainfalls spoil the crop, two species of organ-pipe cactus bear plentiful and nutritious fruit—first the *pitahaya dulce,* cloying to this palate, then the *pitahaya agria,* tart and refreshing. The tribes went on a two-month binge and for a season were truly happy. According to Father Baegert, whose memoirs are sometimes referred to as "the black book" of Baja California, the tribes were so enamored of the pitahaya that they picked the seeds out of their feces and ate them again, as well as tying string to their favorite pieces of meat, pulling them out and eating them over and over for sheer pleasure—practices Baegert referred to as the "second harvest." Because of a susceptibility to European diseases far exceeding that of mainland Indians, as well as their classically Stone Age culture, it has been suggested that the people of the peninsula were of wholly different stock from other Mexican cultures and had no contact with them. While it is futile to speculate how far they might have developed if left alone, their societies seemed static and may have been the most primitive in the Western Hemisphere when the Europeans arrived. Concludes Father Baegert, who could not personally have survived the desert without his imported technology, the Baja California natives were "stupid, stubborn, dirty, uncouth, ungrateful, lying, knavish, lazy, gossips, children to the grave," but "if they were directed from infancy by Europe they would progress in manners, arts, and sciences."

Legend has it that word of what eventually became Baja California first reached European ears when Moctezuma mentioned to Cortés an "island of pearls somewhere to the north." However Cortés heard about the place, in 1529 he pledged to the Crown that he would discover the island with its "precious metals" as well as find the passage beyond it leading back to the Atlantic, since it was obvious that the north would offer a passage symmetrical with the Strait of Magellan. Unable to attend to it right away, in 1533 Cortés dispatched a boat whose pilot, Fortun Jiménez, looking for a quick landfall to the north after murdering the captain, became the first European to set foot on the peninsula when he landed in the La Paz harbor. He introduced himself by trying to snatch pearls from the local tribe and was promptly murdered with his band of twenty. A year later Cortés set off with three ships full of men, women and horses, intent on founding a permanent colony at La Paz, to be called Santa Cruz. After a year of disasters in which he lost many men and animals, he withdrew, consoled, at least, by a pearl worth five thousand ducats. Baja California's European epoch had begun.

The next century and a half of European contact is a litany of sporadic, ill-planned, disconnected, mostly nefarious forays, largely but not exclusively Spanish. The explorer Cabrillo sailed the Pacific coast in 1542, as did the explorer Vizcaíno in 1602, although he failed to set foot in the central desert that now bears his name. Rumors of an island of precious metals to the north hung in the air, spurred by the name "California," which first appeared in connection with the North American coast in the diary of a sailor who accompanied the explorer Francisco de Ulloa in 1540. The place name "Californe" is found as early as the eleventh century in the *Chanson de Roland*, but as "California" it had been popularized in a novelistic romance, *The Exploits of Esplandian,* by Garci-Ordoñez de Montalvo, science fiction of its day, first published in Sevilla in 1510. California was an island "very near the side of Terrestrial Paradise," whose only inhabitants were women and whose only metal was gold. It must be remembered that when the name stuck to the peninsula, it was not Baja California; it was the *only* California. Even as explorers tried to square the fabled island of wealth with the reality of this California, they pressed for a passage around it and gave their fictitious waters a name, the Gulf of Anian.

The most organized visitors to the peninsula, in fact, were pirates, most of them British, who considered Spanish galleons en route between Mexico and Manila to be Baja California's chief resource and who justified their activities by saying they were only rescuing what had been stolen by the pope. Sir Francis Drake made use of the harbors and in 1587 Sir Thomas of Cavendish took a Spanish galleon at Cabo San Lucas, near the peninsula's tip. Another visiting celebrity was Alexander Selkirk, the model for Daniel Defoe's *Robinson Crusoe,* who was taken to Cabo San Lucas by pirate Woodes Rogers in 1709 after being rescued from his literary island.

It might be wondered why Spain, busy consolidating an empire that stretched from Mexico to Chile, left a twelve-hundred-kilometer peninsula to pirates and pariahs. The answer lies in the strange social parallel between Spain and the New World. In 1518, when Cortés began his conquest of Yucatán and Central Mexico, and in 1531, when Pizarro reached Peru, Spaniards encountered civilizations as complex as their own, so stratified that they resembled Spain in a distorted mirror. Astride the huge, obedient, miraculous animals that were horses, sheathed in the brilliance of their armor, discharging fire, the conquistadors rivaled the local god-kings in display and surpassed them in technological dazzle. In a transport of luck, they even arrived as gods predicted in New World legend. The Spaniards had little need to destroy a subdued and awestruck population when, with a bit of manipulation, they could replace its kings with themselves. Some native leaders had to be disposed of, but more were merely demoted, flattered and surrounded with Spanish glitter, leaving a well-ordered hierarchy in place for the milking.

While Spain claimed vast reaches in two continents, its primary objective was not terrain but wealth that could be shipped back home, preferably gold. As long as there was a working Indian population to turn out the necessities, there was no immediate need to dispossess them of the land they tilled so well. In regions where native populations succumbed to European exploitation, as particularly occurred in certain islands of the West Indies, Africans were imported to replace them and the system continued. As long as they could, the conquistadors sent back the gold that enriched—and eventually bankrupted—the Spanish Crown. Their reward was to found a colonial aristocracy, propped by a lesser Spanish officialdom and flanked, to be sure, by the Church. There were uprisings, setbacks, rebellions, but during its first centuries in the New World, Spain managed an amazingly smooth consolidation of scattered, stratified societies, binding them to a Crown that awarded titles only to Spaniards and took its financial slice.

Baja California, whether island or peninsula, was nominally Spanish during this extended period, and Cortés had put in his year trying to colonize it. But Baja California missed the founding epoch in Mexican, Central and South American history. The peninsula had no organized society to take over from the top; it had no organized society at all. Instead of celebrating a god-king, the inhabitants expressed joy by throwing dust over their heads. Exactly which Indian picking seeds out of his feces was a conquistador to replace? Baja California did have its pearls, but in an age awash with gold, pearls were paste. Baja California's harbors and coves served mainly to nestle British pirates who preyed on Spanish galleons, and the land itself was unspeakable. But the peninsula did have a resource of little interest to the king's exchequer. Baja California might be a nightmare of all things burning, barbed, illusional, inedible and vile, but if it had human beings, however depraved, it had souls.

The idea, then, was not to colonize the peninsula but to Christianize it, and the idea came not from the Crown, which saw scant glory and no gold in the project, but from the powerful new Society of Jesus, commonly known as the Jesuits. Founded in 1534 by the Basque Ignatius of Loyola, the order quickly became one of the major forces in Europe, founding colleges, leading the intellectual thrust of the Counter Reformation, and founding missions—first in India, then the Congo, the Far East, Morocco, Mexico and Peru in a network that circled the globe. Jesuits abandoned the special garb that distinguished other orders, maintained firm lines of command, and forged themselves into a structure both flexible and monolithic. As confessors to the crowned heads of Europe, they didn't hesitate to use political leverage in the pursuit of divine ambitions. In most areas of their missions, Jesuits acted in alliance with a separate civilian authority that commanded the soldiery. In Paraguay and Baja California, Jesuits were given civil and military as well as religious power, designing and executing laws that regulated all aspects of life. With its vast New World empire, Spain's influence over the Vatican was considerable and occupation of the peninsula by a friendly party was in its interest. In 1697 the Jesuits were issued a papal bull licensing them to begin conversion of Baja California's population.

Spain was eager to promote the Jesuits, if only to establish its presence on the peninsula, but by the end of the seventeenth century the Crown was bankrupt from trying to extend itself in Europe on the spoils of Mexico and Peru. The Jesuits had Spain's political and moral support but financially they were on their own. The order set up the Pious Fund for the Californias, whereby wealthy communicants in Spain and Mexico backed the endeavor with private donations, hoping, no doubt, for a bit of celestial advancement. The conversion of Baja California was thus strictly a volunteer effort. Politically answerable to Spain, Baja California Jesuits included Germans, Italians, mainland Mexicans, a Croatian, a Bohemian and a Honduran. For nearly two centuries after the first padres reached Baja California with Cortés, its inhabitants were spared the missionary trauma. When it finally happened, it was driven less by the rapacity of the Spanish Crown than by the single-mindedness of geographically diverse but fanatic believers.

The episode began in 1683, fourteen years before the official edict, when Padre Kino reached La Paz. He constructed a small chapel and survived a minor attack by the local tribe—only to be betrayed by his own militia, which invited the tribe to a banquet, fired a cannonball into their midst, and set off the very insurrection Kino was trying to avoid. He moved his operation 160 miles north to San Bruno, where the Indians were reportedly more cordial, and was driven back to the mainland a year and a half later by starvation and scurvy. To his close friend Juan Maria Salvatierra fell the honor of founding Baja California's first permanent mission, not far from Kino's second failed attempt, in Loreto in 1697.

All of Baja California's thirty eventual missions faced the task of transforming nomadic, Stone Age tribes into settled agricultural polities grouped around a chapel. Before Jesuits were sent to Baja California, they spent five years in mainland Mexico learning such disciplines as construction, irrigation, agriculture and the making of cloth. The padres initiated contact by passing out food and learned, with breathtaking speed, the local languages. For many tribes, at least at first, it was like *pitahaya* out of season, and they eagerly clustered around the padres, accepting baptism as readily as they did the ministrations of their own shamans. The missions were pitched at the peninsula's rare springs, which the padres fed into mazes of dams and canals that seemed to multiply water itself. People unused to work of any kind were placed on a strict schedule and told when to do what. Skin that had gone bare was shielded in cloth, some imported, some made on the spot with spinning wheels and looms. One mission even imported a master weaver from Sinaloa. Everything the Indians did had to be conveyed by example, and under Jesuit tutelage the native men raised chapels and even sizable stone churches such as those at San Ignacio and San Javier, built of igneous blocks a meter thick. From imported seeds sprang citrus orchards, vineyards, vegetable gardens, date palms from North Africa, pomegranates from Spain, mangos from the Philippines, sugar cane from the Caribbean, corn and avocados from the Mexican mainland. From supply ships came goats, cattle, sheep and domestic fowl. Stone Age people who said they felt asphyxiated when they couldn't see the stars at night were made to sleep under roofs and to become, for a time, imitation Europeans.

Some of the cultural misunderstandings during the early period took a colorful, even comic turn. When Father Ugarte threatened one tribe with the flames of hell, they were enchanted to learn of a place where they would never be cold and asked him how to get there. Another tribe kept laughing during the litany, and when Ugarte learned that he had been given obscenities when he asked for religious words, he set about relearning the language from small children. Father Salvatierra, a better psychologist, turned local custom to advantage by describing heaven as endless fields of pitahaya. A playful historical novel called *The Journey of the Flame,* by Walter Nordhoff, writing under the name of Palo de Fierro Blanco, is faithful to the flavor if not the event. Father Ugarte, writes Nordhoff, led by example to the degree that he challenged the natives to excel him in tilling fields and piling bricks, even working local dances into his routine. Salvatierra's arrival coincided with a twenty-five-year remission from the annual plague of grasshoppers due to a timely appearance of insect-eating seagulls, allowing him to temporarily upstage the local shamans. After grasshoppers were almost forgotten came a fresh plague that particularly decimated the new crops planted by the padres and left the traditional plants untouched. Christianized Indians died off by the score, unregenerates survived, and the shamans were back in business.

Most of the padres' setbacks were less picturesque. Itinerant tribes, once offered free food and set to work, made increasing demands that the padres could not satisfy, resented the novelty of labor, and predictably rebelled.

Foreseeing the difficulty of making obedient workers out of preagricultural nomads, the padres had recruited a small number of soldiers, under strict command, mostly from the state of Sinaloa across the gulf. When Salvatierra was robbed and attacked, he barely prevented his military wing from executing the culprits. There were increasing disputes between the clerics, who favored persuasion, and the secular militia, which wanted vengeance. Floggings and executions took place, often without the padres' knowledge or consent, heightening tensions between padres and soldiers as well as between pro-padre and anti-padre Indians. Christianized tribes were attacked by the unconverted, who envied the luxuries of the missions, and intertribal massacres ensued. When padres tried to turn the polygamous, fish-eating tribes of the cape into meat-eating monogamists, they suffered such martyrdoms as incineration and beheading. Less than two generations after their founding, most of the missions were in ruin, and in 1734 a mixed Spanish and Mexican soldiery was dispatched from the mainland to restore order. They executed rebel leaders and one by one rebuilt the missions—missions that began to collapse one by one behind them.

The ambitions of the Jesuits, battling dread terrain for the souls of Indians who often repelled them, are summarized by Pablo L. Martinez in *A History of Lower California* in his remark that martyrdom was "a role which all the missionaries sought, openly or in a concealed fashion." It is ironic that they were defeated, finally, not by ungrateful pagans or even the desert itself but by lies in Madrid. During the seventy years that the Baja California Jesuits labored in isolation, on borrowed money, it had become the age of deism and the Enlightenment, and such figures as Voltaire and Pascal and Diderot were attacking Jesuitism as reactionary, mercenary, even dangerous. Although Baja California's placer gold was still undiscovered and from the beginning Salvatierra had refused to allow the Jesuits to become involved in pearling, rumor trickled back to Spain that the Baja California Jesuits were amassing personal fortunes in gold and pearls and weren't kicking in their 20 percent to the Crown. In response, the king sent a certain Captain Mendoza to sniff out the situation and report back.

Pablo Martinez is probably correct that if the Jesuits *had* indulged in pearling and enriched the Spanish coffers all along, they probably would have received royal assistance instead of a frame-up. As it turned out, Mendoza himself set the Indians to pearling, pocketed the proceeds, then reported to the king that the duplicity of the Jesuits was all true. In 1768 the Jesuits received an edict from a dim-witted Charles III that any Jesuit who did not leave the peninsula within twenty-four hours of receiving the order would be executed, as would anyone granting a Jesuit asylum. All Jesuit property was to be confiscated. At that point the entire mission system was maintained by sixteen Jesuits. They were summarily sped to the mainland, marched across Mexico on foot to Veracruz and shipped back to Europe.

It was not, to be sure, the end of the Baja California missions. After the Jesuit expulsion, what was left of them was turned over to the famous Franciscan Junípero Serra, who managed them for five years, founded one more, passed the system on to the Dominicans, and headed toward lusher ground in what is now the United States. Father Serra, beloved of the American California mission circuit, gets particularly bad notice in *The Journey of the Flame*, in which Nordhoff dismisses him as a "great walker" and charges him with sacking Baja California's missions of their grain, cattle, hides and wine, leaving a marginal population to sink so that he could found his earthquake-prone operations up north. Because the Jesuits were thought to have abused their ecclesiastical authority, all power over land, cattle and produce passed to the military, and Indians lost faith in Franciscan and Dominican padres who couldn't reward them with food. The Dominicans proceeded to found nine more missions, including the great church at San Ignacio, and missionaries held what amounted to governmental powers until the Secularization Act of 1855, issued by a Mexico then independent of Spain, ended missionary authority.

It might be asked of that whole doomed epoch what had been accomplished. A minimalist might reply that the padres at least established that they were converting a peninsula, not an island. That two-century controversy, along with its place in Baja California history, is a minor scandal in the history of cartography. Baja California's peninsularity was first established by explorer Francisco de Ulloa, who was dispatched by Cortés in 1539, sailed to the delta of the Colorado River and found no outlet to the Pacific. Another explorer, sent by the viceroy of New Spain the following year, confirmed Ulloa. In 1602 the cartologist with the Vizcaíno expedition, which failed to reach the northern end of the gulf, took it upon himself to draw Baja California as an island. From then until 1771, maps show an appalling alternation between fat peninsulas and islands that stretch nearly to Alaska. In the middle of that period, between 1698 and 1702, Padre Kino—who once published his own map showing Baja California as an island—made no less than six trips from mainland Mexico to the Colorado River by horseback, all confirming peninsularity. He sent his journals to Europe and published fresh maps. In 1721 a Jesuit padre, Juan de Ugarte, heard in Loreto that someone had sailed around the island of California and wanted to decide the matter "once and for all." At great difficulty and expense he built a boat and sailed it north, dispatched a land expedition for good measure, and sent his findings to Europe. In 1737 a German Jesuit cartologist who had been a teacher of Kino reviewed all the evidence, including the testimony of Kino and Ugarte, decided that the islanders had the better argument, and published another erroneous map. So notorious is this lapse of cartography that in 1964, in London, a book was published called *California as an Island, A Geographical Misconception, Illustrated by One Hundred Examples.*

How, one asks, even in a land of mirages, can error so endure? When California was named, the myth of an island was projected upon it. Cartologists in Europe worked with what was sent them, and some trusted sources in the New World sent islands. Kino and Ugarte weighed in with firsthand evidence but Sir Francis Drake, whose legend was growing, had referred to the island of California. The padres turned out to be better mapmakers than most explorers, and when Father Serra looted the abandoned Baja California missions and headed north to found new ones, he knew, at least, that he was on firm ground.

While Baja California can boast thirty missions in all, nothing close to that number ever functioned at the same time. The tribes they ministered to, leaving no record, surely suffered ills we haven't even imagined. The grandly named Camino Real, or King's Highway, that linked them was named for a series of monarchs who didn't support the effort economically, later demanded a financial cut of what turned out to be nothing, and finally sabotaged the whole enterprise; the highway itself was never more than the frailest track, and those who seek it today are perhaps deceived by its name, or romanced by its obscurity. A few solid buildings and interesting ruins remain, but the more common adobe structures have melted into the weather—or, like the castles dismembered after the Moorish expulsion from Spain, they have been felled by scavengers seeking treasure that isn't there. More impressive, perhaps, are the irrigation systems, a few still in operation, others choked with debris that rockets in stony inlays across the desert. Deftly engineered, they nourished domestic plants and animal species whose descendants sustain a new Baja California population.

The overwhelming legacy, however, is the decimation of the Indians themselves through European diseases and destruction of the culture that kept them alive in the desert. Authorities vary, but it is estimated that during the seventy-year Jesuit occupation the native population dropped from 50,000 to 7,000 individuals. In 1800 the population of Baja California consisted of roughly 4,500 Indians and 750 Spaniards and mestizos. By the end of the nineteenth century there was a relict population of a couple of hundred Indians, racially and culturally doomed, their forebears having been obliterated by smallpox, measles, dysentery and syphilis. One might be generous enough to lay the blame for contagion, particularly the latter one, more on the soldiery than the padres, but it was the padres who brought them there. It is further ironic that syphilis, which often prevented tribes from reproducing at all, was the worst offender, for syphilis was actually a New World disease transported to a previously uncontaminated corner by Europeans. The padres, of course, predated our knowledge of contagion and in no way saw themselves as agents of destruction—though the shamans didn't hesitate to blame the padres and their new religion. The padres saw the die-off as God's revenge on barbarism. They even took a kind of craftsman's delight in the death of converts, rejoicing that their souls, as Padre Clavijero put it, "fluttered away to Paradise."

Walter Nordhoff, in his introduction to *The Journey of the Flame*, puts the irony gently when he says, "They felt God had called upon them to save the souls of millions of Indians, who did not know they had souls, and always politely resented having souls thrust upon them." The irony loses wit when one reads the ever-bilious Father Baegert: "Though the majority of baptized adults could not by any effort be made to practice what they promised, there were some exceptions and one must consider, besides, the infants who were lucky enough to perish quickly before they had a chance to sin. The more than 14,000 young Californians who have been sent to heaven during the last seventy years is reward enough for the effort of the missionaries." Hastening their flight to heaven was the destruction of their own culture without their being taught a new one. They planted, harvested, hulled, ground and baked the miraculous new plant that was corn, but strictly on orders, mechanically, sometimes out of sequence, without being taught the cycle itself or the principles of agriculture or cooking. They were made dependent on clothing without being shown how to make, repair or use looms and spinning wheels, or what plants to feed the machines. Adults did go back and forth between the missions and the desert, but children were required to live at the missions through early adolescence, missing the very years when the culture was passed on, most crucially the rites that marked passage to adulthood. Once the padres left, the Indians had no idea how to sustain the clothing and agriculture they had become dependent on, nor how to return to being hunter-gatherers in their harsh desert. But even full knowledge that they were committing cultural genocide would not have deterred the missionaries, convinced they were rescuing an unregenerate race from eternal flames. It was a case of a theologically abstract culture trying to impose a blissful afterlife on people whose languages were literal and, in some cases, contained no future tense.

By fending off secular pioneers who might threaten their authority, and by confining their ministration to people whom their diseases were killing, the padres effectively put themselves out of business. A few settlements hung on, but by the end of the missionary period at the beginning of the nineteenth century, history came almost to a stop. The whole ecclesiastical effort is encapsuled by an incident in Santiago in 1723 when Indians, seeking refuge from a hurricane, ran for shelter to a half-built mission that collapsed on them. It also has an analogue in one of those gags popular in the fifties: a box containing a small machine is switched on; for a few moments gears grind, cogs screech, the box heaves and shakes; then a hand from the machine's own interior reaches out and switches the whole apparatus off.

The end of the missionary era, then, is a historical fault line, a low point in the population of the peninsula. The soldiers brought in by the padres were never very numerous, but with the disappearance of both padres and Indians, they were the only ones left. The padres, knowing they would have to live with the consequence of their choices, had picked their protectors carefully for vigor, intellect and loyalty, and favored married men who wouldn't compromise the Indian women they were trying to convert. While trying to keep the peninsula exclusively religious, the padres thus imported a breeding population of civilians whose succeeding generations they could not control. They had no alternative but to let surplus sons of the military colonize uninhabited spots with water, homesteads that became the oldest ranches on the peninsula. By the nineteenth century, when missions were left without padres, the soldiery inherited the mission lands, or took them forcibly, and the remote ranches gradually gained titles from secular authorities. Harry Crosby, in *The Last of the Californios,* asserts that even in the middle of the twentieth century, most of the ranching population of the sierra descended from people who were on the peninsula by 1800.

But the sierra never did support a large population, and development along the coasts awaited immigration from the mainland. A sign of the peninsula's future was the founding in 1811 of a permanent town at La Paz, site of several failed missions and abandoned since 1749. Pearls, long eclipsed by gold, at last came into their own. Especially favored were the so-called black pearls found in the La Paz harbor and northward along the coast, which weren't black in the manner of obsidian but were dusky and lustrous, pellets of wet smoke. When Loreto was wiped out by a storm in 1828, La Paz became the political as well as the pearling capital. Gradually, throughout the peninsula, a mestizo population began to immigrate across the water—mining, fishing, trading, serving as intermediaries between the outside world and the interior ranches.

After Mexico gained independence from Spain in 1821, the government became swept up in the nineteenth-century rage for progress and actively encouraged colonization of its uninhabited territories. A law was passed in 1863 modeled after the American Homestead Act of the previous year, but ceding roughly forty times the act's 160 acres of land. It was expanded by a more sweeping law in 1883, under the reform movement of President Porfirio Díaz. The new land grants, called *colonias,* required a minimum population in each square kilometer over a period of ten years, but lacking on-site inspection, the law was flagrantly ignored. The government lacked funds even to survey the land properly, and one law was loose enough to allow a company to keep a third of whatever land it purported to survey.

The result of so many reckless laws in a land of impressionist maps and absentee supervision was, predictably, a bureaucratic free-for-all. Grants were extended on the whim of the nearest minor official, leaving the grantee free to draw his own lines. Titles were conferred, canceled, redrawn, accepted by local authorities and voided in La Paz, or accepted in La Paz and rescinded in Mexico City. When the Mexican government felt a need for large infusions of cash, it encouraged outside investment, much of it foreign, but Americans were discouraged, principally because of Mexican bitterness over losing so much territory after the war with the United States in 1848. Many grants were extended to Europeans who turned out to be just as rabid for minerals to ship home—and just as bored by colonization.

The greatest burst of population came with the discovery of gold in 1872. Americans and Mexicans converged on the northern ranges of San Pedro Mártir and Sierra Juárez, and a town called El Alamo grew to eight thousand prospectors overnight. Americans from the East Coast booked passage to the California gold rush around South America, jumped ship on the cape of Baja California, thinking to save money by walking the rest of the way, and died in the intervening deserts. The boom was a windfall only to ranches that sold beef to the miners, and many of today's most successful spreads in the north began during the gold rush. The gold played out fast, but the onyx mine we had visited at El Mármol in the north and the silver mine at El Triunfo, south of La Paz, became long-term operations. And a copper mine at Santa Rosalía, with backing from the Rothschilds, was run by the French from 1885 to 1954 and had been revived by the Mexican government when we first encountered it in 1968.

American investment may have been discouraged, but the peninsula was subject to intermittent schemes devised in the United States. American whalers were the first to suggest its annexation. President Jackson proposed to buy it for five million dollars. Presidents Buchanan and Garfield were both interested, and J. C. Fremont, territorial governor of Arizona, thought it would be just the spot to relocate troublesome Apaches. In 1847, during the war between the United States and Mexico, American ships took command of La Paz and the cape, hoisting the Stars and Stripes, leaving local politicians in place and offering American citizenship. A number of inhabitants, tired of receiving laws but no support from mainland Mexico, actually welcomed the American presence in hopes it might improve conditions. Mexican historians claim that La Paz was shelled and burned, with great damage to property and a citizenry in flight; American historians claim there was only token fighting, with a single token casualty. In formulating the Treaty of Guadalupe Hidalgo, which concluded the war in 1848, the United States first demanded both Upper and Lower California. Mexico objected that the loss of the peninsula, inasmuch as it faced mainland Mexico across a narrow body of water, "offered great embarrassment"—a phrase that suggests more interest in saving face than in retaining a spike of desert. Americans, equally uninspired by the peninsula, acceded without objection, even adding some land in the north so that Baja California wouldn't become, this time from a political standpoint, an island. In the wave of Mexican nationalism that followed the loss of so much land in 1848, some 350 Baja Californians who had sided with the United States were granted refuge in Monterey, California, lest they be murdered by local patriots.

The sovereignty of Baja California may have been decided in 1848, but in 1853 the peninsula was invaded by a private American citizen, a twenty-nine-year-old Southerner named William Walker. Having learned from the recent war how easy it was for the United States to provoke incidents and seize Mexican territory, Walker, claiming that some American merchants had been expelled illegally, landed in Cabo San Lucas with forty-five volunteers and ran up the flag of his newly invented Republic of Sonora. Sailing north to La Paz, he sacked the larger houses, seized government records, lost six men in battle, and proclaimed a slave-owning constitution called the Code of Louisiana. Besides personal glory, Walker hoped to get his conquest annexed to the Union, tipping the congressional balance in the South's favor. Chased by a Mexican ship, he sailed north to Ensenada and held the town for three months with reinforcements. When he tried to march his men east to take the state of Sonora for which his republic was named, he was deserted by most of his crew in the desert and was finally seized by U.S. officials for violating neutrality laws. Once out of jail, he set off with another army to take Nicaragua and came to permanent grief. The Walker caper was only the oddest annexation attempt, for private American armies continued to harry the peninsula well into the twentieth century. As recently as December 1941, in the wake of Pearl Harbor, Senator Reynolds of North Carolina, chairman of the Armed Services Committee, proposed that the United States annex Baja California to protect it from Japanese submarines. Even in the fury against Japan, the idea met with little enthusiasm from either side and has not surfaced since.

As those who love the peninsula as it is have frequently pointed out, retention of Baja California by Mexico has kept it from being overwhelmed by development like U.S. California. In 1888 President Díaz divided Baja California in the latitudinal middle, along parallel 28, into northern and southern territories to be run by a succession of presidential appointees, most of them generals from mainland Mexico. A mixed lot, one personally planted trees along the La Paz waterfront while another was a fanatic teetotaler whose dry laws we ran afoul of on our first trips. Baja Californians resented the imposition of outsiders but could do little about it. The border area in the north, which included the southern extension of the fertile San Luis Valley, was pulled into the agricultural mainstream, fueling towns like Tijuana, Mexicali and Ensenada, and leaving the actual peninsula to fend for itself.

Through that long stasis in the south, few events stand out. At the turn of the century, a mayor of La Paz experimented with the cultured pearl on the nearby island of Espíritu Santo, but his pearl beds were destroyed by his political enemies during the revolution in 1914, and the Japanese brought the idea to fruition. In the late thirties, the beds of pearl oysters stretching from the La Paz harbor northward for 250 miles all died within a period of four years. Popular legend held that they were dynamited by the rival Japanese, though now it is generally accepted that the oysters, weakened from four centuries of exploitation, were attacked by a parasite. In 1954 the shores of Scammon's Lagoon, midway down the Pacific coast, were converted to ponds of brine that would eventually become the world's largest evaporative salt operation. And gradually the peninsula's isolation was breached. In 1964 La Paz was linked with the mainland by ferry service, allowing free flow of people and goods to the southern end of the peninsula, and in 1973 the south was linked to the north by the pavement that replaced our beloved track through the dust. Back in 1952, the peninsula's populous northern half had become the state of Baja California—as if the peninsula ended at parallel 28. The rest of the peninsula, now Baja California Sur, didn't achieve statehood until 1974, a year after the highway's completion.

As the peninsula, seen from Mexico, became the states of Baja California and Baja California Sur, in the United States it was turning into a phenomenon called "Baja." Popularized by backroad car races called the Baja 500 and the Baja 1,000, and abetted by the Anglo-Saxon habit of dropping syllables, Baja became something Americans did in a place called Baja California. Baja was American four-wheel vagabonds living on the edge. Baja was also coastal resorts with airstrips where American executives trolled for trophy fish. Baja became the hotel-and-condo palisade that overtook the cape. Baja was a motor home on the new paved highway: bicycles in front, boat on top, jeep on the trailer hitch. Increasingly, Baja was kayaking, whalewatching, scuba diving, mule treks to cave paintings, newly sanctified as ecotourism. More aerobically, Baja was surfing and windsailing. Baja was a voluntary adventure for foreigners in a land where Baja Californians were trying to hang on.

In the phrase "Baja California," the adjective "Baja" merely means geographically lower or southerly. Used alone, as a proper noun, "Baja" takes on such connotations as low, menial, short of stature and inferior in quality. Alarmed that the identity of Baja California was menaced by Baja, in 1982 the state government of Baja California Sur banned use of the term "Baja" as a substitute for "Baja California" in all official business, even as it continued to encourage the tourism that gave the abbreviation currency. In April 1993 *El Sudcaliforniano,* Baja California Sur's leading daily, delivered a series of attacks on some teachers who planned to use the term "Baja" in the name of a new state-funded kindergarten in Cabo San Lucas. The teachers were, said the paper, training a new generation to use insulting, contemptible, anti-Southern Baja California language, as well as breaking the law. They were naming a school for a place where Mexican restaurants and hotels discriminated against Mexican clients because foreigners tipped better. The teachers were like La Malinche, the Indian woman who translated for Cortés on his way to slaughter the Aztecs; they were helping outsiders kill indigenous culture. *El Sudcaliforniano* knew that "Baja" was one more projection, this one by gringos, on the homeland of its readers.

As a land to account for, Baja California is full of the kinds of blanks that invite projections. Its history begins with a few primitive weapons of unknown fabrication. At some point appeared a culture that painted some 250 sophisticated murals and vanished. The first Europeans encountered a Stone Age people with seemingly no contact with predecessors or contemporaries. Sporadic attempts at Spanish colonization, unrelated to each other, left hardly a scar. For a century and a half, padres recast Baja California as a land of doomed sinners, exterminated them in trying to impose their concept of salvation, and almost brought history to another full stop. From the padres' soldiery and from mainland Mexico came a replacement population whose traditions comprise what now passes for the Baja California heritage, currently threatened by cultural domination from the north. Just as the peninsula is split by volcanic ranges, merciless deserts, the vastness between sources of water—so has it been sliced by time into cultures that have said nothing to each other, have turned their backs on each other, have no more in common but that they played out their lives on the same platform. The chronicle of Baja California is not the record of proliferating and braided cultures that makes most human history a kind of plant life. On the peninsula the image isn't evolutionary but geological: a series of unconformities, of layers deposited in widely separated times, with whatever happened between them— if anything—absent from the record.

Perhaps that is why I am drawn to the Telstar postcard of the peninsula, in which space technology and the dyer's hand have met but not quite coalesced. Accurate but off target, a hard-edged mirage, it embodies a land whose layers don't quite mesh: perhaps it is the peninsula's last great mural. The card also caught my own disparity. It was Baja I had set out to visit, and over the decades I pelted it with jeep trips, backpacks, boat tours, mule treks, the kinds of excursions brochures call adventure travel. But beyond Baja lies a peninsula full of towns, ranches and desert where people love and abuse the land, endure and die. To approach the goal of conjuring the peninsula whole in my mind, I needed to pass through Baja to Baja California.

VINTAGE BRANDY

3

ventually the peninsula needed no spokesman but on that first trip, when Katie and I were novices from the north, it was an extraordinary gringo who extended an initiation. A third of the way down we took a side road to Bahía de Los Angeles, then the peninsula's best-known attraction between the border and La Paz. The bay deserved its fame. Twenty-five miles in diameter, its unity with the gulf was disguised by peaks that rose from the sea to form islands, continuing the arc of ranges that ringed the shore and giving it the appearance of a giant lake. Jagged, cactus-spattered slopes plunged to brilliant beaches and electric blue water, crowned by a cloudless sky. The light was blinding and there was barely a sound.

We entered this vision through five kilometers of garbage, generated by a resort that catered to that recent cultural development, the flying sportsman. Clustered at one end of the bay were an air strip, a motel, a dining hall and a chapel, all owned by one man. Flying sportsmen from the States swooped in for the week or the weekend in their Cessnas, rented fishing boats and guides, patronized the motel and food operations, ignored the chapel and posed with dead marlin. A fragrant few were strays off the highway like ourselves, and we took a room primarily for the hot showers.

In two days we were veterans of this outpost of progress. We knew the ramshackle two-street town that supported the resort, with several dogs for every person. We kept clear of the owner's formidable wife with her crew of terrified kitchen girls. The room baked in the sun, but when a Cessna revved to take off, we ran to slam the window so our refuge wouldn't choke with dust. Meals on a strict schedule disclosed the clientele. We met a young pot-smoking couple with a baby and a sailboat, dreaming their way down the coast. We met a biologist conducting experiments with sea turtles. We watched the flying sportsmen, boisterous in the morning, reeling without lures by dinner. During one lunch we heard a stranger say to the biologist,

"Those snapping turtles can really abbreviate a finger." Katie and I, de-bauchees of the phrase, stopped the man on his way out the door. He pro-posed an excursion to an abandoned mine.

Brandy and his son Ken were fellow strays off the road, traveling in a Volkswagen camper and a sand buggy. The buggy was a forerunner of the off-road vehicles later to mash many habitats, a Volkswagen bug stripped to its frame and suspended between balloonlike tires that enabled it to crawl over impediments that stopped a jeep. As we pored over old boilers and col-lapsing buildings of a silver mine, what we really studied was Brandy. Slightly younger than Katie, he had been haunting the peninsula for two decades and was an Old Baja Hand. With piercing blue eyes, shaggy auburn hair, an auburn moustache twisted to rakish points, and a rakish wit, he cut a vital figure—except that he was also chronically short of breath, carried oxygen tanks in the sand buggy, and sometimes had to retreat to the car and breathe through tubes up his nose. As a young flier for the Marine Corps he had crawled out of a crash that permanently scarred his lungs. Every job he had taken since—breathing exhaust fumes as a test driver in Detroit, inhaling nightclub smoke as a manager of a jazz band—masochistically worsened his condition. Usu-ally he traveled the peninsula alone but this time he had brought his eigh-teen-year-old son Ken, who had never tasted the wilderness nor driven a car. Brandy had towed the sand buggy behind the van until they reached the *cuestas* that had terrified Krutch, at which point he demonstrated the gears to Ken and said, "Drive." We didn't question his approach to driver educa-tion but we did ask if he was taking enough precautions for someone with lung damage. "I don't expect to last a lot longer," he said, "but in any case I've lived on the edge so long I've come to enjoy the view." The crowning touch was that Brandy was a fan of the folksinger Katie Lee, owned all of her records and dreamt of meeting her someday. He couldn't believe that in a trap for flying sportsmen, over a turn of speech, she had ambushed *him*.

Given how exhilarated we were on all sides by the new acquaintance, Katie and I were stunned when they pulled up to us the next morning in their two vehicles, yelled, "See you down the road," and roared off. Where in this eight-hundred-mile gape of desert would we see them again? We picked over our failed expectations as we threaded our way south. Several days later, as we were boulder-crawling the straightaway between El Arco and San Igna-cio and thinking that in Baja California the longest distance between two points was a straight line, we saw the sand buggy bouncing toward us. Our relief vanished when we realized it was Ken, alone, headed the wrong direction. What had happened to Brandy?

The story heightened the Baja Hand's mystique. In the middle of the straightaway the camper had broken down and he needed a spare part. He remembered having spotted an abandoned Volkswagen camper three years before outside Santa Rosalía, seventy miles ahead on the gulf. Leaving Ken in the camper, Brandy sped off in the sand buggy and was gone three days. Ken, whose natural habitat was Los Angeles, spent those days in a panic. What if the buggy also broke? What if his dad's lungs failed? If the worst transpired, what did Ken do with the remains? Hornets surrounded the camper, keeping Ken inside in fright, and he didn't know—as Katie now informed him—that they were only looking for water and he could have diverted them by setting out a pan. On the afternoon of the third day Brandy pulled up with the needed part, having pried it from the abandoned camper that remained precisely where he remembered it. Having shown he could live off the land as well as any inhabitant, he installed it and they were off for San Ignacio. Ken was heading back to their campsite for some missing lug nuts and would meet us in town at a place called Casa Leree.

Beauty is relative to setting, and that first arrival in San Ignacio had been prepared by days of volcanic rock, barbed plants, ephemeral settlements, false leads and convoluted straight roads. We reached a brink and looked down on a valley tossing with date palms and a mission that glowed amber and rose. As we descended, the air was lush and sweet. Like hornets, we sensed water. We forded a small stream and stopped the engine. The wind through the palms—the crepe paper of fan palms, the soft plumes of the dates—surged in rustling waves that approached and receded, a surf we could almost drink. We proceeded across a small causeway where a lagoon reflected a ruddy cindercone. The roadbed, buried in fronds, tunneled through trees, among which we glimpsed houses, donkeys and children. We emerged at the mission's small plaza, shadowed by billowing Indian laurels. Ten miles before town we had come upon a flat rock lettered CASA LEREE GOOD FOOD ENGLISH SPOKEN ASK FOR IT. We followed Ken's directions from the plaza, ready to ask for some English.

The gate opened on a large courtyard covered by a five-feet-high grape arbor. We crouched beneath it and straightened our spines in a cool kitchen, where we were welcomed by Brandy. He introduced us to the proprietress, Becky Carrillo, whose English, good or not, was precisely like ours. Plump, bespectacled, sixtyish, with a quietness that drew us close, she invited us to sit and produced beers from the refrigerator. As Brandy gave us his version of the camper repair, Becky studied Katie. "I know you from somewhere," she said at last.

Katie had no recollection of Becky. Becky assured Katie that she had a good memory for faces and never forgot a voice. They compared careers and discovered that Becky had been a secretary for many years at MGM, nine of them years when Katie was in films. Minutes after our arrival in this obscure oasis, Katie and Becky were reminiscing about the old days on Hollywood Boulevard. When Becky left the kitchen to answer a caller at the gate, Katie said to Brandy, "Why didn't you tell us where you were going? In a place this huge we might never meet up again."

Brandy gave a poker player's smile. "This road is a slot. Just *try* and get away from someone."

Becky returned and showed Katie and me to a sectioned dormitory, one partition of which was ours. Overhead was a thatching of fan palms intricate as a carved ceiling. This room, Becky's kitchen and a table under the grape arbor became our midpeninsula headquarters during the three consecutive springs we traveled the MTH.

We took in many of the early Spanish missions on those trips—from San Borja in the north, with its spiral stone staircase and tracery around the door, to the stark, well-preserved mission of San Javier in the south, to the rubble piles that marked most attempts to impose Christianity—and only the mission at San Ignacio seemed civilized. Its harmony of volcanic blocks and maroon pilasters centered the town, and the town in turn seemed to issue from its mouth. Laurels like thunderclouds hid the church from its own plaza, plunging benches, pools and fountains into permanent cool. A bramble of small streets concentrated the town's low buildings. Beyond the inner settlement lay fields, orchards, vineyards and more houses. A system of *acequias* ladled water to outlying fields, cutting pathways through the palms and reflecting transects of leaf-strewn sky. Unlike other peninsular towns we had seen, nothing in San Ignacio was crude and all was of a piece. At dawn I liked to climb to the rim of the desert that stretched beyond the horizon for hundreds of miles north and south, and watch the valley come to life: women sweeping patios, feeding animals, sprinkling streets against the dust; roosters crowing, tiny dogs yapping; men trying to start stuttering trucks.

During our first visit a flea market erupted in the plaza. Clothing, frying pans, mufflers, mugs, urinals, clocks, tires, spatulas, saucers, hinges and rusted keys cluttered the shade of the laurels, supervised by two seedy, suspendered men from the border. Even their truck was for sale, and I wondered what they would do with the rest of their junk if someone bought it. Across the plaza a pair of salesmen we knew from Casa Leree were selling shirts from Yucatán. Shopkeepers remembered us from one visit to the next. I hit it off with an Ignaciano named Héctor, three years older than I, whose family owned an orchard and vineyard off the plaza; swearing Katie and me to secrecy, he led us on foot several kilometers across the desert to a cave where two manos, stones for grinding corn, rested over two metates that had been beaten into the very bedrock, an assemblage that hadn't been disturbed for centuries. We took sick cars to a German mechanic named Frank Fischer, who as a youth had deserted a ship in nearby Santa Rosalía, married and raised a family in San Ignacio, and immured himself in crankshafts and transmissions. One evening I abandoned Casa Leree for sunset at the lagoon. When I arrived, the cindercone seemed irrationally snowcapped in its central basin. Through binoculars I watched the full moon rise like a coin from a slot, saw the Sea of Tranquility slide behind silhouetted cacti until the moon hung over the crater, doubled by the palm-lined lagoon in a symmetry so lush, so tropical, so flawless that it could only be rendered in black velvet.

Casa Leree itself was both *pensión* and social center to those passing through. Breakfast featured *huevos rancheros,* with the eggs and salsa slipped neatly between two fried tortillas. "This is the authentic way of making them," pronounced Katie.

"To the contrary," replied Becky, "it's an idea I borrowed from the American sandwich."

Middays were devoted to books and journals, spiced by such incidents as Katie trying unsuccessfully to talk some truck drivers into freeing a baby fox they had captured on the road, tied to a table leg, and were teasing with a stick. At night, over beer and rum, Katie would break out the guitar she packed in the jeep. Becky accompanied on mandolin, Brandy told stories and I chatted with the shirt salesmen, once getting into a comparison of Mexican and Andalusian slang that was raw enough to drive Becky from her kitchen. Some of the carousing was to postpone bedtime, for Casa Leree was not an easy place to sleep. There was nothing to do about truckers snoring beyond the partition, but when they left the light on, Katie climbed the wash basin, leaned over and unscrewed the bulb. As snoring subsided and we tentatively drifted off, a cat would scamper across the palm thatch, a sensation like floating to earth and hearing your parachute rip. Any of the courtyard's several dogs might erupt in the night, and once Katie flew out of the room and emptied a chamberpot on a persistent yapper.

I was curious what local people thought about Becky: born in San Ignacio, gone to Hollywood forty years, returned to run a *pensión* for passersthrough like us. "My nickname here is La Malinche," she laughed, "as you probably know, the Indian woman who translated for Cortés on his way to destroy the Aztecs. They respect me anyway, probably because I don't care." Asked why she kept the grape arbor so low that guests had to strain their backs to get in from the street, she said, "It is well that people humble themselves a little when they enter someone else's house."

To the extent that we set off for Baja California with preconceptions, we saw ourselves immersed in a remote splinter of the Sonoran Desert, wallowing in dryness, absorbing a land free of our kind. Every campsite, even on the MTH, was fresh habitat to explore and there were periods when we camped for days on empty beaches, collecting shells, hiking arroyos, sometimes avoiding even each other. On the other hand, we fell in with the Old Baja Hand. Through Brandy we met locals and fellow travelers who appealed to his gregarious nature and who deepened our knowledge of the peninsula. At times, too, we felt that we saw so much of humanity that the landscape we came for was being crowded out and we were losing our purity of purpose. An example was our exit from San Ignacio. Normally we would have camped out after a few days in town, but we had impulsively agreed to meet Brandy and Ken, along with the shirt salesmen, at the Hotel Central in the upcoming town of Santa Rosalía.

Traveling alone from San Ignacio, we plunged back into the desert through stands of an elephant tree called *copalquín,* gleaming like fountaining ghosts against fields of ropy lava. We shifted into compound low at the aptly named *Cuesta del Infiernillo,* the Descent of the Little Hell, which was far more challenging than the three *cuestas* we had dreaded farther north. Even as we scouted and signaled to maneuver the jeep down stone steps that seemed too high for our wheelbase, we kept an eye on Las Tres Virgenes, a complex of smooth volcanoes receding serenely to the north. At the *cuesta*'s bottom we returned to the peacock blue of the Gulf of California. Our reward for pressing dutifully past this array of marvels was to keep our date amidst one of Baja California's greatest anomalies: smog.

Copper had been discovered in the coastal mountains in 1868. A French mining company backed by the Rothschilds opened a mine in the 1870s and pitched the company town of Santa Rosalía in a narrow valley that opened on the gulf. Using wood brought by ships that hauled copper to the American Northwest, the French raised hundreds of similar two-story buildings in even rows. The linear designs, with expansive balconies, were considered architecturally advanced for their day, and stores in the same style were fronted by covered wooden sidewalks. Santa Rosalía had been literally stratified, with Mexican miners jammed into the close-set housing in the tight valley while their French overseers saw over them in their expansive homes on the hill. By the time we arrived, the town was almost exclusively Mexican and the housing had been naturalized, with each building painted a distinct pastel and most of them engulfed in flowers and vines. Towering over all was a shaft that Gerhard and Gulick identified as North America's second-highest smokestack, exhaling a black pall that sealed the valley like the lid of a casserole, baking the population in heat and soot.

Santa Rosalía's crowning eccentricity was a church once thought to have been designed by Alexandre Eiffel, who built the famous tower for the Paris World's Fair of 1889. Eiffel's involvement has been thrown into doubt, but it is known that the Boleo Mining Company, needing a church for the town, bought a European pre-fab that was made of galvanized iron because it had been destined for Africa, where insects would have devoured one of wood. A barn with a peaked roof, scalloped eaves, cut-out Gothic windows and an erector-set cupola with bell, it was, when we first saw it, painted the greenish turquoise popular on pickups and illumined inside with neon tubing. The exterior has since gone through tan and grey paint jobs and the neon has been replaced with conventional bulbs, tempering a vulgarity once sublime.

By the time Katie and I whipped through town and found the block-long wooden hotel, Brandy, Ken and the shirt salesmen were ravenous for dinner. Caked with dust from the road, we rushed upstairs to the shower stall across from our room. Katie, showering first, yelled halfway through that the water had gone off, soap was congealing on her, and would I *please* rouse someone to get the water back on. I told one of the kitchen girls, who led me to the water tank, showed me the valve and warned me to be sure to turn the water off afterward. Katie finished, then I showered and shaved. I deposited the towel and shaving equipment in the room before turning the water off. During the interval, unseen by me, the hotel manager turned the water off himself. I returned to the valve, thinking to turn the water off, and turned it back on. When Katie heard water across the hall, she remarked that it was a

Mexican custom to shower with the door open. We heard the manager charge to the tank and turn the water off again. Pitying the imaginary bather caught with soap drying, I turned the shower back on. On my return from the water tank, I faced the manager striding toward me like a struck bull. What, he demanded to know, was going on? I explained the sequence as I understood it and he supplied the missing link. Wasn't it funny? I said encouragingly. He glared at me with an infinitely pained expression and stomped back to the kitchen. More than ever we felt we belonged in the desert.

Traveling with an Old Baja Hand didn't prevent an unexpected crisis at the end of our stay in Santa Rosalía. Somewhere in the cactus between El Arco and San Ignacio we had crossed from the northern state of Baja California to Baja California Sur, which would remain a territory run by appointed governors for another five years. The teetotaling governor's dry laws were still in place, banning the sale of alcohol from Saturday noon to Sunday night so that workers—including Santa Rosalía miners—couldn't cheat their bosses with Monday-morning hangovers. Bars functioned normally but liquor stores had to keep a six-block distance from schools and churches, essentially banishing them from the peninsula's tiny towns, and anyone transporting liquor had to pay a stiff annual fee of $160. We were leaving town on Saturday afternoon and wanted some rum to flavor our sunsets. I presented our dilemma to a group of men on the street, who told me of an operation so flagrant it was about to be shut down. Ken and I took off in the sand buggy and had no trouble spotting, one block from a school, a painting-supply store with several shades of rum and tequila. Because it felt naughty we bought more than we intended. It fascinated us that in a landscape that had survived two-thirds of the twentieth century little touched by humanity, several thousand people were crammed into a grid of wooden buildings in a coastal trough, prey to arbitrary laws and steeped in the grime of nineteenth-century industrialism. We floored it south with our booze.

It was by racing and lingering with Brandy that we found a flawless balance between solitude and socializing at Bahía Concepción on the Gulf of California, two-thirds of the way down the peninsula. A desert fjord twenty miles long and several miles wide, Bahía Concepción was a marine intrusion between igneous ranges. Along its snaking, backtracking coast, luminous blue water paled shoreward through ribs of turquoise and aquamarine as a bottom of white sand rose and broke into blinding crescent beaches. Coves were separated by volcanic outcrops and it was to round one of them that the MTH disappeared underwater at high tide. Except for a couple of ranches, this weave of desert and sea was uninhabited.

A friend of Brandy's named Bill Lloyd had moved permanently to a cove called Coyote Bay on the margin of Rancho El Coyote. A few years back Bill had been an executive in Detroit. When his doctor warned him that the automotive wars were about to kill him, he moved to Baja California, married a woman from Rancho El Coyote, slapped up a two-room reed shack and fathered two children. He seldom planned more than a day at a time and those plans always included polishing off a bottle of rum, which he began after his wake-up cold beer. Nursing a series of two-hour drinks that maintained a genial well-being, he made pocket money by taking travelers from the MTH on fishing expeditions in his skiff. The greatest challenge in Bill's life was to lubricate himself in a semidry territory—buying rum from travelers, trading it for boat trips or, when desperate, driving in to Mulegé, the nearest town to the north, on a weekday.

When we visited Bill we always camped at the other end of the beach so that socializing required a several-minute barefoot commute. The day's cycle began with a faint whitening behind the mountains across the bay. As the sun climbed toward the horizon, sea and sky melted together through fusions of lilac, lavender, then orange that paled to tangerine, glassy smooth or broken in close-stitched arcs by schools of dolphins. We waded with our first coffee, suspended in pastels. Once the sun broke free, the sky's brilliance turned the water deep blue. Swimming around a point, we discovered a beach like a hidden topaz where our tans deepened in the torpor. Middays, drained of color, were so numbing that we read the same sentence over and over before giving up. Interruptions were rare: a kid showing up from Rancho El Coyote to stare at strangers; mad honking from the MTH when the shirt salesmen held their beers in salute as they headed south. When the sun dropped over the mountains behind us, the range across the bay turned rose, then ghostly, a drift of pumice, while water gave light back to the sky in coppery greens. Before bedtime we always took a last swim, setting off sparks of bioluminescence with every stroke. We spun nebulae with our hands, kicked off burning fountains, flew the breaststroke like firebirds, parodied the Milky Way with galaxies of our own.

One day Brandy asked a curious favor. Gloria, Bill's wife, was frightened by Brandy's pet tarantula, which often dozed on Brandy's scalp beneath his straw hat. The day was too hot for Brandy to tax his lungs: would I carry the tarantula across the MTH and turn it loose far enough away that it wouldn't come right back? When I showed a certain reluctance, Brandy assured me that a tarantula bite is no worse than a bee sting, that tarantulas are feared only because they are large and hairy, and—the phrase I nearly joined in chorus—that they will hurt you only if you hurt them.

Skeptically, I let it walk from Brandy's hand to mine. The weightlessness was unexpected because the creature was so large. Its constant movement gave the impression that it had more than six legs, and as I turned my hand so it wouldn't fall, it seemed to envelop my skin in silk. The hair that might have frightened me had the opposite effect, making the creature seem mammal-like, even appealing. As I walked to the MTH, it kept falling to the ground, making me lay my hand in its path to retrieve it. Brandy had no reservations about holding it by one leg, but I was afraid that would provoke a bite, and at last I took off my own straw hat and let it ride to its new home in the crown.

To replenish supplies we drove north to Mulegé, where Bill scored his rum. The buildings huddled on one side of an estuary lined with palms, bamboo and banana tangled with vines. Mule carts, foot travelers and occasional trucks plied the paths on each side of the water and the town had a languid, tropical feel, heightened by our knowledge that malaria had only recently been eradicated. Its isolation also permitted an experiment in penology. Men who had been convicted of capital offenses—murder, arson, armed robbery—and had shown themselves to be model prisoners elsewhere were transferred to a compound over town, where they spent the nights. At the blow of a conch at dawn, the doors opened and the men descended to the town to take jobs and visit with relatives who had moved to Mulegé to be with them. They passed the time as they pleased until dusk, when the conch blew again and they climbed the hill to their cells. The only restriction was that they were not to enter any establishment that sold liquor and if a single prisoner tried to escape, the entire experiment would be terminated. A clerk who sold us canned goods told us that he lived in the house on the hill, which had good food, a fine view and plenty of room for us. We couldn't have invited him to our own favorite haunt, for it was a bar owned by a woman with the unforgettable name of Cuca Woodworth. With an outdoor patio, a ping-pong table, rattan chairs and a view of the prison framed in bougainvillea, it featured a rum drink called El Cepillo—the brush—after Bill Lloyd's crew-cut. Mulegé seemed as sane as Santa Rosalía was demented.

Our days at Coyote Bay weren't quite eventless, for Bill took us in his skiff to remote beaches where we dug for butter clams, to volcanic islands where we donned snorkels and watched polychrome fish circling the mouths of caves, and to a knob of lava so white with pelican guano it seemed glacial. We must have reciprocated with too many bottles of rum, for he slew and marinated his only goat for our last night's feast.

La Paz, the only settlement south of Ensenada that could be called a city, lay 130 miles short of Baja California's tip, but to reach it over 600 miles of lava and grit gave a sense of arrival since the final run to land's end was already paved and the challenges of the MTH had been met. Brandy and Ken, after camping with us for days at Bahía Concepción, had typically packed and peeled off without warning, saying they would meet us in La Paz. The last day of our approach was a particularly grueling haul on virulent washboard across an agricultural plateau where we were often blinded with the smoke of fired fields. After sundown we came to a brink and saw a horizon of lights shorn by the sweep of a bay. Soon we were gliding on our first pavement in three weeks, immersed in a network of duplicate streets and small buildings. On exactly which block would we find Brandy and Ken? Feeling abandoned once more, we had a sulky dinner, then stopped to plot our next move over a nightcap on the terrace of a waterfront hotel. On a whim I asked whether Brandy and Ken were registered. They were. Asked to explain why he had left our meeting in La Paz to chance, Brandy replied that it wasn't chance at all. "Everyone who comes to La Paz winds up on the terrace of La Perla."

Brandy had even planned to use the hotel as a convenient rendezvous before he led us to more suitable digs on a back street. El Sombrero Trailer Park was not a park for trailers but a compound of thatched umbrellas, tables, chairs and hammocks, where for three dollars a day one could camp out in the city. The owner, Rudy Velez, was the brother of Lupe Velez, known in films as "the Mexican spitfire." Lupe had been married to Johnny Weissmuller, had famously dated Gary Cooper, suffered an early and tragic death, and left her money to Rudy, who used it to start El Sombero. Katie, who had known all the Hollywood gossip about Lupe, now heard the family version. I, in turn, marveled that we were traveling with one of Katie's fans, had stayed with a woman who recognized Katie from her speaking voice, and that Baja California was the longest peninsula on a very small planet.

Brandy, Katie and I took extended sorties through town in the sand buggy.

Only the road through town was paved; the rest was a dusty mesh of small board-and-batten houses with iron or thatched roofs, dominated by wind-mills that hauled up water for abundant foliage. Clouds erupted from the buggy's wheels as Brandy careered around sinkholes and pits. His vehicle was a fresh species in less-traveled streets, where we were stormed by de-tachments of kids and barking dogs. When a melee thickened, Brandy drove back and forth to encourage it. Katie perched over the gears with Brandy's movie camera while I crouched on the passenger side with one leg dangling out, and at one point a running dogfight developed as a terrier defended my leg from yappers that tried to snag it with their teeth. The epics of C. B. de Mille were current targets of parody and Katie swung the camera while I yelled en-couragement to the dogs and Brandy shouted from the wheel, "In line now. Kids from the left! Dogs to the right! Roll it! Dogs fall back, kids around the corner! Now forward! Charge! Gun it!" And finally, speeding away, "Cut!"

As irresponsible travelers, our own tiny pack with a moving territory, we seldom knew what day of the week it was and in La Paz we were caught again on a weekend without cocktails. When I paid for sunglasses at a drug store, I asked the cashier if she knew of anywhere I could buy rum.

"Not until Monday morning."

"Surely there's some place I can buy it now."

"See that girl in white at the end of the counter?" I nodded. "Ask her."

I got in line behind several disheveled old men who plunked down five-peso pieces and left with small bottles of clear liquid in brown bags. When it was my turn, I asked for a bottle of rum. The clerk produced the same little bottle.

"Is this really rum?" I asked.

"Yes."

"For drinking?"

"Yes."

I deposited five pesos and the cashier giggled as I walked out.

Katie and Brandy looked skeptical when I returned with the brown bag, pulled out the bottle and popped the cork. I let a couple of drops touch my tongue. The bitterness in my mouth was succeeded by the sensation of an electric eel diving down my throat and boring through my intestines, itali-cizing each twist. I passed the bottle to Katie, who took a sip, began to choke and passed it to Brandy. He bounced a drop meditatively on his tongue. "Perhaps it could be disguised with something. Maybe fish heads." We used grapefruit juice instead and faked a normal cocktail hour. When I attempted to walk off a vicious hangover the next morning on the waterfront, an American I had never met came up to me. "I don't know whether you've heard the news," he said. "Last night Bobby Kennedy was shot."

The following spring Katie and I repeated the entire trip, crossing the border with Brandy, visiting favored people and places while adding new ones, stretching another round-trip to the cape into a two-month creep. We would have done it all over again with Brandy the following year, but by then he was confined to the Tucson Veterans' Administration Hospital and spent his days in a cranked-up hospital bed with tubes up his nose. On his nightstand he had stood a Kleenex box on end, lettered, in caps, WOULD YOU GIVE THIS MEDICINE TO YOUR CHILD? Required to repeat his entire medical history daily to med students practicing their interviewing techniques, he recorded it. As soon as the questioning began he punched PLAY, then leaned back ashen on the pillow as the tape nattered on and his eyes bore into the student du jour with blue fire. Unable to join us, he lent us his new toy, a stripped Volkswagen bug with a glittering fiberglass azure-flake shell and a high-pitched clamor. It was so minimal that instead of a spare it was rigged with a device that re-inflated a flat with energy from the spark plugs, allowing the driver to speed to the next repair shop. Brandy, unfailing ironist, called it Wind Song; Katie called it the Blue Fart.

We tested our new mobility on our first day across the border, crossing Laguna Salada—a salt flat forty miles long, fifteen miles wide and below sea level—to reach a palm canyon in the Sierra de Juárez. We were roaring back across the flat when we noted that the Blue Fart was burning more gas than anticipated. As we fretted over the fuel gauge, we felt the car wobble. We stopped and found that air was escaping from a tire. We pressed on until the tire went flat. Turning off the engine to save gas, we hooked up the clever pump. The motor wouldn't restart; it seemed the battery was dead. We couldn't push the car to fire the engine because the tire was immobile, and we couldn't inflate the tire because the usually screaming engine was silent. We were a tiny multiple catastrophe surrounded by blinding, featureless, unearthly whiteness.

The rule in such situations is to remain with the vehicle until you are found—but who would find a speck in Laguna Salada? We carried water for a day's drinking, not long-term survival. It was midafternoon. I wanted to seek help on foot, Katie wanted to stay put, and an hour later we followed our separate paths. Under a straw hat, with a quart of water and a parka in my daypack, I started hiking toward the highway between Tecate and Mexicali, fifteen or twenty miles to the north. Walking without landmarks was like treading water and I felt blood pounding in my temples. The temperature was in the eighties and the Sierra de Juárez was hanging in its own reflection. I looked back at the sand buggy, expecting it to shrink and finally vanish. Instead, it grew taller until it resembled a shimmering phone pole. I kept hearing the faint buzz of insects—the sound, I concluded, of my pulse banging my tympanum. After an hour's walking I thought I heard the insect change gears. I turned around and saw, advancing rapidly toward me, the strangest mirage of all, a 1956 Buick. A middle-aged couple drew up and pronounced a polite *Buenas tardes*. They were from Mexicali and owned a ranch on the far side of Laguna Salada, where they retreated every weekend. As far as they knew, they were the only people who regularly crossed the salt flat. They were on their way home when the lady in the blue sand buggy caught their attention by flashing the sun toward them with her pocket mirror. They would tow us to Mexicali, have a trusted mechanic fix our car, and see us safely back on the road.

I rode in their sedan back to the sand buggy, watching the phone pole shrink to the Blue Fart. Katie had been discovered by hornets, those water-mad insects unaccountably condemned to the desert, but hadn't wanted to waste any water by setting it out for them. They didn't sting but merely externalized her own buzz of fear. The couple towed us calmly across the salt flat. By the time we reached the highway, night had fallen. The road to Mexicali was a major truckway and the buggy had no lights because of its dead battery. While the couple towed and Katie steered, I trained a three-battery flashlight out the back, lest we be crushed by the civilization we had miraculously reached. The couple found us a mechanic and lodging for the night, and the next morning, repaired but shaken, we returned to the peninsula in this azure-flake glitter as blue as Brandy's eyes—as if, from his hospital bed, he had engineered our abandonment as a prank, complete with its last-minute rescue.

If Brandy, still trying to eke out a bit of joy by torturing med students, was doomed, so was the track through the desert where he had initiated us into his secrets. The Main Transpeninsular Highway, that fraying thread from the north to the cape, was about to be replaced by asphalt, a substance that would not blow away. At Casa Leree, in San Ignacio, I met a young couple from Mexico City who had arrived in a small plane and were taking aerial photographs for highway planners. I didn't hide my dismay. The man asked me to put myself in the place of an Ignaciano trying to get his wife as quickly as possible to the hospital in Santa Rosalía over hours of primitive road, including the *Cuesta del Infiernillo,* implying as tactfully as possible that my preservationist attitude was selfish. I, in turn, argued that the accelerated pace would provoke new ills, encourage the young to leave, and aggravate the need for hospitals. It is a classic argument that neither side ever wins, and it left me certain that the highway would go through because highways simply did.

Our fears were confirmed at Coyote Bay where, during our second visit, Bill Lloyd told us that the road had already been surveyed through his beach. He was temporarily holding it off, alleging it would damage some unexamined petroglyphs, but he was only buying time so he could raise money from the States. We had wanted to believe in his idyll on the beach—the shack, the small family, the nourishing rum, his romantic exile out of Somerset Maugham—but he talked of building a pseudo-Samoan resort with a panoramic bar and restaurant under a palm-thatch dome and Kon-Tiki-tacky huts dribbling exotically down the beach. Once it was complete he would hire others to manage it while he moved to the far side of the bay and lived just as he did now.

"And how long before a road catches you on that side too?" I asked.

"On a dead end to nowhere? Not in my lifetime."

It was just south of Coyote Bay that we encountered the road crew itself for the first time. Men and machines were poised over a beach still more beautiful than Bill's, with a cluster of palms by the water, and rather than go around it they were planning to blade straight through the middle. Speeding past muttering curses didn't prove so easy, for we had a flat tire before we cleared construction, their mechanic fixed it on the spot, and the foreman pledged to buy us drinks in Loreto—our destination to the south—that evening.

All the way to Loreto we were condemned to the improved road, for it had obliterated the MTH. To either side the crew had bulldozed a corridor five times the width of the roadbed, ending that immersion in desert that the slow track imposed even through the windshield. Nor were we compensated with a smooth ride, for asphalt was still years away and the surface bristled with rocks angrier than the worst washboard. Straight, interminable, boring, the highway turned the cactus into a wash of khaki that would only blur with speed. We settled with relief into a *pensión* in Loreto, only to be invaded by the road supervisor, who had spotted our vehicles. He bought us the promised drinks, then insisted he had to buy the sand buggy to commute to work with. Next he grabbed Katie's hand. We left, claiming a pressing social commitment, and returned only when his truck had vanished.

What the highway would bring was illustrated by the advances that greeted us at Cabo San Lucas, a fishing village at the peninsula's end. Pavement reached the cape at San José del Cabo, hugging the gulf side of the southernmost mountains, then washboard continued around the cape and returned by the Pacific—in Brandy's phrase, "circumcising the tip." In 1968 two luxury hotels were already installed in Cabo San Lucas, which pavement had not yet reached; one was grafted to the very rocks that ended the peninsula in an arch like the leap of a dolphin. An elderly couple who lived on the cape told us that the ranches around them, subsistence operations largely free of the monetary system, eventually borrowed from the banks. When they defaulted, the banks seized the property and sold it to developers. The empty beaches were waiting, the mountains behind them provided a stage set, and the cape only lacked that sublime ingredient—infrastructure—to turn into a glamorous, lucrative, generic Riviera. How long, we wondered, would it take continuous pavement from the California border to sentence the peninsula's vast intervening coastline to the fate waiting at land's end? How long before all of Baja California would turn into that American grail, "Baja"?

We had reached Baja California the first time with the sense of entering a timeless landscape. Changes in the desert itself are measured in millennia and the settlements we found were small, unobtrusive and far between. It didn't strike us that we were witnessing the end of a distinct and relatively brief period in the history of the peninsula. The first tracks for cars penetrated the desert in the 1920s, initiating the phase when adventurers from the north came to explore, to be the first English speakers to reach someplace new, to hone their lives with alien grit. Mexican traders, also from the north, brought pickups full of merchandise to ranches and communities cut off from the world's innovations. On our first trip, to the amusement of both sides, we had traveled in tandem with the shirt salesmen, who always set up in some prominent location and handed us cold beers as we pulled into town. What was ending was that brotherhood of travelers from all social strata, intending commerce or adventure, who abandoned themselves to the

MTH. The half century of Old Baja Hands, who knew each other, knew the peninsula, knew what wrecked car to rob, and formed the cultish readership of Gerhard and Gulick, was doomed by pavement, even if its veterans still plied the peninsula. On bad roads, people with nothing in common but the same obstacles stop, trade information and get to know each other; on good roads they pass each other, annoyed and anonymous. What we had taken for a timeless way of life was merely the frontier of the machine age, a charmed half century that flourished between no roads and good roads.

Our close call in Laguna Salada assured us that even with pavement on the horizon we could menace our health and experience the new. Continuous asphalt down the peninsula's spine still left all the fraying tracks to the side that would take years to exhaust. There were coastlines to reach, mountain ranges that fended off the intruder, and what changed was the rhythm of experience. On the old track, even in cars we had experienced a slow, evolutionary sense of one thing modifying itself into another; with the highway came the modernist disjunction of speeding from one sensation to the next—even if each destination was another patient crawl over lava.

Katie and I had tasted enough of the peninsula that we were committed to it, and we had reached that point of partial knowledge when the rage for completeness takes over. A desert cut off by the sea was appealingly finite. Over the years we would fill in the blanks, not on leisurely, seamless peninsula-long expeditions but on targeted jaunts to specific destinations, usually in other company. We would keep gathering pieces to reassemble inside. The goal of trying to ingest a peninsula remained, but the tactics had changed.

GUINEA PIGS FOR TURKEYS

4

After the three epic spring journeys with Katie Lee fell two years when I traveled the peninsula only vicariously. Brandy and the Veterans' Hospital survived each other and Brandy returned with Katie to the MTH in various of his patched vehicles. What I heard from Katie was how that Old Baja Hand kept impaling his cars on rocks, then stood aside panting while Katie pried them off; how he had chronic flat tires, then retreated to his oxygen tank while Katie wrestled with his spastic jack. On one of those trips Brandy proposed marriage, reminding Katie of all the widow's awards she would receive from the Armed Services when he died.

"I may have done many questionable things," Katie objected, "but I have never married a man for his money."

"Would you deprive a dying man of his last chance to screw the government?" he replied.

They were married in a Las Vegas chapel under a bough of plastic roses. Brandy cried during the ceremony but Katie insisted on keeping it secret to maintain the appearance of impropriety.

As Brandy's health deteriorated he seemed to stand aside and watch with the rest of us, as if it were occurring to a stranger. When 1973 arrived, he announced that he didn't expect to live out the year. He rented a house for the winter on the outskirts of La Paz, a concrete bungalow garnished with fruit trees. Katie had committed much of January and February to singing gigs in the States and I flew down to tend Brandy in her absence. Winters in La Paz tend to be dry, cool and sunny, but that year the rain pounded relentlessly, the wind drove it into the north windows and the cold bored inside. Every day in a small beehive fireplace we burned ironwood—hot and smokeless, just as the soot-blackened cutters on the MTH had boasted—and I rounded up food and medicine. Dr. Santa Ana checked in daily, attentive and serious. Mortality seemed to accompany even my chief diversion, which was to explore the surrounding desert with the man who brought us wood. Ironwood was already scarce and he hatcheted around the trunks of mesquite, smashing their life-giving layer of cambium so that the trees died on their feet. He then collected firewood from trees whose demise he had precipitated a year before. *Limpiando el desierto,* he called it. Cleaning the desert.

Brandy's blood pressure rose, his skin paled, Dr. Santa Ana's look darkened and I tried to penetrate Brandy's indifference to what was happening to him. Even within a life of chosen adventure he had put himself needlessly at risk and I finally accused him of having a death wish. Rather than defend himself, he merely sighed, "But everyone I have it for is going to outlive me."

Katie returned from her gigs; Brandy entered the Hospital Salvatierra and succumbed five days later. Even though Brandy had prepared us for this from our first meeting, the end was so abrupt that I flew home unable to distinguish my emotions from a raging flu I had caught in the hospital corridors. Katie marked Brandy's grave in the La Paz civil cemetery with an arrangement of seashells they had gathered together. In December of the year that Brandy didn't plan to finish, a dedication ceremony attended by President Luis Echeverría was held at a heroic abstract sculpture of an eagle where the new highway crossed from northern to southern Baja California. The pavement that replaced the MTH was now complete.

The nearly simultaneous deaths of Brandy and the primitive track he had by heart put a seal on an era, but another means of exploring the peninsula opened up the following year. A couple of Phoenix friends who had never been to Baja California stumbled upon a magazine ad for a company called Baja Expeditions doing boat trips out of La Paz: did I want to check it out? We found ourselves on a small chartered cabin cruiser with just three other passengers and three crew, and spent five days chugging northward and back along the Sierra de la Giganta, an escarpment of volcanic ash that stretches along the gulf north of La Paz for over two hundred kilometers, rising from the sea like an impenetrable wall. Our fellow travelers included a honeymoon couple, a retired librarian, the Mexican captain, his assistant and the founder of Baja Expeditions, Tim Means. The trip's onboard enigma was the way Tim commanded our party of nine with a lack of speech that approached nonpresence. With snarled black hair, bituminous eyes, Zapata moustache, a thick-set frame and a crocodile's display of even, improbably numerous teeth, only a ruddy complexion kept him from looking Mexican. Tim was a storehouse of information, but it pained him to dispense it and the mountains retained their mystery. Though my own metabolism moves somewhat faster than Tim's, I liked him in some way that involved connecting with that languid rhythm.

Up close the Sierra de la Giganta's two-hundred-kilometer facade broke into spires, tilted mesas and lopsided pyramids pierced by interior darkness like a splintering mansard roof. Anchoring off the coast, or within the bays of uninhabited islands, we hiked to a ruined mission, clambered a canyon of wild figs and ate mangos at remote ranches. Toward the end of the trip I struck out alone across the island of San Francisquito, intending to return along the shore, and found my route blocked by high tide. As dusk thickened, I scrambled up and over a series of ridges and small valleys, and by the time I reached the last brink, I could see our lighted boat in the harbor's arm, as well as ten feet in front of me, and nothing in between. The sky had been opaque for three hours by the time I reached the beach with blood on my hands. I yelled for a skiff, unsure what reception I would receive. The honeymooners were too self-involved to notice, my friends were too drunk to care, the captain bawled me out, his assistant assisted by glaring at me, and Tim merely shrugged that I appeared to trust the desert and could be assumed to know what I was doing. On the strength of that near mishap I was promoted from a Baja Expeditions client to a hanger-on.

Baja Expeditions, at that point only a year old—with its original charter scrawled on a cocktail napkin—still peddled that oxymoron, the planned adventure. To be tended by guides, even mute ones, curtailed spontaneity. Unchosen travelmates often chatter of politics and Thai food and previous adventures while the present adventure passes unattended. Worse are the surprises left in. On our five-day boat trip, for instance, I shared the bow with the retired librarian in bunks aimed at each other in near collision. The librarian suffered from a condition called apnea: instead of regular breathing or even regular snoring, she wheezed unpredictably, blew like a calliope and, more terrifying, would cease making noise altogether. I would count the seconds, sometimes more than sixty of them, and think, "Now what? She died." Then she would gasp like a surfacing whale and, without waking, resume the cycle with some shocking variant. I saw the Sierra de la Giganta in a stupor of passive apnea.

But Baja Expeditions was just refining its lineup of trips by skiff, passenger boat, burro, kayak and bicycle, and the misfires needed to be weeded out. Volunteers, paying their expenses but returning no profit to the company, were occasionally useful as stand-ins for tourists on jaunts that hadn't been tried. Since the itineraries were only roughed out ahead, they were open to misadventure that kept travel lively, and in return for the bumpy ride we promised not to sue. In the parlance of the time, we were guinea pigs for turkeys.

My favorite test run—for a trip that proved too difficult to repeat—was a ten-day trek through a central chunk of the Sierra de la Giganta. The recent five-day boat trip with my friends, when we ventured ashore now and then but mainly watched from deck as layers of ash paled from daybreak's peppery fire through chalky noons to dusk's violet, left me full of questions: Were there waterholes, settlements, hidden oases? Did people live there? What were the birds and mammals? Did that geological attic have a history or was it a blank page? Because the route was so daunting, the venture was semicommercial and some of the guinea pigs were paying turkeys.

Logistics proved more daunting than expected. Ranchers promised burros and mules, perhaps out of politeness, then backed out. None knew Tim's entire route and separate guides were lined up for each half of the trip. When it was discovered that the first guide had slashed off the ear of the second guide in a barroom brawl in La Paz, their midtrip encounter looked socially unpromising. Compromising, we canceled half the trip.

The starting point was so far over back roads that the turkeys weren't let out of the truck until after dark. We spread out sleeping bags by a small reservoir above a ranching community and Tim threw a goat roast in appreciation for our campsite. He had arranged for a goat to be slain the previous day and it had awaited us suspended from an overhang. Shortly before our arrival it was pulled down and eaten by dogs and another had to be sacrificed at the last minute. The kitchen was set up in a towering, hollow, freestanding rock out of Hieronymus Bosch, giving preparations the air of a performance in a bandshell. Amidst a barbarous glow created by tin-can torches filled half with water and half with gasoline, local men mingled freely with guests, women lining the wall formed an animated fresco and children disported throughout. After the guests had the stewed vegetables and finger-scalding goat rolled into tortillas, a matron delivered an effusive speech of thanks and with a single motion the women peeled off the wall like a human centipede and disappeared below the dam. A young man asked if he could borrow a flashlight to fetch some tequila. I produced my pencil-sized reading light. Never having seen such an instrument except in the hands of a dentist, amid much laughter the young men took turns peering into each others' mouths and saying "Ah!" A guitar was produced and passed to an old man who groped for chords while the men sang all the ranchera songs they knew, then sang them over. "The second set is always better," whispered one of my new travelmates. Recovering my flashlight, I made my way to my bedroll, where I heard one more drunken chorus, then a burst of firecrackers, then silence.

It is always disconcerting to wake up in a place you have seen only by dark. Granite boulders were poised over our heads, held in place by a matrix of ash. Unlike the usual volcanic jumble, the cliffs here soared in straight lines, angles and wide parabolas, as if we were at the bottom of a gigantic shipyard. A teenager drove a herd of goats over a ridge and almost over my sleeping bag on the way to the reservoir, shepherding a tumult of shouts, bleats, tinkling bells and cloudbursting hooves. An old man pulled a few rocks aside to start water flowing in an irrigation canal. Painted in scarlet on a rock over the dam was a huge number 9 and more numbers and arrows glared on the cliffs below, where forty people lived among orchards, reed houses, pools, waterfalls and intricate stone walls. Government engineers had recently descended upon them and painted ciphers around their habitat, indicating where earthen dams that had been improvised over generations were to be replaced with rock retainers covered by wire mesh. The engineers assured the inhabitants that the government dams would preserve the topsoil.

As we loaded up we got a good look at our guides. The ear-slasher, with a pistol on his hip and impenetrable dark glasses, was hollow cheeked, intense and withdrawn, while his younger brother—in a flashy shirt and turquoise choker—seemed more like his son. Cursing, hefting, bracing their boots against the burros' flanks as they tugged on lash ropes, they hoisted our kitchen onto wooden pack frames, a box on each side with duffels in the middle, until each burro resembled a mountain ready to avalanche. There were three mules to ride—for our guides and for a woman subject to asthmatic attacks. The rest of us walked.

This was my first extended look at the sociology of adventure travel, and I was surprised at the maturity of our group; perhaps it was principally older people in good shape who had the time and means to hike the world's backcountry. Among us were a retired commercial pilot, a retired military officer, a florist and a railroad engineer. There was an electronics marketer who tapped a basketless ski pole ahead of him like a sensor. There was a computer programmer with long grey hair, two-week beard, a wool cap full of buttons from antinuclear campaigns and T-shirts with survival messages, who sat cross-legged and played his inverted Sierra cup like a bongo. In changing flowered shirts was a securities counselor and sometime real estate agent who surfed. The only woman besides the railroad engineer's asthmatic wife was a young Santa Barbaran with a subversive sense of humor—lean, adventurous Nora, in whom Tim showed great interest. I was the only non-Californian. Our party, which sometimes stretched half a kilometer, may have been the greatest cavalcade the Sierra de la Giganta had seen since the demise of the padres, for it was still being talked about when Tim and I returned to the area fourteen years later.

Bit by bit, in the abandon that comes from plodding all day, Tim told me what had led him here. He had grown up in Phoenix, swimming in the canals and hunting deer on the outskirts of town. When Frank Lloyd Wright caught him with a rifle at the architectural school of Taliesin West, the architect listened fascinated to the fifteen-year-old's reasons for shooting deer. An uncle tried to ground Tim in Phoenix by securing him managership of a Jack-in-the-Box while he was still a teenager and Tim pursued a degree in petroleum geology while supervising hamburgers. During a geology convention shortly after the Santa Barbara oil spill, he was horrified that those attending were oblivious, concerned only with job security. On a geology fieldtrip in the Grand Canyon he gave a note to a student to take back to his professor saying that he was not hiking out halfway at Phantom Ranch, as planned, but was dropping out to become a river guide. After a stint as a Colorado boatman answering all questions—How deep is the water? How dangerous are the snakes? How many people drown a year?—with "It varies," he dropped out of river politics to become a wholly unsupervised guide in Baja California.

Occasionally talking, mostly looking and trudging, we made our way across long dusty flats like caked oatmeal, up switchbacks of loose rocks and over boulder-strewn ridgetops. The vertical geometry I'd noted at our first campsite also prevailed horizontally, for we found ourselves in a complex of high flat mesas inscribed by canyons that fell away in straight lines and gradual curves, leaving the topland sliced into pentagrams, rhomboids, lopsided figures that mimicked regularity. Seen from the canyon bottoms, some lava flows were layered as evenly as if they had been deposited by shallow seas while others rose in pocked, elephant-hide verticals. Here and there water broke the surface, channeled through the infrequent ranches or pooled around springs. In a hanging valley where a few of us strayed, ducks, grebes, sandpipers, turtles, oleanders and palms converged on an oasis the size of Walden Pond. The aura of water was transported to the high mesas by leaves—waxy and leathery to minimize evaporation—generated by plants that shed them during drought and grew them back after the next rain.

The geometry so smooth to the eye translated into climbs and plunges. Our party, self-absorbed, was often too strung out for one end to communicate with another. We soon saw that for the ear-slasher the only line from here to there was the forced march, with just enough pauses to tend animals, ingest food and water and eliminate same. "I've looked into that cave," he would say when diversion threatened, "and there's nothing in it." Scenery was a nuisance, stops for mere rest unmanly. National stereotypes were precisely reversed, with the guides under internal pressure to race to the next camp and the gringos wanting to poke, hang back or collapse on a rock. The paradox was brought home to me one afternoon when we were settling into a campsite for two nights and I scouted for the perfect spot. I found it under a solitary tree with pale green trunk and oval leaves, a *zalate,* the peninsular fig. By the time I returned from the luggage pile with my duffel, the guides had hacked it apart and fed it to the mules.

Halfway through the trip we became fixated on water. A pool we had just passed was pronounced undrinkable and we had polished off our canteens. The ear-slasher promised us sweet water at the bottom of the next descent and we kept up with his stride. We heeled obediently across a dry lake. Kilometer after kilometer powdered our boots. The sun hammered down and I conjured another Walden, full of wild palms and waterbirds. We rounded a bend, started up an arroyo, and someone let out a whoop. There, catching deep blue sky, was water.

The closer we came to the pool, the quieter everyone became. Set into dark rocks and backed by an igneous cliff, it was scenic on the far side. On the near side a gentle slope of dust and cow chips slid into the murk. The middle was dark as oolong, with an au gratin effect at one end. The railroad engineer dipped a cup and drank. I got out my plastic tumbler, dipped, inspected a brew not much darker than one we had survived at the last campsite, and gulped. I dipped, drank again, rested a moment, then tossed off one more glass.

At that point a discussion erupted over whether the water was safe. The engineer remarked how tasty it was. The florist pointed out that overhead the sky was a brilliant blue while reflected in the water it appeared to be full of thunderclouds. The investment counselor, the youngest and strongest who had paid for this trip, collapsed under a mesquite in the dust. The rest of us dove into the lunch bag. There was a serious run on fresh oranges. When we were halfway through our tortillas, salami and cheese, a longhorn steer appeared at the pool, glared at us, ambled to the igneous side, waded in and began to drink. We watched edgily to see if he would add water as well as subtract it. After a several-gallon draught the steer posed nobly, started toward the bank, then paused. One of our lunch crowd, anxious to clear the pond of danger, lobbed a pebble just behind the steer. Plink. We sat riveted as the tail went up, the rosette bulged, and a substance the color of Pernod dropped to the pond and fanned into the murk. The animal strolled magisterially off. Our next drink, an hour later, was rich with purification tablets.

"In light of this afternoon," I asked the ear-slasher's brother, "how safe do you consider this water?"

"Much better than the last campsite," he replied cheerfully. "This pool has a spring at the bottom and the water is constantly renewed, while the last one was old rainwater the animals have been drinking in for a year. This water only seems bad because you caught a bull in the act."

"By the way," remarked the investment counselor in another tongue, "in case anyone cares, the Dow Jones today hit 993."

"What would be your source?" asked the painting contractor.

"A transistor radio with earplugs. I left my girlfriend in charge of my stocks, but I still like to keep track."

"You mean when you were lying in cowshit this afternoon, you weren't just resting, you were following the *market*?"

"That's right," the investment counselor replied. "Also, George Raft died."

We woke next morning to a surprise chill. Tim discovered a congealed lizard, tried to stroke it to life, then set it on his jacket in the sun. Before breaking camp we hiked to a ranch the ear-slasher remarked was only a kilometer upcanyon. The dust gave way to limestone shelving; a clear stream splashed through pools and dells and small waterfalls; slickrock glistened with smooth ledges; black phoebes called from the rocks; waterweeds swirled like emerald finger paintings. We drank in confidence from cool sweet water. Scrambling through vines, we reached a compound of thatched-roofed open sheds and tight cinder-block buildings. No one answered our call, so we let ourselves through the gate. The wooden buildings were full of hand-carved furniture I longed to pull out and test for a few days. It was hard to believe the guide had led us to the camp we now called Aguacaca when this oasis lay waiting. Was utopia also a nuisance?

When we returned to camp, the lizard lying on Tim's jacket had come to life. Tim played with it, then let out a yelp: it had dug its fangs into his finger and wouldn't let go. All grabbed for their cameras as Tim, grandly stoic, held out his hand with the nine-inch lizard clinging by its teeth. As soon as it dropped, we hit the trail.

We threaded the Sierra de la Giganta through stretches of dust that found new muscles to harrow in our ankles and calves. Frosty nights aggravated colds and bronchial conditions. One afternoon someone let out the whoop that signaled water. Water it was: the Gulf of California. At last exposed to us, plunging north from a brink, was the full facade of the range we had been immersed in for the last week and a half. Nearly smooth on top, it sloped through creased alluvials of burnt rose, eggshell cinders and corrosive green. Rather than tapering into the gulf, it broke in a scalloped cliffline beyond which swept a sea of lapis. Amid swirling calms full of mica glints, islands followed the shore like dolphins arrested midflight. The horizon dissolved in vapor. This was the scenic consummation, and with the help of five spontaneous leaders, we maneuvered the entire party—mules, burros, bipeds— side by side for one of those victory photos that looks like the grin of some prehistoric mutant.

We began a murderous descent, hooves and boots skittering on loose rocks as we tried to keep an eye on the view. Dropping while seeming to tread in place, submerging into the vista, we lost half the elevation of the Grand Canyon. Our reward was to be lulled by the waves at last, to watch the islands breach from eye level. The water sizzled toward us as if clawed from beneath by tiny fingernails: a school of minnows simultaneously chased by other fish and strafed by pelicans. As I enjoyed the seascape with its Darwinian touches, I became aware that I had been unconsciously scratching for some time. When I satisfied my foot, my armpit itched, then my calf, then the back of my neck. As I walked to the campfire, I felt my lower lip swell. Exploring for further effects, I found a band of welts on the back of a thigh and another on my neck. I asked the ear-slasher's brother whether some plant might produce those symptoms. He replied that it had small hairy leaves, was called *ortiguilla,* and all effects would be gone by morning. The plant book mentioned *ortigilla* as a local variant of *mala mujer,* or evil woman, a familiar plant whose vast hairy spadelike leaves were so blatantly nightmarish one hardly needed to be warned in print. By morning the itching and welts had nearly disappeared, my lower lip had subsided and the Dow Jones had dropped to 969.

To get to another seaside camp four kilometers away, we turned inland, apparently on a cutoff, through a claustrophobic arroyo. Hills thrust themselves between us and the gulf, and the trail climbed sharply, leading us over a sulphurous upland of mesas and ridges. A new perspective on the Sierra de la Giganta broke its smooth summit into pinnacles and spires that reminded some of the Tetons. Others grumbled that we shouldn't have been primed for a short hike if it was to be another forced march, and I pointed out that every kilometer we salted away now wouldn't have to be done later. Suddenly the ear-slasher's brother kicked his mule up to me and laughingly confessed: we were lost. The two guides had never been so far north before. He spurred his mule gaily on and began to sing ranchera songs for the first time: getting lost was the solution to everything. Soft sand was meanwhile knotting the thighs and calf muscles of the clientele and I didn't explain the situation to any who hadn't figured it out. It struck me how fortunate we were that half the distance had been chopped off the trip. The arroyo led in and out of a chasm that I thought, ironically, our party would have found scenic on some milder occasion. We spotted the sea at the end of another arroyo, a kilometer off. The marchers were too numb to cheer but one of the burros, as if propelled by our thought, made a dash for the beach. We caught up trudging. We were just where we hoped to be, laughed Nora, except that we had described an eighteen-kilometer horseshoe over an alluvial plain instead of a four-kilometer walk along the coast. I picked a campsite on the edge, hoping no one remembered my glib little remark about salted kilometers.

At this point Tim took over the selection of the route, and at the small settlement of Tambaviche we reached the most curious artifact of our journey. The wide beachside valley was dominated by a massive stone house with a steeply pitched roof, a chimera where any structure at all was the exception. As we approached, the house proved to be a hollow shell with no panes in the windows and no floor for its second story. A large *pitahaya* cactus, its roots thirty feet from the ground, leaned rakishly from an eave like the plume on an eccentric hat. I had been told the story of this house in La Paz and now heard it repeated almost verbatim from one of the inhabitants of the handful of shacks behind it. In the 1920s, went the account, a fisherman too poor to own a boat found a black pearl of immense size and value. Even after being cheated by the merchants of La Paz, he had enough money to build the mansion and to establish a sailing fleet that plied the coast between

La Paz and Tambaviche. The pearl, it was said, found its way among the British crown jewels and was stashed in the Tower of London. When the fisherman died, his heirs couldn't decide which among them should live in the house, or how to share it, or even how to sell it. The structure fell into disrepair and was raided for materials to build the shacks that sprawled behind it. The man who told us this story was the fisherman's grandson, as were most of the men at Tambaviche, as were more descendants scattered from La Paz to San Diego. The perfect fit between a story I heard in two places convinced me that it was the authentic version and perhaps even true. Years later I went to the Tower of London hoping a dark pearl would gleam back from some scepter or coronet, further confirming the tale and evoking the husk of a desert mansion, but among the diamonds and emeralds and sapphires was no substance so base as a pearl.

A two-hour jaunt remained to our trek's end, and on a sudden inspiration Tim asked the storyteller to give us a lift in his skiff. Those of us who chose to piled into the fiberglass boat, one of hundreds turned out in a La Paz factory by an American named Mac Shroyer whom Brandy had introduced me to years before. We found ourselves skimming the foam propelled by a noisy, reeking outboard. The coast slid mutely past, unlearned by muscle. We beached well before the first foot soldiers heaved in, and the airline pilot was seriously miffed. "If I hadn't walked the last mile," he quivered, "I just wouldn't feel right."

I felt a pleasant flush of malice. "Really?" I heard myself reply. "This is the first time I've hit camp without aching feet and I feel wonderful."

The next afternoon we were skiffed to a passenger boat scheduled to return us to La Paz, becoming rank intruders in a party of marine biologists from La Jolla who were collecting some rare sort of sea worm. By now the sun had passed beyond the Sierra de la Giganta, turning its peaks, promontories, clefts and arroyos into a dusky silhouette, a blank face. Was that geological blowout really veined with orchards, waterholes, goats, turtles, wild figs? The range returned to being the long, secretive wall that had baffled my imagination from the water: the whole journey might have been a delusion, a shared myth . No, for there was a single, solid anchor glowing back: the great ruined house at Tambaviche, a tiny salmon-colored square in a dark valley.

A trip with no paying turkeys, without even Tim, was thrown together to visit the Sierra de San Francisco in the midpeninsula, north of San Ignacio.

The year before, Tim and two friends had arrived in the area packed for a trip by mule to the cave paintings, but without formal plans. The three had overindulged in a restaurant on the paved highway, driven ten miles north on a side road and collapsed for the night. In the morning they were discovered by an elderly man named Tacho Arce, who asked what they wanted.

"To see the cave paintings," said Tim.

"When?" asked Tacho.

"Now."

Their expedition—led by Tacho, a rancher and trader who knew the caves better than any other living person—was so joyful that Tim considered guiding paying customers to the paintings. Unable to return the following winter because of conflicting trips, he dispatched six surrogates, all with ties to the peninsula, and I got another look at the sociology of guinea pigs. Accompanying me were Nora and her cousin Beth, women in their early twenties who had first reached La Paz in their sailboat; Mary Shroyer, who kept books for her husband's fiberglass boat factory in La Paz; a young La Paz-raised hellion named Scott; and a veteran of Tim's previous cave trip, also named Bruce, whom our guides rechristened Cruz to distinguish us. Paying basic expenses, we were to return with advice about food, equipment, scheduling and prospective customers.

I had flown to La Paz for Tim's previous trips and hadn't yet traveled the paved highway. A friend from San Diego, ready for novelty, offered to haul me to San Ignacio in a refurbished U.S. Mail delivery wagon, a model the government had withdrawn because it was overtall, top-heavy and tended to tip over. The vehicle dramatized the perils of the narrow, unbanked new pavement. The desert had been bulldozed toward the highway on either side so as to elevate the roadbed, leaving no shoulder and increasing the probability of rolling if one pulled off to avoid an accident. Cactus that had crowded the MTH with its spikes and scents, sometimes turning the track into a tunnel, now kept its place beyond and below us as we followed a causeway through the void. The gangly mail wagon and the paved tightrope were a mutual disaster, and as we threaded the forest of *cirios,* bending to the ground because nature had grown them too tall for their height, the peninsula seemed a general botch.

We reached San Ignacio at a cautious crawl and after a seven-year absence I faced more change. Between the lagoon and town the Mexican government, flush with new oil money, had constructed a rambling hotel called El Presidente, part of a national chain built on the premise that if you raised a hotel, guests would come. Casa Leree had closed and Becky had moved to Florida. Frank Fischer, the old German mechanic, had died. His son Oscar Fischer, who spoke only Spanish despite his name, had replaced the garage with a six-room motel—in which my friend deposited me before aiming his mail wagon back north.

At Oscar Fischer's I continued to read about the cave paintings we were to visit. Their greatest mystery, after their origin, was their neglect. Several Jesuits, writing accounts in Europe to fill free time after their expulsion in 1768, described them accurately and recounted Indian legends about their creation. A century later a French industrial chemist named Léon Diguet, an employee of the El Boleo mining company in Santa Rosalía, visited many of the caves between 1889 and 1895 and published a monograph on them when he returned to France. In 1962 the mystery writer Erle Stanley Gardner, who learned of the paintings from a man who grew up in the sierra, launched a high-profile expedition with helicopters, reporters, photographers and one archaeologist, and turned it into a cover story for *Life* magazine. The paintings weren't systematically cataloged until the early 1970s, when a California schoolteacher named Harry Crosby undertook a series of expeditions guided by none other than Tacho Arce and published a coffee-table book called *The Cave Paintings of Baja California*. What was remarkable about these ventures, and several others, was that each seemed independent of the other. The cumulative effect of this publicity was a growing demand to see the paintings, as many as twenty people a year according to Tacho when we joined him in 1977.

On a clear October midmorning—after the tedium of reaching Santa Martha, the last ranch accessible by vehicle, then repacking supplies and loading burros and mules—we were at last atop hand-stitched leather saddles and moving. In the wake of September rains, the desert was tangled and lush, the cactus thigh-deep in weeds. Having pictured authority in the lead, I was surprised to find five riderless burros in front and the pack team driven from behind by Tacho and two young cousins. We turned from our canyon into a steep side valley that broke into switchbacks near a pass. We got off and walked, letting the animals plod without us, and were suddenly overwhelmed by a sweet, violent stench. We spotted a dead burro just off the trail. One of Tacho's cousins held his hand over his mouth with a look of desperation. I asked Tacho what had happened.

"He died only a week ago."

"Something loose on the trail?"

"No, he just stepped wrong and slipped."

Having just read a Crosby effusion on the infallibility of burros, I was not reassured.

Thus was our initiation into the Sierra de San Francisco. One by one we admitted that the cave paintings were only a pretext for exploring this volcanic range with its remote ranches, for fielding whatever chance tossed us. We rose early and started late, sipping coffee while animals hobbled for the night were found, brought back and saddled. We were amazed at how far a mule with its front legs bound could wander; once, to our disbelief, a mule hid so far off that we weren't underway until three in the afternoon.

Particularly at the trip's beginning, our transportation was our chief focus. It was possible, by kicking, yelling and lashing with the crop, to coax a trot and even a rare gallop out of a burro, but when the effort ceased the animal would lapse into its familiar stride, leaving rider more exhausted than beast. We developed strategies. I encouraged a trot by posting madly; it seemed my burro couldn't bear to walk a post. Nora and I evolved a system whereby she reached back and bopped mine in the head, mine kicked hers in the back legs and we bluffed our way uphill. One burro rounded bends as if posing for time-lapse photos and Scott would ask, "Is he moving? Is he moving?" Once when Nora was screaming "Burro! Burro! Burro!" and swatting its flank, to stony indifference, without warning the beast lunged forward. Nora rose straight in the air and landed, unburroed, into some spineless foliage, hurt only from laughing so hard. When the same thing happened to Cruz, he was pitched into a cholla and spent the next hour tweezering out needles. Although we guinea pigs rode a mix of burros and mules, Tacho and his cousins rode only mules, brooked little insurrection and kept the animals moving with smart whipcracks against their chaps.

Man and beast progressed over plateaus and ridges, down and up canyons three to four thousand feet deep. Entire hillsides were turned to mint by a ferny growth that suggested northern moors. At high points we caught glimpses of the Gulf of California, hovering in smoky turquoise over fold after fold of green. *Palo blancos,* their ivory trunks fanning into a mist of alfalfa, lined the arroyos, climbed the slopes and embroidered the horizons. Over stretches where chunky lava stopped all growth, our nine persons, nine burros and five mules threaded the rubble like ants through instant coffee. I had the impression that our weeklong migration rounded a series of ridges rayed from a central mesa but I may have been wrong, for our only map was in Tacho's brain. It was Tacho whose spirit and bearlike person hovered over our trip, paunch spilling over his scorpion belt buckle, teeth like bleaching caprock, eyes slitted with mischief, sheer drive erupting with information and jokes and exhausting stamina. Local volcanics had been creating Tacho for sixty-seven years and showed no signs of relenting.

Each day we stopped at one or two of the little ranches tucked in the mountains, often unnoticed until we were unexpectedly within them. These were the outposts created by descendants of the soldiers brought in by the padres, who wound up surviving both padres and Indians to become the oldest families of the peninsula. Water from their wells, springs and impounded rains was sluiced into orchards, vegetable gardens, and animal troughs. Few of the inhabitants had witnessed a more urban existence than San Ignacio or Santa Rosalía. Sewing machines and hardware reached them by truck and then by mule, and transistor radios brought them Radio Obregón with news that might as well have been pure invention. At the most impoverished ranch, set haphazardly in a bare field, the family was light complected, the father stoop shouldered and sickly, the women unkempt, the buildings in disrepair. The children's eyes were liquid and squinty and the little girls' dresses—that unfailing barometer of social health—were filthy. Pondering the effects of inbreeding, we arrived next at a ranch wedged into a tight canyon. Palm logs split lengthways, hollowed and joined end to end, channeled water seamlessly throughout. A pool like a hand mirror caught bits of the three houses, the storerooms and corrals. Each building, a joinery of stone, wood and thatch, was a tight ship drifting in marigolds, zinnias, dahlias, morning glories, geraniums, sunflowers, bougainvillea. The potted stick of a night-blooming cereus awaited its burst of glory. Hanging from the rafters amidst coleus and philodendron was a cradle of hand-hewn slats. The mother gently pushed her suspended child while the grandmother sliced garlic on a windowsill that doubled as a cutting board, enabling her to work and converse. When we asked the grandmother how many lived there, she seemed baffled by the question, then counted relatives in groups of four that we added into sixteen. The family had lived downcanyon before being washed out by a flash flood and moving to the present site in 1943. The ranch was thus only twenty-five years old but was surely built on techniques already refined in the area, based on methods imported from the mainland which may, in turn, have been modified practices from Iberia that built on skills from North Africa. . . . Gone was all thought of inbreeding and we left instead debating the ranch's name, *Salsipuedes*. Did it mean "leave if you can" or "leave if you can bear to"?

Our days were livened by small, memorable events. I heard an unholy screeching from the burro in the lead and came upon the contents of a food box sprawling on the ground, with the strawberry jam rolling toward a cliff; a cinch had broken and had to be repaired on the spot while we collected our commissary. A rattlesnake crossed the trail between two mules and slipped under a bush; Tacho, who had lost a grandchild to a snake, fired into the foliage until the creature stopped moving, then pulled it out fat and limp, hung it on a *pitahaya* cactus as if to warn other snakes, cut off the rattle and handed it to Scott. We spotted two white goats that had clambered up a wall they couldn't get back down: would they die and fall or fall and die? At one ranch we came upon a man who had been blinded by a fever and who stood all day on a porch in dark glasses, impassively braiding four strands of hemp: it was his rope, it turned out, that we had been using on our trip. At another ranch we caught up with a pair of freshly shot mountain lions we had been hearing about. Their skins, dry and shriveling, were suspended from a mesquite tree. "We kill them and kill them," I heard one old man say, "and still they keep coming."

The animals we most focused on, after those we rode, were those we ate. A goat was slaughtered for us when we began the trip at Santa Martha, and three meals a day we worked on it. We roasted goat ribs over hot coals and tore the meat off with hands and teeth. Tough, salty, stringy, it was also tasty and satisfying. We mashed it with rocks and fried it with onions, peppers and herbs to make *machaca*. We diced it into Rice-a-roni. We had goat with noodles and goat Orientale. We boiled it into stock for soup. We mixed it with tomatoes and avocados and rolled it in tortillas. As a relief from tough, greasy goat meat we ate soft, creamy goat cheese. One midday we visited a ranch where women offered us olives and dates they had picked and cured. They made tortillas that had to be eaten hot. We proceeded to the orchard, where the rancher shook a mottled sycamore-like trunk, bringing down a hail of guavas. We continued to the vegetable garden, where we devoured watermelon until our faces were bloody with sweetness. When we left the ranch we realized that without intending to eat a meal at all, we had been overtaken by a wholly goatless lunch.

As for the cave paintings, our purported goal, we clambered to all we could. The long, stylized red and black murals depicting lynxes, coyotes, snakes, mountain sheep, vultures with outspread wings, rabbits, deer and creatures we couldn't identify among solid, schematic men and women with their arms outstretched, all looming overhead on dark overhangs, gave the unsettling sense of life, teeming and frozen, where one expected bare stone. Flat and angular, the figures overlapped with little regard for each other. Animals were sometimes overlaid so thick that to the unstudied eye they ran into a general wash, a midden of forms, the reds occasionally thickening with an effect of dried blood. Figures continued obliviously over stone that fractured at sharp angles—sometimes to interesting effect, as when a hand unexpectedly advanced from a protruding rock—but usually so arbitrarily one wondered how the painter kept track of his subject. The composite effect was of pentimentos, palimpsests, multiple exposures. Only by physically standing in the caves could one sense their sequestration in deep canyons and their impressive scale but, ironically, it was in the two-dimensional photos of coffee-table books—the one by Harry Crosby and another that appeared after our trip, by Enrique Hambleton—that one could trace the designs without the distortions of geology that the artists overran. It raised questions of whether the actual paintings were the point, or whether we were admiring the aftermath of some hunt by sympathetic magic, the capture of an animal by conjuring its image. In any case, we had no idea who produced them, or why. The world of the ranches, though remote from our own, still spoke to us. If the paintings finally addressed our times, it would be through archaeology, symbology, chemical analysis, radiocarbon dating, major digs—and money.

On our last morning Tacho took us to a painting Harry Crosby hadn't seen because it had simply slipped Tacho's mind. We followed through the cactus and underbrush to an overhang with four delicate red mountain sheep and several larger, less perfect specimens. Knowing Crosby would catalog it eventually, I tore a page from my notebook, wrote HI HARRY in block letters, folded it and wedged it noticeably into a crack below the sheep. Our contribution to archaeology was one disposable graffito.

After returning to San Ignacio, all six guinea pigs repaired to the Hotel El Presidente to prepare our report for Tim over margaritas. Beginning with petty complaints, uniformly despised were the Sierra cups masquerading as plates. As one person put it, they were perfectly angled so that when they burned your lip they spilled the soup in your lap. Unused was the freeze-dried food we had brought. Besides bearing instructions that were unreadable to our guides, freeze-dried had no appeal when there were so many inventive things to do with goat. More basically, we decided, our party of nine, with thirteen animals, though small for a tourist group, had been unwieldy, and the necessity of sticking together had curbed our freedom. Our visits to the ranches felt like invasions, and surely the ranchers' welcome would soon wear thin. Pleased with our own memories, we came up with a flawless recommendation to Tim about the trips: don't do them.

Before leaving the hotel we invited Nora and Beth to camp with us on the road to the ranch where our trip began, but they were headed north to Santa Barbara, we were headed south to La Paz, and they preferred to stay for one more margarita before sacking out near town. We pulled up the ranch road just far enough to be clear of the highway and camped. As we were drifting off, a stranger drove up and informed us that our two young friends had driven their Volkswagen bug into a palm tree and were in the San Ignacio medical clinic in critical condition. Trusting the obscurity of our campsite, we left our possessions and jumped into Mary's and Scott's cars. In the dark I couldn't find my glasses but it was hardly the moment to search.

As in many isolated towns, doctoring was provided by a medical student who performed a year of government-sponsored service as part of training. The clinic was a two-room bungalow, and Nora remembers being carried into it in darkness and being asked if she would pay to fire up the generator so they could be attended by light. Nora was badly cut on the lip, had a broken arm, a broken leg and two broken ribs; Beth had a fractured clavicle and unknown internal injuries. The young doctor said the girls' condition was beyond his capabilities; our best bet was to take them to Guerrero Negro, on the Pacific coast, in hopes that someone could fly them to the States.

The police appeared at the hospital and summoned us to their one-room station. They asked if we would assume responsibility for the girls' possessions. As soon as we did, they informed us that they had found cigarette papers, indicating that the girls were smoking marijuana. Mary replied indignantly that it implied only that they preferred to roll their own tobacco; outside the station, however, she told us that Beth had whispered to her in the hospital that one of her bags contained peyote.

An injured girl was loaded into each car, along with the doctor and a nurse, and the party sped to Guerrero Negro. Useless without my glasses, I stayed in San Ignacio and mustered a taxi to retrieve our possessions from the campsite. Even in my myopia I was sure I had found the spot, but there was nothing to find. I had the taxi drop me off at Oscar Fischer's motel. The night guard couldn't be roused. I hiked to El Presidente and found the door padlocked. I was shivering in my T-shirt, the margaritas were curdling into a hangover, I was terrified that we had just assumed responsibility—to already suspicious police—for luggage bearing dope, and I felt like one of those

Graham Greene characters who loses all his familiar supports in the first chapter.

As we were walking earlier through the dark in search of the clinic, I had paused at a crumbling and roofless adobe building behind Oscar Fischer's to relieve myself and idly noticed a decaying mattress. To this refuge I retreated. When I pulled the mattress into a wall's shadow to hide it from the glare of a full moon, part of it fell away. Several palm fronds lay strewn in the building and I pulled them over me for whatever warmth they might provide. With no hope of actual sleep, I recited mentally all the poems I could remember, and recited them again. The world imperceptibly lightened and I heard the familiar sounds—dogs, roosters, radios, combustion—of San Ignacio waking up. Feeling ridiculous and not wanting to be seen crawling from a collapsed building, I waited until all nearby sounds of pedestrians, children and even dogs came to a lull before venturing out. I walked straight into Oscar Fischer.

He asked in stupefaction what I was up to. I recounted the whole episode, including my inability to rouse his night guard. But why hadn't I beat on his own door? he demanded. It simply hadn't occurred to me to rouse someone at what I estimated to be three in the morning. He took me to his kitchen for food and coffee, then gave me a room at the motel. I bought a razor and shampoo in the plaza and tried to soap off the night.

Too edgy to sleep, I returned to the plaza so that my friends could find me when they returned from Guerrero Negro. And if I was to be arrested, I wanted to get on with it. As I sat under the laurels, an old man in a jacket large enough to be a cape made speeches to the air. Several young boys followed him, hid behind benches and under the foliage, then leapt out at him shouting *Guaco! Guaco!* As I lost myself in a blurred vision of this scene, Oscar Fischer settled next to me on a bench.

"What does *guaco* mean?" I asked.

"It's that crazy diving bird at the lagoon. The kids call the crazy old man *guaco*, mostly because he hates it, and they spring out at him the way that bird springs from the water." The boys were impersonating black-crowned night-herons.

Visions of the plaza held me until late afternoon, when Mary and Scott pulled in from Guerrero Negro. They had been luckier than they could have hoped. Scott had gotten on the shortwave radio at a hotel and reached a couple of American doctors, despised flying sportsmen, who had flown their Cessna to Bahía de los Angeles for some fishing. They had encountered an

American with a medical emergency, were speeding him to San Diego and were detouring to Guerrero Negro to refuel. Could they take Nora and Beth too? asked Scott. No, that was too much weight. Being doctors, Scott begged, couldn't they at least look at them? The doctors landed, took one look and ordered the girls into the plane. Even as we spoke, Nora and Beth were presumably being attended in Scripps at La Jolla.

We proceeded as a group to the police station to claim their possessions. The police made no further mention of dope and turned over the bags. When we went through it later we realized that the peyote looked like old leather, bad patching material, and we tossed it back into the desert from which it came. We drove to our campsite and found our belongings gone, with one set of unknown footprints among our own. With the man who informed us of the accident our only suspect, we let it go.

While Mary and Scott stayed in Santa Rosalía to handle papers on the wrecked car, the two Bruces took the bus to La Paz. This was a continuation of my first trip on the paved highway and I trained my astigmatism through the bus window. At Coyote Bay, where Bill Lloyd was going to pitch his Polynesian resort, trailers cheek to cheek walled off the water, pocked with turquoise privies in back. We reached La Paz to learn by phone that Beth's internal injuries included a punctured lung and a ruptured spleen and that she was lucky to have survived. I flew home, pulling my eyelid back to bring gate numbers into focus. Nora, at least, kept her sense of humor, for at Christmas she sent me a woodcut showing a two-personed sleigh hitting a palm tree and, inside, the inscription "Baja Humbug!" Attached was a present made in the hospital: a denim workshirt appliquéd on the back with red and black mountain sheep from one of the caves.

Baja California, a thin peninsula for its length, shows a split personality: the gulf side rugged, volcanic, burning with color; the Pacific side flat, fog-bound and cool. I preferred its mania to its depression and generally kept to the gulf side or the mountainous spine. But on the Pacific side, in coastal channels and bladder-shaped lagoons, lay one of the peninsula's great spectacles, the breeding waters of *Eschrichtius robustus*, the California grey whale, teasingly known as the "desert whale."

Making the longest known migration of any mammal, grey whales spend half their year in transit between summer feeding grounds in the Bering and Beaufort Seas off Alaska and the Pacific lagoons of Baja California, where they breed and, thirteen months later, give birth. The grey is the most coast-hugging of all whales: fifty-foot adults can maneuver in water that barely floats them. Much of their behavior has yet to be decoded, but it is believed that the salinity of the upper reaches of the lagoons, twice that of the sea, helps support newborns who emerge fifteen feet long and weighing a half-ton.

It is ironic that the English name for the largest breeding waters, Scammon's Lagoon, honors Captain Charles M. Scammon, who followed the whales to their calving grounds in the 1850s and simultaneously studied and slaughtered them. Other whalers, seeing him return to San Francisco with a quick and spectacular catch, followed Scammon, developing a variation on bullfighting whereby they killed the baby, then harpooned the charging mother head-on. Because of the mothers' furious attacks on whalers, grey whales—who now allow themselves to be "petted" by whalewatchers—were known at the time as "devilfish." With the arrival of the first factory ships in 1913 came another wave of slaughter. Because they followed the coast and bred in confined water, greys were the easiest whales to close in on.

In 1937, when the population had shrunk to three hundred individuals, the International Whaling Commission declared the grey whale protected and banned further taking. In 1971, after a national and international campaign by environmentalists, President Luis Echeverría declared Scammon's Lagoon a whale refuge, making Mexico the first country to establish such a sanctuary. In 1979, Laguna San Ignacio was declared a second whale refuge. When I first visited grey whales in the late seventies, they had returned from the verge of extinction to an estimated population of seventeen thousand and were considered fully recovered.

Commercial whale trips to Bahía Magdalena, most southerly and accessible of the calving areas, hadn't been tried before Tim began them, but they were so popular from the beginning that Tim hardly needed guinea pigs. Bahía Magdalena was actually a three-hundred-kilometer waterway consisting of one large bay flanked by narrow, deep, swift-moving channels created by barrier islands. Among the four calving areas, Magdalena ranked third in actual number of whales but first in sheer roiling concentration. The channel north of the bay quickly became, and remained, the whalewatching destination of choice. Groups of a dozen whalewatchers were bused from La Paz to Puerto López Mateos, a scruffy town pitched twenty years before to service a fish cannery. Parties were then skiffed two kilometers across the water to Isla Magdalena, a forty-kilometer island of sand dunes whose only settlement, a fishing camp, lay thirty kilometers to the south. Awaiting the whalewatchers—set up between dunes—was a dense cluster of musty olive-drab tents that suggested an encampment from Rommel's North African campaign.

For a while I went whalewatching almost yearly, largely drawn to peripheral activities. I loved hiking the two kilometers across Isla Magdalena to the Pacific. Between the dunes grew tiny gardens, almost orientally composed, of waxen plants and grasses whose windblown blades drew targetlike circles in the sand. The surf of the open Pacific pounded louder as one walked west, accelerating with one's own heartbeat, until from the final dune an expanse of combers boiled toward the beach, cold and powerful, inviting moody walks along the edge. Still more I liked to ride a skiff into the mangroves that lined the shore, their roots in muck black as pitch, their leaves sometimes brushing the gunwales on both sides. Herons, egrets, cormorants and frigate birds eyed us from their perches, hoping we weren't true, and flapped off at the last minute. Strolling from camp, I could lose myself in the green heron hunting with its head lower than its back, its yellow legs so bent that its forelegs lay flat behind its enormous feet. Inching forward like a cartoon sleuth, it jabbed its javelin beak forward with each step, then drew its head back as the body caught up so that the bird advanced in a series of disjointed, cubist jerks, leaving a delicate, seamless zipper in the sand.

If the rust and turquoise of the gulf seemed afire, the Pacific lagoons, even at midday when we were out in the skiffs, appeared to be dozing off. Dunes from the barrier islands floated the horizon in sable clouds as the mangroves lining them drowsed over dark stems. As if from the unconscious, a form of sunblistered rubber would surface and unroll itself, bit by bit, stupendously, like a sea serpent. A hole in its surface would explode a sigh, geysering a rank mist. In another direction, the triangle of a head would sluice from the water, its huge round eye staring out mournfully. A heart-shaped tail would flash as a creature unexpectedly submerged. From the stillness came the rush of their colossal breath, the smack of their flukes.

The sense of a dreamworld didn't last long in the skiff because whalewatching, which involved imagining the animal from seeing only bits at a time, assumed the nature of a tease, and everyone wanted pictures to take home. So that no one's view would be obstructed, an elaborate etiquette had evolved whereby those in the bow lay low, those in the center sat and only those in the stern were to stand. Conversation swirled with the jargon of whalewatching. Whales that rose for a look were spy-hopping. They didn't breathe, they blew; they didn't circle, they gyred; they didn't jump, they breached. Flukes were never called tails. The swelling calms whales left when they submerged were lily pads. The male member at full extension, a prodigy I have seen only on film, was a Pink Floyd. Even with the tiering of passengers for clear views, in the excitement of action photography people swung to where the whales were, which was sometimes behind the standers. Telephoto lenses leered like voyeurs. Once in a while a whale would breach— would leap entire from the water and fall with a resounding whack—and any photographer's dream would be to catch the desert whale in full flight. As it was, most of the photos of heads and flukes and backs were, to continue the terminology, blob shots, and I'm sure that if I ever looked through my rangefinder at a whale in the sky, I would have been too stupefied to press the shutter.

I found that whalewatching by skiff, particularly among whalewatchers on fast film, was not an experience I wanted more than once per trip, but I did show up annually. Whalewatching was a pretext for camping on the island, for hiking the sand, for floating through mangroves and ambushing birds. In 1977 the *Don José,* a twenty-passenger boat with cabins that Tim commissioned from a La Paz boatyard, became a mother ship that sat in the bay or moved around it slowly and sent out skiffs. In the salon were a library of peninsular lore, an endless supply of coffee and beer, and ongoing Scrabble rivalries. Some of us still camped on the island and only boarded when the mood struck. For Baja Expeditions die-hards—clients, former guides, guinea pigs emeriti—who had formed an evolving social nucleus, whale trips became a way to get together and, discreetly, party. One winter, when Tim and Nora realized that twelve of the twenty passengers on an upcoming whalewatch were friends or relations, they decided, on six weeks' notice, to get married.

Woodcut invitations showing romantic pelicans were dispatched and the swarm of people who could be summoned to an obscure island on short notice was impressive. Tim's parents from Phoenix were already signed up for the trip, as were the Shroyers from La Paz. Nora's mother sewed a wedding dress and her father, an amateur potter, threw souvenir cups embossed with whales. Tim recruited an old hunting friend who had since become a preacher to perform the ceremony. Extra tents were pitched at the island camp and Tim hired a second bus to haul guests from La Paz to Puerto López Mateos. Kurt Vonnegut, who had survived a mule trip to the caves with urban one-liners, sent a telegram to the effect that his doctor wouldn't let him forsake the tranquility of New York for the tensions of Baja California. With his usual reticence, Tim waited until the bus ride to inform the eight paying strangers that, by the way, they would also be part of a social event.

Joining the two busloads were guests who arrived over the next five days after traveling by car, truck and private plane to reach López Mateos landing strip, where Baja Expeditions guides waited to ferry them to the island. A friend of Tim's who raised goats on one of the gulf islands arrived with three of his goats for the wedding feast. In his pickup along with the goats were two hitchhikers as surprise guests. The widowed Katie Lee showed up with an Australian boyfriend she identified as a souvenir from a recent trip around the world. The preacher, whose luggage was lost on the way, was forced to spend the week in the polyester pants he arrived in. Strangers met while chopping heroic fruit salads or picking bones out of grilled fish. Under a blaze of constellations bottles were passed around driftwood campfires while Katie and a Nigerian scuba diver sang folksongs. Guests fed the goats oatmeal from their breakfasts.

A wedding site was prepared in a hollow between the dunes several kilometers down the island. Those who had fed the goats were a bit horrified to see them slaughtered and dressed out by the preacher and the groom on the morning of the wedding. Guests changed into finery, everything from cleaner T-shirts to caftans and ankle-length batik. Midafternoon, eighty people boarded the *Don José* for a short cruise to the wedding.

We debarked at a broad swale between the dunes. Several dozen white gladioli, brought by one of the guests from a floral shop in La Paz, were clustered on the dunetops. Tim and Nora remained on board to change, and from our sandy perch we watched them descend to a skiff, two figures in white. Tim made several spins with one hand on the outboard and the other on a white top hat. When he ran the boat onto the beach, Nora climbed out the bow, hiked her full-length gown over her knees, and hauled the skiff onto the sand. Tim climbed ashore in a white swallowtail tux that matched the hat and set off his Zapata moustache, giving him the air of a riverboat gambler. Both were barefoot. Nora produced a bridal bouquet from the bow and they walked with their respective parents to a gladiola-trimmed clearing. The preacher, whose actual religion no one had inquired into, stood before them with goat blood on his polyester and delivered a long, nearly incoherent harangue about Adam's rib. Onlookers gasped as a pair of white seagulls swooped unexpectedly toward the ceremony and veered off. After the kiss, the guests dove into a punch of fruit juice, champagne and—was it dark rum? Even the goatfest didn't stabilize its effects. One guest slipped through the dunes with another's girlfriend; a disgruntled old flame of Tim's was skiffed away by a guide. A fog gathered and thickened.

Tim and Nora, committed to continuous trips for the next several months, remained at the wedding site for a one-night honeymoon while the guests were corralled back to the *Don José*. The captain was sober but the fog inside the rest of us matched the weather as the boat, at its slowest possible speed, palpated back along the coast. No one wanted to get off to grope for a tent through the fog. Of the eight paying strangers, six joined the celebration and two remained very quiet. Their cabins were respected but the rest of us lay sideways two or three to a bunk, or sprawled in the salon or on deck where stupor overtook us.

The aftermath had its own flavor. A fisherman made off with Tim's rented top hat, and when Tim returned the rest of the suit, the La Paz rental company called to complain about serious strain on the fabric, along with an in-explicable amount of sand in the pockets. All who attended received follow-up woodcuts of a pair of pelicans grinning with anatomically incorrect teeth. A dozen years later one of the guests stumbled upon a *National Enquirer* publication called *Weddings of the Rich and Famous,* with Liz Taylor, Princess Di and Arnold Schwarzenegger in nuptial drag on the cover. Inside, in a break from stardom that featured marriages in unusual places—in the bas-ket of a balloon, on a cliff in Malibu, in front of the meat counter where the lovebirds met—was a photo of Tim and Nora's wedding on what was re-ferred to as a "whale-sighting trip." We tried to determine from the angle who might have taken it but the identity of the guest who sold out to the *Enquirer* was lost in the fog.

PORT OF ILLUSION

5

Most of those jaunts to lagoons and caves and remote ranges during the seventies and eighties began with a flight to La Paz. For reasons I couldn't isolate, La Paz had taken hold of me and I routinely arrived a few days early to prowl its dusty streets. After three agonizing arrivals over roughly a thousand kilometers of sand, ruts, drop-offs and clinking lava, it seemed unsporting to swoop effortlessly into the La Paz airport. Through the window of the banking plane loomed the uninhabited sand spit of El Mogote, shagged with mangroves, fanned like a wing protecting the inner bay. Beyond the water's raw sapphire stretched a busy meshwork of leaves. Straightening for the runway, the plane skimmed a desert where cows grazed and *cardón* cacti, huge on the ground, stood in their faded khaki like toy soldiers. At the plane door I was smacked by heat, dryness, lightness in the lungs, quickening of the pulse. Untempered by transitions on land, La Paz by air wasn't arrived at; it was uncorked.

One year I flew to La Paz five times. The following year, free of wintertime commitments in the States, I loaded up the jeep, drove down the already disintegrating new pavement and stayed a half year. The migration became an annual event and the buoyancy that struck me when I walked out of the plane became the air that sustained me. Renting small houses in various parts of town, I was poised to visit other parts of the peninsula when whim or an invitation struck. Meanwhile, as a part-time resident, I began to examine what there was about the town, ordinary in so many aspects, that mesmerized.

Gradually I realized that in various ways La Paz didn't add up. Riding the inside curve of a promontory that hooked into the Gulf of California toward the north, the town caught sunsets across a bay where, intuitively, the sun ought to rise. Its geographical contortion was clear on the map. What most baffled was that La Paz had grown from a population of 35,000 when I first saw it to 160,000 without changing, for me, its careless appeal. Gone, granted, were most of the windmills and the board-and-batten houses with corrugated metal or thatched roofs that had made the La Paz I first knew seem like an overgrown village. But La Paz was still a cross-stitch of trees and one- to three-story buildings in a ratio that favored trees. It sprawled toward the back, up an inclined plane that rose into ranches, cactus and, eventually, limestone peaks. The streets in the old part of town angled and veered as they followed geological features long since flattened, warping its grid into triangles and trapezoids, abetting dislocation, and since the center had little distinguished architecture, the replacement of an older building with a newer of the same size maintained the aura of randomness among Indian laurels. The beach along the waterfront was considered too urban and lean, its sand too close to traffic and its tides too polluted for the international bathing set. La Paz was one of those places that bored the tourist while whispering to a struck minority: here you must live.

My question then became, what propelled its growth? The answer I usually received was that La Paz was the capital of Baja California Sur. That made it the capital of a handful of towns, few of them sizable, of ranches, communal farms, fishing cooperatives, and of the cape region where tourists found beaches more to their taste. At 4.7 inhabitants per square kilometer in 1989, Baja California Sur had the lowest population density of Mexico's thirty-one states, and the various levels of government—state, county, city, military, education, garbage dump, cemetery—never exceeded 30 percent of employment. By 1940 most of the pearl-oyster beds that sustained La Paz's most romantic industry had died of plunder and disease, and conventional fishing was shrinking from overharvest. Because Baja California Sur was commercially at the end of the line and every importation cost more, in 1939 La Paz was declared a free port. When ferry service across the gulf was initiated in 1964, Mexicans from the mainland arrived to shop for goods from the Far East and the United States unavailable in the rest of Mexico. Boutiques full of watches, pocket calculators, perfume, pen sets and silk fans crammed the downtown maze, but even as the same merchandise became available in the rest of Mexico and free port status was gradually phased out, the town continued to grow. Living in the city, one noticed a cement factory here, a flour mill there. An enormous phosphate mine forty miles to the north was worked by men bused daily from La Paz, but even when the mine was privatized in 1994 and most of the workforce was laid off, the town didn't shrink. What sustained La Paz was like dark matter in the cosmos, present only by inference. Like any place worth inhabiting, La Paz was a riddle to solve.

Looking for clues, I began with the basic building block of La Paz, a dense, fine-grained stone glowing from pink to lavender. Recognizing its disguises became a game. Used as it fractured, it was most commonly set in jigsaw patterns with a thin binder of cement. Finely worked, stone met stone with a mere webbing of cracks. Sometimes it was varnished to bring out the colors as if it were wet, which turned its patina to plastic. Rounded pieces set swimming in painted white fill created a garish collage, while eight varieties squared into blocks and close-set produced a crazy-quilt facade for La Paz's cathedral—terrible architecture but wonderful geology. Entire buildings made of the stone were the exception, but nearly every establishment worked it in. Barriers of it hid middle-class homes of cement. It provided retaining walls, decorative panels, planters, mausoleums. Piles of it lay around town, spoor of abandoned projects or proof of intent to resume work. A geologist at the University of La Paz told me it was tuff and breccia, volcanic ash that had settled and vitrified, tinted by iron, manganese and assorted trace minerals. To the common *Paceño* it was *cantera,* rock from the quarry, or *laja,* flagstone. Dense but easily split, at once fragile and tough, it might fracture into meaning, and I traced it to its source.

A steep residential street in a poor barrio in back of town continued into a hillside that had been pitted and gouged. I saw a bright yellow truck in the distance and expected to reach a gate where a guard would turn me back or allow me to proceed under supervision. There was no gate, the truck dove onto a subsidiary road, and I reached a cluster of men sitting on a pile of *cantera.* Because it was Saturday and nearly noon, they were preparing to knock off for the weekend. When I mentioned that I was interested in the quarry, a man leapt to his feet and offered to show me around.

"My part is over this way," he said.

"Your part? Doesn't some company own this?"

No, he explained, the government owned the hill, which was worked by a cooperative of about a dozen men who divided the rock among themselves, and each had his patch. He pointed to a farther section where another cooperative, roughly the same size, operated a quarry reached by a different road. From patch to patch the stone varied from rose to lilac, a nuanced arc of the spectrum. Within a compact stone the texture varied from coarse to fine-grained, chunky to smooth. We reached a salmon-colored pit.

"Isn't this a beautiful color?" he asked.

"Yes. How do you get it out?"

He struck the cliffside with a small iron bar, and in a burst of dust, rocks gushed to our feet, precut by their fractures. He had two piles, one worked so that it had smooth faces on two sides, and the other heaped as it fell. It was lifted into wheelbarrows and pushed to trucks that couldn't reach the pit. There was no marketing; customers simply showed up with a truck, looked over the colors and consistencies, and struck a deal with a co-op member. You could also order *cantera* through a contractor, but why pay the markup if you could come yourself?

The way the rock had nearly fallen on my guide unnerved me, and I asked if the work wasn't dangerous. "Yes, a man was killed last year by falling rock. Another fell onto a rock pile and broke a leg."

Could this rock that saturated La Paz all come from a few men poking a hillside? There had been a previous quarry by the bay, said my guide, these two had been running for twenty or thirty years, and there was one more quarry farther from town. That was the scope of it.

Thanking my guide, I wandered to other small pits where men were jabbing or chipping or smoking and waiting for noon. Each was exuberant about his stone's particular tint and texture and boasted of its use in luxury buildings: for patios, for intricate floors and walls, for varnished panels. When I asked one man if the rock was volcanic, his smile fled and he said, "No, this is not porous, this is *cantera*." Out of this improvisation came the basic building block of La Paz.

Laced by vitrified ash, the La Paz I first knew was personified for me by a celebration that took place every weekend in one of the outer barrios. Most of the streets then resembled frozen whitewater, with transverse waves, upwellings, holes and tongues of passage on which drivers passed each other indiscriminately left or right in a kind of slow-motion river running. A major obstacle in the middle of one of those streets was an ancient Chevy sedan without wheels. Each Saturday around noon, six old men lodged a case, or two or three, of beer on the car's shady side and climbed in. Throughout the afternoon they worked their way through the cans. Children and grandchildren brought them food. They threw the empties out the windows and left the car only to urinate, often in public view. They enjoyed the pleasures of drinking and driving without the danger, and perhaps the scenery even accelerated as the day wore on. However cursed they may have been in surrounding kitchens, they were elders of the barrio and their Saturday spins were not criticized in public.

For Rubén Sandoval, a native Paceño who had spent his young adulthood in Paris and returned to become chairman of the humanities department at the University of La Paz, the escapades of the six elders—the defenestrated litter, the car at the center—represented a town already debased. When he was born, in 1948, La Paz, with about twelve thousand inhabitants, was still small enough that everyone knew everyone else. On hot nights people sat in front of their houses until midnight telling stories about each other. If you stole a chicken or pig, you had to slaughter and cook it quickly before it was recognized. There was little money but the bay was so rich with marine life that Paceños scooped up clams with their hands. Anything planted grew, and people planted dates, coconuts and wild figs. Crab has since become a luxury food, but when there was nothing else to eat, Rubén's mother would send the children to the shore and they would whine, "Do we have to eat crab *again?*"

Rubén remembers the La Paz of his youth as "almost a communist society." One person would provide seafood, another flour, another fruit, and all got divided up. There was no delinquency and the jail languished for tenants. There was not even litter, for people found a use for everything, valued cleanliness in poverty, sprinkled and swept the dust. Poor women made dresses for the town's few society ladies because there was no finery in the stores. But even the poor dressed well, took time to dry meat and fruit, made cheese, concocted *dulces* for dessert. In such a static, stratified society, the minor tension between the uncommon rich and the common poor surfaced mostly as pranks. Each class proposed an annual carnival queen, and the judges, being rich, always picked their candidate, leaving the poor one to be princess. Sometimes the princess's retinue took revenge by burning the queen's float.

Rubén dates the transformation of La Paz to the coming of the ferries from the mainland in 1964 and, to a lesser degree, to the completion of the paved highway in 1973. When strangers from the mainland arrived to go shopping, Rubén noted a vulgarization among the locals. Everyone now had cars, used and unmaintained. Instead of dressing well, people bought cheap clothes, threw them away and bought more. Traditional cooking ended when people found shortcuts at supermarkets. Imported middle-class consumer-ism replaced the "communism" of Rubén's youth.

The La Paz I first saw in 1968, four years after the first ferry, was already damaged goods by Rubén's standards, but the chord it struck within me has resounded from other immigrants over the changing years. Elma Vidaurri— a woman from Mexicali who had lived in various parts of Mexico and the United States and had become the city's prime distributor of room deodor-izers—said that when she first flew into La Paz in 1972 and saw the bay, the palm trees, the little town, it mirrored some image already within her. "I found precisely what I was looking for," she says, "without even knowing I was looking." In 1984 Brazilian pianist Jeni Bergold and her Mexican hus-band, Antonio Rosales, having lived in the Mexican interior, were consider-ing Ensenada for a new start. They pulled in on Friday night, just as Ameri-can college kids were beginning their weekend debauch, and they were appalled. Instead of turning around, they ventured down the peninsula. As people dropped away and the desert unfolded, they became more and more excited. They arrived in La Paz at night, and as they strolled the waterfront among the palms, the shadows, the nondescript buildings, they knew that all they lacked was jobs and a house. This sense of La Paz as a place inwardly foreknown had been anticipated for us newcomers by John Steinbeck in 1941 when he wrote, in *The Log from the Sea of Cortez,* "We had never seen a town which even looked like La Paz, and yet coming to it was like returning rather than visiting."

Perhaps La Paz, however foreign, seemed like home because home is a nest, not a showplace. Before the ferry arrived and La Paz grew, it did have natural divisions: the waterfront, the commercial core, Rubén's neighbor-hood of tiny fishing shacks called El Esterito, the boatyard area called El Manglito. When migration began, the government extended utilities and sold lots cheaply, requiring only that the buyer do something—anything—with the land. Up went houses, laundries, taco stands, service markets, photo studios, motorcycle repairs. Neighborhoods grew vibrantly and chaotically and many operations, modestly begun, were upgraded until they received that final blessing—to be hidden by a wall of *cantera.* Visitors are often struck by the anarchy of upper- and lower-class houses among beauty salons, beer outlets, churches, muffler dispensaries and karate studios. Whether you are exhilarated or maddened by such vigor depends on whether you can toler-ate the all-night truck repair next door or strike a deal on work hours, for tol-erance is the Paceño substitute for zoning.

Tolerance can shade into criminal negligence, as occurred during Hurricane Liza on September 30, 1976. The government had bulldozed a token dam of earth and sand across an arroyo behind town and then opened the arroyo to settlement, building two middle-class housing developments in the middle of the drainage. When the deluge hit the mountains, the dam was breached by a twelve-foot wall of water that buried an area four to five blocks across and three miles long before pouring into the bay between the new slab of the Hotel El Presidente and the ramshackle Abaroa boatyard. Because so many recent arrivals from Oaxaca and states to the north had not so much as registered their presence, many of the victims were impossible to identify and one could only guess at their numbers. It is believed that more than three thousand people were lost, many of them buried in common graves that stretch in five surreal parallel planters in La Paz's civil cemetery, and many more became part of the La Paz substratum. I poked around La Paz during the winter of 1977 and realized roads were clogged with grit and blockaded, but I didn't appreciate the scope of the disaster until I flew out of La Paz and looked down at the massive double exposure, an alluvial ghost over the city's grid.

Who were all these strangers drawn, sometimes fatefully, to La Paz? The common answer was that they were midlevel professionals: engineers, doctors, professors, teachers, many of them escaping the pollution, congestion and crime of mainland Mexican cities. La Paz received a traumatized infusion of such people after the Mexico City earthquake of 1985. Antonio Rosales, himself a teacher, pointed out that somebody had to provide housing and services for incoming professionals and that anyone in Mexico who found work tended to import the rest of the family. According to Lorella Castorena, a sociologist at the University of La Paz, a great number of Oaxacans, some of them indigenous people speaking Zapotec and Mixtec languages, migrated to La Paz after attempting life in the States, finding in La Paz ample job opportunities and a more open life than in their crowded homeland. La Paz also had one of the lowest out-migration rates in Mexico; people who moved in tended to stay. All of this had doubled the population every decade since 1950.

Still, how could 150,000 people on a desert shore keep themselves decently clothed, housed and fed? The answers came pouring in. Besides the obvious—bureaucracy, overfishing, flagging tourism—every bit of merchandise that reached the small towns and ranches from the outside world passed through the port of La Paz. Ranchers hit town at regular intervals to shop and raise hell away from family. Although no longer a free port, La Paz was still a galaxy of successful tiny businesses. One Korean owned four identical import shops because small operations were taxed far less than large ones. One office manager, when asked where she bought her shirt, said, "At Target, in the United States," but her secretary replied, "It was made in La Paz, in my brother's maquiladora." Remote from American markets, La Paz had five maquiladoras by 1994, all making clothes, and electronics sweatshops were said to be on the way.

Did I know, furthermore, about the Escuela Normal, the vast teachers' college that dispersed instructors throughout Northern Mexico? Had I noticed the chile-packing plant five blocks from where I lived? And had I seen how the road beyond the *cantera* quarry passed through one repair operation after another? One Sunday, in fact, returning from an excursion, I had engine trouble and was passed from one ranch to another trying to solve the problem. These ranches, I noted, didn't tend cows or chickens; they tended refrigerators, washers, driers, cars, and were *machine* ranches. La Paz, capital of a frontier, had more cars per capita than any other Mexican city, and there was gainful employment in giving machines their last rites.

As with everywhere else on the globe, there was also the hidden economy of drugs. La Paz did not seem a center of narcotraffic, either for production or epidemic use, but parents worried about children, and some of the state-financed, low-cost outlying developments, or *colonias*, were menaced by drug-inspired gangs of teenagers. Newspapers reported major drug busts at Pichilingue, the port eighteen kilometers outside La Paz that received cargo ships and ferries from the mainland; quantities too large for local consumption were hauled north on the highway toward Tijuana and the United States. Airstrips on ranches outside La Paz were increasingly used as transfer points for drugs en route from Colombia to the United States, turning the peninsula into what Paceños were calling a "trampoline." A cartoonist for one of the La Paz dailies, asked if any subjects were off-limits, replied that there were only two: the military—possessed of humor in no known country—and drug dealers. Whether the humorlessness of drug dealers coincided with grimness in uniform was not a subject of public speculation.

All of these pursuits, and many more, might be enough to propel a city without industry farther into the cactus, and the government itself financed new housing projects. But the growing inventory made La Paz less credible than two explanations of how money itself was treated. Alejandrina Hernández, a woman from Mexicali who knew she had to establish her veterinary practice in La Paz as soon as she saw it, said that nobody in La Paz saved and that the same money circulated over and over. As soon as a sum came in, it was spent on new curtains or a *cantera* wall. And according to Rubén Sandoval, what fueled La Paz wasn't money but the promise of money. It was bank loans, credit cards, twenty years of installments, a mirage of payments projected into the future. Debt, perhaps, was the massless, elusive dark matter that sustained La Paz.

The majority of those inflating La Paz might be mainland Mexicans looking for a fresh start, but sprinkled among them were foreigners looking to recast their lives. Well-positioned to track the non-nationals were Americans Mac and Mary Shroyer, who had arrived as adventurers in a small sailboat. They had been struck that La Paz had no predatory tourism, no wrenching difference between the rich and the nonrich, and they decided that they had to make their living chartering a boat from La Paz, "for whoever wanted to go somewhere." They gave up jobs as California schoolteachers and moved to La Paz with two small children in 1967. Chartering led to boatbuilding and finally to the establishment of what became La Paz's first marina. To a non-yachtie, any marina looks like a floating trailer park, and Mac admits that by assembling primarily Americans and Canadians into a tight quad, the marina was precisely the opposite of what happens on land. In most other Mexican cities with a gringo population the English speakers gather in compounds and enclaves, but in La Paz they are dispersed as randomly as bakers and dentists.

"To begin with," says Mary, "La Paz eliminates those who come just for the weather. Unlike Cabo San Lucas, it's open to north winds in winter that make it too cold for sunbathing, and it doesn't have the cape's cool winds from the Pacific to temper the summers. It is a climate of extremes and lacks the broad white beaches that tourists love. A few have actually arrived at the marina, decided they didn't like boats, and moved onto the land, but they're the kind of American with something to do. Outside the marina, Americans in La Paz don't gather in groups."

As an American living in La Paz I didn't try to expand my own American friendships—that being almost the only social option at the other end of my life—but I vaguely wondered whether there wasn't some interesting American network I was missing. One night I had a clearer look than I expected. An American I did know hoped to start a branch of "the salon movement," an attempt by that monthly compilation from alternative magazines, *The Utne Reader*, to regenerate the lost art of conversation. *Salonniers* were to discuss some topic that had been pondered upon, and ours was to be "community" in general and "the American community in La Paz" in specific. From various standpoints the fifteen assembled testified that Americans in La Paz, as a community, did not exist. Minor socializing and sporadic contact fell well short of any sense of belonging to a group. Perhaps prodded by the evening's format, a few expressed pious sentiments about the need to "pull together more," but the truth about Americans in La Paz was better expressed by the fact that the salon itself never reconvened.

According to Mac Shroyer, "Even as a place to vacation, La Paz appeals basically to the Mexican tourist. The free port is over, but there is still a tradition of coming to shop and working in a little beach time. Northerners who want to party and shout their orders in English may find that the service people, while friendly, aren't really geared to that. La Paz may be too Mexican for them." The 1992 statistics bear him out: in La Paz, Mexican tourists outnumbered foreigners more than three to one, while on the well-packaged cape, foreigners outnumbered Mexicans more than five to one.

Strewn through La Paz, unfussed-over as Americans, were French, Germans, Brazilians, Argentines, as well as Chinese and Japanese, some of whose ancestors arrived in the last century to mine, farm or fish. There was also a Mexican old guard—what might be called Before the Ferry—of families that considered themselves the *real* Paceños. Residents not born in La Paz, who constituted, with their progeny, 70 percent of the population by the early nineties, generally found themselves excluded by the old families, even though they were Mexicans themselves. Their sheer numbers reduced the old clans to exclusive cliques. Such social nuances only surfaced gradually, for they were masked by a broader La Paz style.

It is risky to generalize about any society, particularly one that values individuality, but from observation, and from Paceños' own self-definition, a profile emerges. Paceños avoid the instant, back-slapping camaraderie of the mainland, regarding it as shallow. They practice frank eye contact that includes a quick sizing up of strangers. Instead of saying good morning, a shopkeeper may simply look up to ask, visually, what a customer wants—not intending discourtesy but directness. Paceños sometimes compare themselves to the cacti that surround them, standing in the open, visible in full clarity, and barbed. A Salvadoran who settled in La Paz despite finding greater human warmth elsewhere in Mexico invokes a parable from Erich Fromm about that mammalian cactus, the porcupine. In winter the porcupines huddled together for warmth and stabbed each other, but when they went their separate ways, they began to freeze. Like Fromm's porcupines, Paceños found their level of comfort in gathering just close enough not to draw blood. Such literal prickliness might imply coldness, even xenophobia, but the apparent rigidity is contradicted by the two qualities most prized by Paceños: improvisation and tolerance.

Before the side streets were paved in 1994, improvisation was most brazenly demonstrated by the river runners behind the wheel. Improvisation also shaped La Paz's basic building block as individual co-op members fractured the rock of their preferred tint into the size of their choice and set their own price. For Republica Welding and Used Parts, improvisation was expressed in a *cantera* wall whose undulating top was filled with an ingenious filigree of gears, valve springs, catalytic converters, mufflers, cooling fans, gas caps, exhaust manifolds and tailpipes, not to mention a gleaming hubcap gate and a side door from a Buick sedan. Within these streets and walls was freedom for Alejandrina, the veterinarian, to walk to the waterfront every day and do exercises facing the mangroves of the still wild sand spit of El Mogote, less than a kilometer across the water. To Iberê Gewehr, another Brazilian pianist who migrated to La Paz, to live in Mexico City would be like smoking three compulsory packs of cigarettes a day, whereas by living in clean-aired La Paz he could smoke his three packs a day voluntarily. For Maria Eugenia Ortega, from conservative Puebla, La Paz offered license to build a five-sided guest house next to her palm-thatch A-frame. If the neighbors didn't like it, they could raise the *cantera* wall of their choice. "La Paz," says a biologist from the mainland, "is an exile for volunteers."

La Paz's improvisation was founded on tolerance. Elma Vidaurri noted that Paceños with money to travel were more likely to go to Europe than to mainland Mexico or the United States, leavening the town with ideas they brought back. Rubén Sandoval ascribed La Paz's openness to its having been a port touched by the world. A good example, said Rubén, was the Paceño attitude toward homosexuality. Among the traditional families there was complete acceptance of human variety, related by blood or not; if someone yelled obscenities from a car at a presumed gay, that person was likely to be a newcomer uncivilized by La Paz. As in the rest of Mexico, La Paz social life centered on the family. And with total acceptance for each member, regardless of temperament, there could be no intolerance, for the extended family encompassed the globe.

This individualism, so satisfying to the Paceño, may be invisible to the visitor, for the building lots of La Paz, skinny and deep, are often blocked by walls flush with the sidewalk. The pedestrian will catch occasional glimpses through an open door, all the way through a room of stiff-backed furniture to the deep greens of a garden in back, a vignette so brief that it can only be savored, fadingly, in the afterimage. Each vista is another turn of the kaleidoscope, and only an invitation will reveal the full banality or the imaginative depths within. A facade of turquoise dolphins and sea horses opens on the winter quarters of a Dutch family that migrates annually across a shaded riverstone courtyard to their Japanese-style summer house in back. A blue door gives way to the bright studio of an artist from central Mexico, beyond which his family lives in a cool recess of dark paintings. Bland driveway doors open into a deep courtyard with an aviary of tropical birds and an antique car collection, behind which a leading lawyer shares his office with two hundred ballcaps and a wall of kitsch figurines. And I finally gained entry through a snarl of utility meters into a warren of white grillework like petrified lace. The owner, a sixty-three-year-old Paceño, had the outer layers of his face peeled in his late twenties, had not voluntarily ventured into daylight since, and looked a pale forty-eight. While we discussed Strauss operas, his brother reclined in a summery off-the-shoulder dress in the next room and shot us an occasional sultry glance while watching the soaps.

On the rare occasions when visitors ask me to show them the real La Paz, I let them walk the plaza and the waterfront on their own, then drive them up an unpaved street to a dull bungalow of wood and *cantera*. A tug on a spark plug, ringing an iron casing, summons an assistant, who opens the screen door and seats us in what looks like a chem lab pitched in a Bedouin's tent. Shelves of flasks, beakers and vials stretch past a painted curtain of harem scenes. Soft Arab music floats from a speaker. The visitors' eyes pan a collection of international beer cans and wine bottles, abalone shell constructions, a clock without hands, three antique cash registers, bouquets of peacock feathers, and a portrait of the owner in full military regalia, staring at you with a ferocity that may not be serious.

With apologies for keeping you waiting, Salvador García Pineda enters peering through his bottle-glass specs, stripped to the waist if it is hot, toweling his thick black hair: a professor's head on a torso from a proletarian mural. Welcome! Sit down! My guests and I gather at a table made from a tree felled in a hurricane while Salvador pours us, in plastic cups, sips of the date, kumquat and damiana liqueurs he has made on the premises, or his dry red wine. He might set out a plate of salted shark meat to refresh the palate.

Salvador, the phenomenon I have chosen to represent La Paz to my friends, is by local standards a newcomer. Born in Morelia, he worked in a chemical company, a leather company, a glass factory, the Moctezuma brewery and the Sauza and Cuervo tequila distilleries. He opened a string of boutiques featuring rabbit-fur fashions, then organized a tortilla home-delivery service. Along the way he became a scholar of pigments, solvents, chemicals, fuels and fermentation. Bored with mainland Mexico, he arrived on the ferry in 1980 bearing a load of straw hats to sell on the beach. Paceños, it turned out, already had their hats, and he took a job as a schoolteacher.

A connoisseur, Salvador rebelled at the cost of French and German wines on a peninsula where padres had introduced the grape four centuries back. He bought grapes in the small town of Comondú, to the north, and to make his wine regional he added an extract of damiana, an herb that grows in the arid regions of Mexico. Friends, recognizing how the wine's afterglow feathered the back of their mouths, refused to keep accepting gifts and insisted he go professional. A year after his arrival, Salvador had created a wine for La Paz. Immersed in *One Thousand and One Nights* at the time, and impressed that the hero appreciated wine as well as women, Salvador named his product *El Jeque,* The Sheik.

Once my friends have been wined and have sampled Salvador's exotic liqueurs, all of them distilled from native plants and species introduced by the padres, a tour of the premises begins. The room behind the *cantera* is a sanctum of hoses, cement sinks, thermometers, funnels, Bunsen burners, and plastic buckets that open to a reek of fermenting kumquats. Across a bedroom that contains little more than the sheik's unmade bed and a sign that says "Safe Sex" is a storeroom with the forty or so rolled canvases of sheik scenes that Salvador has commissioned from local artists. A door opens on Salvador's next world, his backyard zoo.

In a cage to the right, one of four peacocks expands its tail full of eyes. "There is only room for one male to display at a time, but they've got it synchronized," says Salvador, fluttering his eyebrows significantly and emitting a soprano giggle. He opens the door to a wire hut. "These pigeons like their home so much that I let them come and go." A pair of penned geese function as watchdogs. Climbing the walls of the yard are dusty pyramids of green and amber bottles, brought by local children and waiting to be sterilized for Salvador's brews. And dominating the yard is a cottage with reed walls and a palm-thatch roof. In its pungent shadow one makes out several dozen suspended wooden cages with metal trap doors on top. It is a hanging garden of rabbits. Salvador lifts them out one by one, rabbits auburn, mottled, chocolate, thick-haired, glacially white with pink eyes. Handing one to a visitor who fondles or recoils, he explains, "I give them to children so they will learn to love and care for animals. Also," he adds in a peal of giggles, "when I get hungry I eat them."

Returning to the hurricane-felled table, my friends are usually in a buying mood, particularly for bottles of El Jeque. The label, made of palm bark stamped with the product's name, allows space for a dedication that Salvador works in careful calligraphy. Then he embellishes the bottle's neck with the date in gold script. A smaller piece of bark covers the cork, and a sliver of ribbon holds a furled paper with remarks about the wine. "Notice how I've folded the cap to look like a turban," says Salvador, fluttering his eyebrows, "and angled the paper like a sheik's rifle." Suddenly it becomes clear that, in the dismembered fashion of a Picasso, a bottle of El Jeque is meant to *be* the sheik.

Salvador is, of course, like no one else on earth, and old-guard Paceños would resent the presentation of an After-the-Ferry nut as their representative citizen. But Salvador embodies, almost to the point of parody, the Paceño virtues of improvisation, individuality and indifference to public opinion. When La Paz was left several months without toothpaste because of a distribution snag, Salvador made a gumbo of five wild plants with antiseptic qualities that was, while it lasted, a regional *toothpaste*. That is Paceño.

"*La Paz,*" goes the lyric of the best-known song about the town, "*puerto de ilusión.*" Port of illusion, in Spanish, means port of dreams as well as port of deception. The visitor lost in the illogic of unrelated habitations, scrambled businesses and concealing walls might decide that the disorder of La Paz finally runs together into blandness, while the person who has entered that disorder might stare in fascination at a drab door, knowing the depths of flavor it can decant. Rubén Sandoval, with the double perspective of the born Paceño who frequented philosophical circles of the Sorbonne, applies Diderot's speculations on the influence of landscape on behavior to La Paz. Of course the Paceño is freer, less materially bound. Mountains are enormous and the sea is infinite. Between two immensities, what is left but to invent the small phenomenon that is you?

CURSE OF THE ADORERS

6

One winter I moved into a particularly vibrant and chaotic neighborhood, renting the A-frame with palm-thatch extensions before it was supplemented with the one-room, five-sided guest house. That architectural hybrid perfectly reflected an outlying barrio of open fields, housing for phosphate miners, an acupuncture clinic, walled-in private houses, a gutted bus, a storage yard for phone cables, and a collapsing kiln tended by an owl. My landlady, Maria Eugenia, a compressed, energetic woman from Puebla who was always incubating five plans at once, told me that the original A was no more than inwardly leaning pieces of sheet metal that shaded a rabbit hutch when she bought the property. She converted it to living quarters, installed a loft, added a thatch to shade the front and projected another thatch in back over a kitchen-and-bath addition. Doing construction herself gave her such unexpected clarity that at the end of each day she wrote out her thoughts—the present and its projections—most of which still seemed valid several years later. "Did you know that Jung built a house and experienced the same kind of focus?" she asked. "When I read that I recognized it, because I too felt very rooted in myself."

Maria Eugenia had moved with her five-year-old daughter into a trailer in the front yard, renting the A-frame to help an older daughter, now eighteen, through school in Switzerland. Calls from Geneva and Berlin, Milan and Hong Kong converged on her tiny quarters. When I said that I felt bad about living in the larger house while she lived in the trailer, she said, "Don't. I actually prefer living in a space so small there's no room for mistakes. Stay in the A-frame or I'll rent it to someone else."

With bookshelves over the john and fishnet thrown rakishly over the palm thatch to keep it from blowing off, the A-frame reflected Maria Eugenia's improvisational nature. Eight steep steps led to a loft with bed, above which, at the apex of the A, a child's cot perched like a crow's nest. Here, propped on pillows to counter the inward-leaning walls, in a stew of binoculars, legal pads, pencils, coffee cup and bird book—seeing but unseen behind a triangle of tinted window—I read, wrote and spied on a half-secret world in back.

Beyond a small field, once plowed and now running to seed, spread a panorama of beehives, scattered work buildings, a chicken coop, a weather station, a palm-thatch pigpen, and a string of goats that were herded from one end of the spread to the other. Commanding the center was the dormitory complex of El Convento de las Adoratrices—the Convent of the Adorers—behind which rose the cupola and cross of the convent's only public building, a chapel that fronted a street on the far side. Lark sparrows enlivened the field, a lone cattle egret befriended the pigsty, and the first time I glimpsed scarlet I thought it was a cardinal. Emerging from the trees surrounding the convent door, it was a nun. A black wimple spilled down her back, a white robe swept her ankles, and a brilliant red scapular glittered from shoulders to sandals, fore and aft. The splendor of this tricolored plumage made spying on the nunnery less like voyeurism, more like birdwatching.

Within a few days I knew the outdoor routine. Every morning, just after dawn, a stout man in a T-shirt that said "Bass Lake" ambled through the back entrance, sometimes with his teenage son. Greeting him on their way to the goat pen were two or three elderly nuns whose tenderness seemed almost allegorical as they bent to nursling goats that tugged ravenously at the nipples of baby bottles of milk. Punctually at seven, a young nun in a pale blue uniform emerged from the convent with what looked from a distance like musical staff paper and took readings from the weather station. Another young nun in blue gathered eggs from the coop. Bass Lake, helped by his son and a few stray nuns, herded the goats across the open driveway from the pen to the fenced field.

Already I had favorite goats: the black one twice as large as the others and the strange brown and white one that looked like a fawn emerging from a sheep. As the day progressed, younger nuns in blue uniforms hung washing. Bass Lake tended bees, directed irrigation water here and there by rearranging dirt with a spade, repaired fences. Sometime midmorning the oldest nun would stroll out with a walking stick, coming to a full stop to confer with the sister who walked with her—not for secrecy, I surmised, but because she was deaf. The nuns never left the premises in less than full regalia, whether driving their blue camper, a curry-colored station wagon or a sporty red coupe. A drivers' education car showed up late afternoon, and I imagined the instructor telling the assembled, in a turn that would work as well in Spanish,

"The foundation is good driving habits, so I want you to begin by trimming your right sleeves. . . ." Two clotheslines threaded the palms, with black, white and red habit parts blowing aside to reveal white nightgowns and long white underwear on the line behind.

One Saturday morning I saw a half dozen neighbors gathered around a reddish object suspended from a beam in front of the convent. The binoculars revealed it to be a goat, tied by its back hooves and skinned. Bass Lake stood chatting with a coffee cup in one hand and a machete in the other. Now and then he handed the coffee cup to his son, hacked off some goat and tossed it into a turquoise plastic bin. When the neighbors left, Bass Lake dismantled the goat in earnest, handing the head to the boy, who took it like the ace of hearts to the convent door—thence, I liked to imagine, to a satanic soup, or perhaps the indoor dogs.

A nun emerged and spoke to father and son. They repaired to the pen for another goat, which they dragged toward the beam with a rope as it bawled and dug in its heels. Having sometimes thrived on goat until my floss ran out, I forced myself to follow a scene the vegetarian reader is advised to skip. The men wound the rope around the goat's torso and back legs, pulled tight, and suspended the animal upside down from the beam. It continued to thrash and attempt to lift its spine, even after the man slit its throat. The man rapped the goat on all sides with a stick, to speed the draining of the blood or to free the hide of dust. When they were halfway through the skinning, a nun emerged with a plate of cookies under a plastic wrap, which she handed to the boy. He carried the cookies to his house, beyond my field of vision, while the man finished the skinning and tossed the hide in a wheelbarrow— which, I now saw, also held the hide of the first goat. The boy returned for a lesson in goat carving. Two nuns emerged with the indoor dogs, a pair of small spaniels, on leads. The man tossed them scraps. Nuns, dogs and men all left, and again I wrongly assumed the scene was over, for Bass Lake returned with yet another goat—a martyrdom I skipped except to note that it was the morning's last.

When I relayed this scene to Maria Eugenia, she reported that the neighborhood ran with speculation that the nuns were selling eggs, honey and goat meat at the market without a permit. Competitors at the market, it was said, didn't complain "because they are afraid the devil will come after them." A few years back neighbors did protest about the pigs because of the smell and the city took them away, but the nuns kept a few piglets and bred them back.

Interested in seeing these urban ranchers up close, when the bells rang for mass the day after the goat slaughter, I slipped into the chapel that was their one public building. The rectangle of a room floated in robin's egg blue, and light from clerestories mixed with neon tubing to create a bright aquarium. A large bas-relief shell in deeper blues behind the altar framed a gilded globe, with the Americas facing forward. Two guitarists noodled random chords as worshipers straggled in. Circulating through the aquarium were eight nuns, their scarlet dulled by the neon, and what I had taken to be a large key with looping chain on the flank of one of the nuns—perhaps the church key itself—proved to be a rosary with cross. A priest in a green tunic convened the ceremony by saying that we would pray for the same recently departed that we did last week—and I realized that church regulations required that this exclusively female religious domain import a male to conduct its most important rites. Mass itself was relieved by two lively songs for which the congregation stood and sang to guitar accompaniment, one a *huapango* beat, the other a *paso doble*. Below the altar stood a small crucifix whose Christ hung so low from the crosspiece that the Y of his arms suggested a suspended goat.

The pantomime of the convent might suggest that the neighborhood was quiet, and indeed it was calmer than the older, denser parts of La Paz. Much reduced were radios blaring ranchera music, revving motors, repair shops that worked at all hours. Several mornings a week a woman and a man took turns at a microphone yelling *Un! Dos! Un! Dos! Uno! Uno! Un! Dos!* to a school gym class, sometimes followed by band practice, at a school several blocks away. Cars in first gear, with speakers so loud that voices were nearly unintelligible, cruised the streets raving of discounts or all-star shows or proclaiming, "Five people hover agonizingly between life and death after hitting a cow last night at kilometer 34—read about it in *El Madrugador* [The Early Riser], your newspaper," its exhaust distributing a blue cloud like a pall of sleaze. Next door lived a blacksmith who worked amid showering sparks in his backyard, and his hammer on iron rang unpredictably through the A-frame. But none of these distractions had the thought-obliterating persistence of the convent's three outdoor dogs. The nuns' dorm was clouded in trees, but through the binoculars I could make out a shepherd mix and two lesser hounds pacing a mysterious shelf just below the second story. Barking pealed from the convent as if from a bandshell.

Sounds withstood by day become intolerable at night, and the usual prescription for insomnia—plugs and pills—was no match for the convent. Maria Eugenia, equally incensed, decided to put a stop to all noise after bedtime. She persuaded the blacksmith to take in for the night his schnauzer with a yap like high-pitched vomiting. Enraged at drag racing on the highway several blocks off, she phoned the police that if they didn't stop it, she was going to the waterfront to commit an act she couldn't predict. Within half an hour the combustion ceased. A week later, ranchera music from distant public speakers two-stepped all night, spinning and spinning the same few chords like a hamster on a treadmill. Maria Eugenia called to complain. Nothing happened. Two hours later she called back. The police reported that they were getting an awful lot of calls from one woman. Next morning Maria Eugenia called talk radio to complain on the air of the noise *and* the uncooperative police. "I would like," she told me, "to proclaim my property a private anarchy." I admired the sentiment, but that seemed to me already the status of every lot in La Paz.

I left town for two weeks, didn't think once of noise in the barrio, and returned to find that Maria Eugenia had had a rough time: the phone and water had both been accidentally cut off, she had gotten sick, and as she lay with a rebellious stomach, the convent dogs had raved nonstop. She confronted Bass Lake and demanded that the dogs be taken off the roof that broadcast their barking. "You will have to take that up with the Mother Superior," he said, "and the Mother Superior is away."

For Maria Eugenia, it was war. Neighbors knew, she said, that Bass Lake had put out laced meat without warning local dog owners, alleging that stray dogs were attacking the convent's chickens and goats. Dog poisoning, it must be said, is not considered as heinous in Mexico as it is in the United States. Once a year the city of La Paz warned all residents to keep their pets inside, then picked up all strays and dispatched them. La Paz was free from rabies, but from feces to roving packs, the dogs created hazards. "We love animals," Alejandrina the veterinarian told me, "but we don't carry on about them like you Americans. They *are* replaceable." I realized their ubiquity when I went to throw something in a trash barrel at the local supermarket, shrank from a stirring inside, then approached to find an entire submerged dog licking a meat tray. But replaceable or not, the acupuncturist and the blacksmith had both lost dogs to the convent, and both were livid. Did the nuns actually *know* what their employee was doing? I asked Maria Eugenia. Maybe, maybe not, she said, but how could the convent, as an entity, eliminate other people's dogs and not take responsibility for its own? She plotted a letter to the police, with a copy to the convent, detailing the barking, the dog poisoning, and throwing in, as an attention-getter, the resurrection of the illegal pigs. All she needed, she said, was a night to sleep on it.

It was a sleep she didn't get, for during the night her trailer was invaded by bees from the convent hives. Fearing they might be killer bees, she grabbed her daughter and fled to her camper truck, there to be serenaded by the yowlers on the roof. At dawn she ventured into the trailer and found more than a hundred bees that had entered through a vent in the hot water heater. "*Es la maldición de las Adoratrices*," she cracked. It's the curse of the Adorers.

Because her word processor was broken, Maria Eugenia took her handwritten letter to a public secretary to type, then brought it to me to cosign. Addressed to the police department, the text read, "It is important that you know that the Colonia Puesta del Sol has been bothered by noise problems such as high-volume radios during hours of rest, as well as dogs on roofs. We ask your support and assistance in ensuring the peace and quiet of this barrio." Copies were specifically directed to the acupuncturist, the trailer park out on the highway, and the convent, with others for general distribution. I learned for the first time that our neighborhood had a name—roughly Sunset Suburb—but was disappointed, as if by a fizzled plot, that the text was so mild. "What about poisoned dogs and illegal pigs?" I asked. "What about confronting the Mother Superior with what her employee is doing?"

"That's for later. We begin with this, and if it doesn't get results, we escalate."

Maria Eugenia spent the day taking the letter around Colonia Puesta del Sol. Her greatest success was at the trailer park, whose owner said he received nearly daily complaints from customers, most of them gringos, about barking dogs. He even offered her poison, which she declined. Her greatest defeat came from the acupuncturist, who despite the loss of his previous dog replied that only the weak complain about barking.

"I train my dog at four in the morning," he stated, "and when he gets excited, he barks."

"You have no business making a racket at four in the morning," said Maria Eugenia.

"That's when reasonable people get up," he said.

"Fine," she snapped, "and I'm going to train my lion in front of your clinic."

Next she tried one of the walled-in houses, which turned out to belong to no less than the secretary of tourism, a significant figure in the La Paz power structure. The secretary's wife was furious at the barking and eagerly signed the letter. When Maria Eugenia reported her encounter with the acupuncturist, the woman laughed. "I know all about it. He used to train his dog in front of our house before dawn. Our dog is meaner than his, and one morning we let him out. The acupuncturist hasn't been back."

The woman in the adjacent walled-in home was also sympathetic, and by the end of the day Maria Eugenia felt she had some neighborhood supporters. She had saved the convent for last and ran out of time. While she was away, the fumigator had sprayed the trailer and left a note saying that the invaders were pure honeybees, with no African strain. "Come in and see this," said Maria Eugenia. The trailer's back seat, strewn with shriveled bees, looked like a rack of drying raisins.

After Maria Eugenia left for the convent the next morning, there was a knock on my door. I opened it to confront two nuns. Their red and white robes, the black hair in front of their black wimples, their radiant, tea-colored faces were purely dazzling. Were they responding to our noise complaint already? "We're worried about the bees," said one. "We knocked on the trailer yesterday, several times, but nobody answered, and nobody is there now. Did the fumigator come? Did more bees show up? How many bees were there?"

Telling them that the owner of the trailer was, ironically, at the convent right now, I gave what information I had, feeling that two rare quetzals had come to my door. When we finished discussing bees, I said, "By the way, we've been somewhat bothered by the barking dogs on your roof. Would you be willing to take them in at night?"

"We'll be happy to pass that on to the Mother Superior," said the nun who spoke.

As they prepared to leave, I blurted, "Incidentally, I'm a writer and I'm writing about things in Baja California. Would it be possible to visit the convent sometime?"

"Just ring the doorbell," said the nun, smiling, "and the Mother Superior will be glad to talk to you."

I was startled that after Maria Eugenia's mild letter, nocturnal dogs disappeared from the convent roof. I decided to let time pass, to see if the quiet could be trusted, before I rang the convent bell. There was, in any case, much else going on in the Colonia Puesta del Sol. This was an area where La Paz was attempting to cope with its exploding population. In the open field by the kiln, housing for union members was going up in tall, cramped buildings, the owl had decamped, and an American woman I once got a ride to town with remarked, "My, my, La Paz is building the South Bronx." When it rained, the water on the road by the new housing was too deep even for my jeep—though I suspected it had been swelled by a ruptured water main—and the other route involved fording a lagoon by the housing for phosphate miners. Once in a while, city trucks dumped loose sand into the sinkholes, but with nothing to solidify the grains, the sand first impeded traction, then spun out to heighten the ridges, thereby deepening the valleys. Even the secretary of tourism had rough going to his house.

More immediately, the blacksmith had started building a wall of cinder block between his yard and Maria Eugenia's and had gotten as far as her trailer, quitting just short of the A-frame. On the other side, in a vacant lot that included the gutted bus and some large tamarisk trees by the road, a truckful of young men showed up one morning and started another cinder-block wall. In three days they extended it from the street to the A-frame, where they also quit, leaving my view intact and Maria Eugenia's trailer boxed in.

"Who owns the new wall?" I asked Maria Eugenia.

"I don't know," she said. "That's the difference between here and the States. There are no regulations, no limits on what you can do. If your neighbor is absentee, you don't even know who it is unless you plow through the archives at city hall."

"But what's the point of building a wall and stopping?" I asked.

"Another difference. Americans wait until they can finance the whole thing, then they do it all at once. Mexicans start when they have enough money to start, and if they don't get more money, or they get interested in something else, the unfinished thing just sits there, or crumbles."

At last the owner of the vacant lot showed up, saying something vague about raising a small apartment building in back, near the gutted bus. "I don't understand why everybody is putting up these walls," said Maria Eugenia. "They give me claustrophobia."

"I'm just a dentist, lady, not a psychiatrist," he shot back, making her laugh in spite of herself.

I too was prey to claustrophobia, and even though I usually left the property during the day, around sunset I grabbed my binoculars and headed on foot toward the bay, either through the South Bronx or past the secretary of tourism's house. Once across the highway I entered the neighborhood where I had lived twenty years before. This was the no-man's-land where I had accompanied a woodgatherer who had hacked at the base of mesquites so that they died on their feet, thereby "cleaning the desert." Now there was no undergrowth left at all. Only the largest trees remained, their extremities shorn, their trunks and crowns still managing a froth of green. Late afternoon, men in pickup trucks pulled up to these amputees with ice chests of Tecate, a beer like fermented dust, and knocked back a few cold ones the way Americans stop at a bar after work. Even though the animated talk over boom boxes belting ranchera music no doubt obliterated much sense of where they were, there was something wistful about the way the men clung to what little vegetation had been spared.

Through the mesquite parties I threaded my way, listening for anything I could pick up over the speakers. What sailed through clearest was the profanity, along with the odd phrase about jobs or prices or sports, but once, when I lingered by some men with boots and high-crowned hats and guts over their jeans, the talk was of wholesale contracts, markups and legal fees, and I realized that these were entrepreneurs, not the manual laborers I imagined. Halfway through this limbo the dismembered trees gave way to a baseball diamond outlined in old tires, where men often brought their young and teenage sons. Near home plate was a flat rock where a father and son smashed aluminum cans with a smaller rock. Overcoming my inhibitions about bringing trash to what was left of the desert, anonymously and in the morning I left bags of my own empties by the flat rock.

The goal of these walks—to see shorebirds—was anticlimactic on this coast where schools, expensive homes and a biological institute alternated with strips of beach, thick mangroves and pickups of adolescents whose rites also necessitated cranked-up speakers, but typically I would see one blue heron, two night herons, one white egret, one snowy egret, pelicans, kingfishers and a pair of Caspian terns. Wandering back to the highway, I tried to retain perspective. Ultimately this desert was being further cleaned for urban infill; better the improvised park of today than the cramped housing of tomorrow.

Accustomed by now to the convent, tormented less by its dogs, I wrote in the A-frame crow's nest, seldom looking out unless motion caught my eye. I did note more Saturday-morning goat slaughters and saw, with a pang, that the hide of the goat that was half sheep, half fawn was tossed unceremoniously into the wheelbarrow with the rest. And one Saturday afternoon I saw a very different object suspended from the beam: the engine of the little red coupe, raised by block and tackle and being worked on by a pair of mechanics. They were drinking, the glasses revealed, not fermented dust but the same brand of beer that I was. The sight was inviting, and the following day I rounded the domain to the front door, rang the bell and explained I would like to accept an offer to interview the Mother Superior. A fortyish sister said that I was welcome to return the next day at noon. When I left for my appointment, notebook in hand, Maria Eugenia called from the trailer, "Have fun interviewing the deaf one."

The doorbell was answered by the same woman, who introduced herself as Sister Cilia. She invited me to sit down and told me that she, not the Mother Superior, would answer questions. Without waiting for one, she plunged in. "We all have our duties. We sell honey to people who come to the door. We take weather statistics every morning at seven and phone them to a government agency. We make habits for other orders as well as our own, make wedding dresses to specification, and dresses for *quinceañeras*—coming-of-age celebrations for girls who turn fifteen. We have a bakery and make cookies, the one thing we distribute ourselves. We also bake the hosts for all the churches of Baja California Sur. And my job is to tend the door. Some days I talk all day, other days I just sit here in silence." This small antechamber, with its white walls, its well-upholstered, anonymous armchairs and table with a few magazines, suggested the waiting room of an expensive, unconsulted doctor.

"Isn't tending the animals another duty?" I asked

"We do have a string of goats, so we don't buy our meat, but they are tended by a man who is our only paid employee."

"And you also sell goat meat?"

"No," she smiled, "just the things I mentioned."

Skipping my question about the pigs, I asked her to describe a typical day.

"The first bell is at five," she said, mentioning a silvery ring—a discreet sound with which one might summon a maid—that woke me if I was sleeping lightly. "I know the rhythm," I said. "It goes ding-duh-ding, ding-duh-ding."

"Each sister has her own rhythm," she smiled. "There is another bell twenty minutes later"—one that often got me when the first one didn't—"calling us to the first service. Then we have breakfast while one of the sisters reads prayers. Then mass, then each of us goes to her duties. During lunch someone reads religious literature, commentary or the life of a saint, and that person doesn't eat. There are various silences throughout the day, different silences, with different meanings at different hours. We have an hour off in the afternoon, when we can nap or do what we like, and another hour of recreation when we can play games."

"What kind of games?"

"Table games," she said, and I couldn't get her to be more specific. "At dinner there is no religious reading and we can chat casually. Then there is another *servicio divino*, a divine service, in the chapel." Every time she used that expression, which was often, for a split second I heard *servicio de vino*, or wine service.

"We go to bed at nine, but we can stay up later to work on personal projects if we like. We're supposed to be quiet, but sometimes we make noise by mistake," she giggled, while I wondered how anyone would notice over the barking.

"I haven't been aware of the Adorers in the United States," I said. "What is the origin of the order?"

Sister Cilia explained that there were few Adorer convents in the States, so it wasn't surprising I hadn't heard of it. There were a few others in Canada, Chile, Spain, and the founding country of Italy, but the country they flourished in was Mexico, with a thousand nuns in fifty convents. The Perpetual Adorers of the Sacred Sacrament was founded in Rome, in 1807. Maria Magdalena of the Incarnation, a novitiate sweeping the kitchen of another order, had a vision through the wall and into the chapel, where the Virgin, surrounded by flying angels, instructed her to found a special new order dedicated to perpetual prayer. Prayer should be sustained around the clock, with sisters taking turns and prayer itself never stopping. Nuns pray for an hour at a time, and eighteen nuns are considered the minimum feasible number to sustain unceasing prayer. The La Paz convent was built for the classic eighteen but currently numbered only twelve, and they had secured a dispensation from Rome relieving them from praying at night. Nuns in La Paz prayed from dawn to dusk, skipping whatever activity—including meals— they would otherwise be doing at the time.

Convents of Adorers were dying in Italy and blossoming in Mexico, Sister Cilia thought, because Mexican convents were more open, less penitential. "There are convents in Italy built for seventy nuns, with only six old ones left. The sisters in Italy communicate only through iron grilles, never show young people what their life is like, and it isn't surprising they have no recruits. The Italians sent a sister to Mexico to find out how we managed to sustain and increase the order. She saw that it was the openness—that young women, for instance, are allowed to stay with us for a couple of weeks with no obligations, just to see what it is like, to learn that it isn't a prison. The Italian sister went back and reported that to the sisters in Italy, but they didn't want to change. Now there is a program to send Mexican sisters to Italy on five-year stints, to populate the huge empty buildings. The Mexican sisters dread it because it's so sad, so lonely. But just in Baja California we have two new convents opening in Tijuana, another in Mexicali, and our first male branch, a monastery, is also opening in Tijuana."

I had to satisfy my curiosity about a few details, beginning with the blue shell behind their public altar. "A nun who was visiting as the chapel was being built, and who thought it should have something of La Paz, suggested it to the architect. The bronze globe in front was actually my idea. It was made in a local foundry, and represents the pearl of the world"—an identification I had missed, possibly because the pearl was set in a scallop shell. And the symbolism of the colorful habits? "White for purity, red for love, black for mortification."

After an hour of conversation I asked if I might see more of the convent itself. Sister Cilia would have to ask the Mother Superior. She returned in five minutes and led me into the courtyard. We were immediately joined by one of the indoor spaniels, who yapped so shrilly I heard nothing else. "Excuse me," said Sister Cilia, "if I don't put her inside, we won't be able to speak."

"Sorry for the mess," she said. "We're going to put tile where the plants are to conserve water. And the roof over that part is falling in. Fortunately some German millionaires, good people, are giving us the money to fix it." Nuns came and went at the periphery, paying no attention, and at the end of the courtyard I saw the kennel. The three outdoor dogs were confined to a small pen. Stairs on either side of their shaded sleeping area led to the roof, the mysterious shelf I had glimpsed through the foliage. I understood how the dogs, with their elevation and their three-wall sounding board, projected their sound straight to the A-frame, and how the only activity left to them was barking. "Why the kennel?" I asked.

"The dogs protect the fourth side of the courtyard," said Sister Cilia, "and from there they can oversee the whole property. They're our guardians." Dogs, I could see, also had vocations: indoors for affection, outside for protection. On the way out, Sister Cilia gave me three issues of a magazine the convent published and said, "I hope we are being good neighbors to you."

Storing the phrase for possible future use, I returned, somewhat sappily, "And I hope, too, to be a good neighbor," hoping, especially, that the A-frame glass was sufficiently tinted to mask my spying.

Returning to the yard, I gave Maria Eugenia a capsule version of the interview. "So they have various businesses going, ask for public alms, take money from Germans, then get a dispensation from the Pope because twelve nuns can't keep up round-the-clock prayer."

"I don't think they're selling goat in the market," I said, but by then the screen door to the trailer had snapped shut, with Maria Eugenia behind it.

As for me, I enjoyed knowing what the silvery bell meant, how the tricolored species spent its time, how the dogs blasted through the foliage. If the secrets, disclosed, were banal, I could still better imagine their life. As spring advanced, volleyball games materialized on Sunday afternoons, with the younger nuns in their blue work uniforms teamed with assorted young men. Whether the latter were family members, parishioners or pickup players from the neighborhood, I'm sure the Italian Adorers would have been scandalized. I, in turn, was scandalized when a hole was breached in the wall by the goat pen, Bass Lake hacked down some old mesquites inside the wall, and the goats disappeared. Suddenly the area filled with spools of phone cable, moved from the storage yard across the street. Did the phone company offer so much for storage that the nuns now bought their meat with the rent money? Were they turning vegetarian? The unplanted field behind the A-frame seemed doubly empty without the mock battles, the sarcastic bleats, the butting and leaping. I read the three magazines Sister Cilia had given me and found them to be full of articles about peninsular history and culture, with less religious propaganda than I expected. I also noted that an article soliciting donations for the new roof included the unlisted convent phone number.

One night, after a period of relative calm, one of the indoor spaniels—surely the one Sister Cilia put inside so we could talk—began to shriek like one of those soprano trumpets used for baroque music. After two hours I got up and dialed the number in the magazine. On the twelfth ring I gave up. When the dog screeched again the following night, I marched to the convent the next morning, prepared to tell Sister Cilia it was time to deliver on the good-neighbor policy. With so many special silences, how about one for sleeping? A different nun answered the door; perhaps it was Sister Cilia's hour to pray. When I explained the problem, the new nun said, "That dog protects us."

"The dog is too small to protect anyone," I objected. "It just barks for the sake of barking."

She gazed at me with a sweet, impenetrable smile as I went on. "We're your neighbors and we were sleepless for hours." I stopped for her to reply, but she was as fixed as the Mona Lisa. "If a dog barks nonstop," I said, "how can you tell when it's finally barking *at* something? It all sounds the same."

The nun maintained her sweet, stonewalling smile and finally said, "I'll tell the Mother Superior about it." When I left, I decided that the Mother Superior was the circular file.

The spaniel did stop, but three nights later the outdoor dogs were back. I dialed the convent with no expectations, but a sister answered. "Your dogs are barking," I said wearily, "and your neighbors can't sleep. Would you mind taking them in?"

"We can't. They're on the roof."

"I *know* they're on the roof. Please take them *off* the roof."

"But they bother us, too!" she said, with a commiseration so surreal that I hung up. But the sisters achieved a miracle, for the barking ceased.

I had taken over from Maria Eugenia in trying to muzzle the night and kept her abreast. "It's ironic," she said, "that those with the most faith feel the most insecure, the most in need of protection. Also the most professionally selfless are the most willing to bother their neighbors. But you must recognize two things. One, they take orders from the Mother Superior, who wouldn't hear a wolfhound bellowing on her pillow. The other is that noise *is* the sound of security for them, because it's their noise. The dogs don't have to be barking at anything. As long as there's barking, defensive noise, harm can't reach them."

Suddenly I saw it. Aimless barking informed the world you were feeding a set of fangs. Danger at night came stealthily, silently, and if you were vulnerable on one side, you raised a wall of sound. Steady, random, firing into the night, barking—or an alarm system, or a boom box—was a lullaby you sang to yourself. It was noisy in La Paz, in the rest of Mexico, in the rest of Latin America, in most of the world where isolation wasn't its own defense. Earlier I had hoped to be repaid for my insomnia with a diverting scandal about poison and pigs, but instead I left the A-frame possessed of an Orwellian revelation. Noise is peace.

BLACK PEARL

7

La Paz, which had produced nothing of global significance since the pearl
beds dried up in the late 1930s, slowly became aware through rumor and
news stories that it was targeted for what was being billed as "the eclipse
of the century," a blackening of the sun that might draw up to a half million
people, four times the city's own population. Furthermore, some of those
people might be, in the root sense, lunatics.

There was no denying the astronomical significance. Although the sun's
diameter is four hundred times that of the moon, the moon is four hundred
times closer to the earth, so one can cover the other like coins of the same
denomination. Of the several dozen moons in our solar system, no other
creates on a planetary surface that perfect fit, blotting the sun while revealing its entire corona. Yet within that congruence lies a bit of play. The duration of an eclipse is extended when the earth is farthest from the sun, rendering the sun small, and when the moon is nearest the earth, rendering the
moon large. The July 11, 1991, eclipse approached the maximum in a far sun
and a close moon, and its duration in Baja California Sur—six minutes and
twenty-one seconds—would be one minute and one second short of the
longest eclipse possible. Solar eclipses occur on earth on an average of every
eighteen months, but most are brief, or visible only at sea, or at uncomfort-
ably polar latitudes, or in countries at war. In North America the most recent
lengthy solar eclipse was in 1806, with the next to occur in 2132.

The astronomical community hasn't been surprised by eclipses for hundreds of years and had been planning for this one at least a decade in advance. Its path would begin just after dawn on the Big Island of Hawaii, cross
the Pacific to arrive in Baja California Sur near noon, then continue its arc
over mainland Mexico and Central America to expire in Brazil. This would
be the first major eclipse to pass over an important observatory, at Mauna
Kea in Hawaii, and Mauna Kea seemed, scientifically, the obvious choice.

But Mauna Kea was likely to be socked in, Baja California promised the clearest weather in the eclipse's path, and many scientists preferred La Paz. The centerline, or core of the moon's shadow, was to pass seventy miles south of the city, but the most serious calibration, such as measuring the sun's expansion and contraction by the moon's edge, is best done *away* from the centerline, making La Paz the optimum spot.

The University of La Paz, perched on a hill behind town, was slated to become base camp for scientific teams from fifteen countries. With funding from the Mexican government, the university acquired six hundred cots, set up banking and postal services, hired round-the-clock medical attention, and provided telex, photocopiers, fax, cafeterias and hourly bus service to town. The scientific community, more attached to its subculture—or super-culture—than to its points of origin on the five continents, was well prepared to converge on La Paz for its six-minute opportunity.

Outside the penumbra of science, eclipses have a reputation for disaster. The word derives from the Greek *ekleipsis,* meaning abandonment. Eclipses were said to have preceded Assyrian insurrections and the destruction of the Athenian navy. According to Chinese myth from the Bamboo Annals, the sun went into eclipse in 1952 B.C. when the sky tenders got drunk. In Amos 8, Jehovah threatens a disobedient Israel with a solar eclipse, along with sackcloth, lamentations and universal baldness. In Pindar's "Ninth Ode," written after an eclipse in Thebes in 463 B.C., pillage of the daystar threatens the loss of man's strength and wisdom, along with war, heat, frost, and a Noah-like flood that might refashion humanity. In A.D. 840, an eclipse caused the emperor of Bavaria to die of fright. One would expect steadier nerves four centuries after Copernicus, but in 1983, in Indonesia, the military chased everyone indoors before occultation, then got chased indoors themselves by their superiors. Closer to La Paz, in a Canadian schoolyard where astronomers had set up their scopes in 1979, the schoolmaster herded all of his students inside to watch TV, then ran outside and yelled at the scientists, "Get in, get in, the eclipse is coming!"

Mexico had its Aztec and Mayan legends involving gods who battle for control of the sky, as well as a heroic Toltec martyr who made an alliance with the Plumed Serpent to rescue the sun. In La Paz eclipse fears took a more contemporary turn. Attendance estimates soared when it was suggested that vans of New Agers, dripping with crystals, would converge for weird ceremonies. It would be the "Woodstock of astronomy." Towns along the way would run out of food, water and gas, or would set up impromptu toll booths. Most of La Paz's six thousand guest beds had been booked up to two years in advance, and the Mexican government floated the idea of allowing only the first twenty-five thousand cars south of Ensenada, or of requiring proof of hotel reservations. Mary Shroyer, managing the Marina de La Paz, says that a roadblock was proposed at Guerrero Negro, with travelers required to get stickers ahead of time. Mary tried almost daily for two months to get stickers but kept being told that they hadn't arrived rather than that the plan had been scrapped. Americans, who like everything lined up in advance, were put off, and some canceled. It was both confirmed and denied that valuable equipment would have to be registered with customs agents. Such mixed signals characterized the official approach. Many Paceños arranged privately to rent their homes to eclipseniks and were supposed to pay the Office of Tourism a fee and open their houses for inspection. The government bought hundreds of tents to arrange in tent cities, to cost sixty dollars a night. The two accessible airports, at La Paz and Los Cabos, could handle only a limited number of planes, and those who flew in would have to stagger their arrivals and departures—spending up to a week in La Paz for their six dark minutes.

The winter before it happened, I sifted rumors and opportunities. My one personal association with solar eclipses was when my father took me to watch a partial solar eclipse on the shores of Lake Michigan when I was seven or eight. I remember how strange it was to watch him hold burning matches under a piece of glass until it was nearly black, then drive five blocks to the lake, hold it to the sky, and make me promise to look *only* through the sooty glass. I remember nothing of what I saw in the heavens, only the strangeness of my father's concern. Then I read Annie Dillard's terrifying account of a solar eclipse in *Teaching a Stone to Talk,* published in 1979, in which the black wall of the moon's shadow races toward the onlookers at twice the speed of sound, making them scream. I decided then that I would travel anywhere for the experience, and I couldn't believe that a solar eclipse of maximum duration and the peninsula of my obsession were poised for conjunction. I wanted to watch the eclipse alone in the desert, to listen to the birds fall silent and watch the lizards freeze. I wanted to watch in downtown La Paz, among the darkened hordes. I wanted to watch the eclipse and to watch Baja California watch the eclipse: wanted Dillard's pure racing shadow and my father's worried hand on the glass.

Baja Expeditions, which had previously sent no more than 300 clients out kayaking, bicycling, scuba diving and whale watching at a time, was planning to disperse 800 people into boats, hotels and a beach camp. Their most curious contingent was a party of 360 Japanese, to be stashed in three La Paz hotels and a convent, who would watch from the convent roof. That option was closed to non-Japanese, but there were also various boats and hotels plus a beach camp for 170 customers south of La Paz, in the centerline, with lecturing astronomers on staff. The edge of the eclipse might be better for experiments, but even off-duty astronomers preferred the deep middle for sheer thrills. So it was to be the Centerline Camp, with time before and afterward in La Paz, to sample its moment in the occulted sun.

When I landed in La Paz, a week before the event, the temperature was in the pleasant eighties rather than the predicted hundreds and traffic was little denser than normal. Gift shops bulged with eclipse mugs, ashtrays, paperweights of black rocks painted with orange coronas, and T-shirts with such messages as "I Blacked Out in Baja" and "Darkness at Noon," but the streets sported only a modest number of tourists and not one crystallized New Ager. Baja Expeditions headquarters was another matter, for besides its own 800 clients to be processed, every foreigner with an independent project had heard that Baja Expeditions was a clearinghouse for information, and they haunted its social facilities. Along with the expected media teams, there was a Canadian film crew that was working on an eclipse tale set in Toronto, had planned to fake the special effects, then decided to catch the real thing in Baja California and screen out the cactus. *The New York Times* had sent its science team to Hawaii, and reporters dispatched to La Paz from the regular bureau were hoping Hawaii would be socked in, allowing them to scoop the specialists. One man planned to watch for behavioral changes at a sea lion rookery and another—in the only twist to eclipse watching I would willingly skip—intended to spend the event underwater, filming fish going to sleep.

Maria Eugenia took a *New York Times* reporter, a writer from *Outside* and me to the Convent of St. Bridget, where she was directing the food operation for the Japanese. Everything needed to be coordinated to the minute, for they would be jetting to La Paz for twenty-four hours, watching the eclipse on jet lag, then jetting back to Japan. Rather than round-the-clock prayer, this convent's service was to keep a retreat of quiet rooms for rent around a shaded courtyard, with attendance at religious services not required but certainly convenient. The nuns had only been contacted at the last minute, when one of the hotels canceled, and Sister Julia Nazareth, from India, was supervising the installation of fifty extra cots, doubling the capacity of the nuns' hostel. Exuding calm, Sister Julia said she was looking forward to visitors from her own hemisphere. Maria Eugenia took us next to the university, where astronomers from Russia, Japan, Czechoslovakia, Korea, Germany, the United States and elsewhere were setting up instruments. On the hour, guides explained which contingent was doing what. Oblivious of the tours, astronomers strolled between trailers and mighty scopes, some of them in bikinis that would raise eyebrows on Mexican beaches, and the fact that they could only be observed from behind a rope made them seem oddly like primates from space.

Amid these pockets of bustle, La Paz residents remained ambivalent and confused. Congratulated on winning the celestial lottery, they were warned that certain materials marketed to protect their eyes were untrustworthy, then assured that no damage was possible during the full eclipse, or totality. Many were so fearful for their eyes that they planned to watch this event— to which zealots were winging from around the world—on TV. The civic cultural center featured two eclipse-oriented art shows, one depicting the eclipse in mythology, the other displaying local art that showed the sun occluded by cactus fruit, the Aztec sunstone superimposed on the sun, and a solar eclipse presiding over an erupting volcano and a city in flames. Remarked the show's curator with some vehemence, "Advertisers want people to watch their commercials instead of the sky, so they're deliberately scaring them inside to their sets. This, in a country where pre-Columbian astronomy was so sophisticated that observations were lined up not just with the sun and moon, but with the stars."

On my last pre-eclipse evening in La Paz, I was one of forty people who went to the Teatro de la Ciudad to see *El Eclipse,* a drama by prominent Mexican playwright Carlos Olmos. The show had run successfully for six months in Mexico City before being brought to La Paz for a one-night stand. A young man pretending to be a photographer who has come to shoot the eclipse is the lone guest at a battered seaside resort run by three generations of women and their lone surviving male, aged twenty-five. One assumes that the newcomer will be variously entangled with the women and fended off by the man, but it devolves that the men had previously met in Mexico City and fallen in love. As the world dims, the dramatic buildup touches on drug money, the influence on Mexico of gringos and the Japanese, the impact of mourning on teen clothing, and whether to sell foreigners some family property. During stage blackout a second-generation woman, secretly pregnant, wears red ribbons under her clothing to protect her unborn from strange rays, another woman watches totality through her late husband's X-rays and local children, offstage, beat drums to help the sun escape from the moon. As light returns the two men take off in the family van, leaving the women without males and without wheels. In a program note, the playwright says he intended to reflect on his characters' intimate contradictions during a night of cosmic terror, and if the experience of actual skywatchers was less turgid, there was no denying that the eclipse was an inspired plot device for throwing characters and themes together.

Not knowing whether La Paz was enjoying the lull before a storm or whether it had spooked a bonanza, I boarded a used schoolbus that Baja Expeditions had brought for the eclipse and bailed out two hours later at their beach camp. The instant village for more than two hundred, including staff, had been pitched just north of Rancho Leonero, a small sportfishing hotel on a secluded bluff. For weeks Walter Hill—he who had brought the goats and hitchhikers to Tim and Nora's wedding—had wrestled with the site, hacking a shaded dining area from a tamarisk thicket, setting up a tank with sixty thousand gallons of water as an emergency supplement to ground-water, raising a resort with cooking, socializing and sleeping areas under the starry sky. He was away when the bulldozer he had ordered to smooth the beach and dune top churned them up instead, and he wound up leveling the area himself by dragging a car bumper from a pickup, a device he re-ferred to as a Fresno. By the time we arrived, ninety tents had been lined up like turquoise barnacles on the dune, with another thirty in a grove of young palms. Shadowy figures looked busy through the mosquito netting of the cook tent, the sun was warming fresh water for gravity-fed showers, a large canvas roof on the beach offered shade between pipes that released a pres-surized mist, and a parachute silk was luffing in anticipation of happy hour.

Yesterday's busload had already settled in, and busloads were to arrive for the next three days until the camp was full for blackout. While jokes circu-lated about "high noon for nerds," it was hard to isolate an eclipse type. Older people in the professions predominated, many of them amateur as-tronomers since childhood. Teachers, a city planner, a river guide, a priest, an off-duty photographer, the assistant attorney general of Illinois and a woman writing for a hometown weekly introduced themselves over tamales. A computer programmer who used the distribution of solar eclipses to ex-plore the world said that during the Indonesian eclipse he wound up touring all day, napping from seven to eleven, and stargazing all night. A concert pi-anist claimed to find similarities in the spectra of sound and light. A retired accountant said he had come "because watching a partial eclipse is like kiss-ing your sister." A resident of Hawaii, in the path of totality at home, cor-rectly guessed his state would be clouded over, and did a brisk business in Hawaiian T-shirts featuring King Kamehameha brandishing a black sun. A bicoastal family had been planning this as a reunion ever since one member saw a total eclipse in Helena, Montana, in 1979. One woman was escaping the penumbra of the Empire State Building and another arrived from Min-nesota bearing a sack of energy bars and two gallons of water, despite having prepaid for all the amenities, because her local paper had used the dire phrase, "Woodstock of astronomy." The camp's champion eclipse chaser was rack-ing up his sixth solar. I felt my greatest affinity with a retired physician who had also been exploring the peninsula since 1968 and had come largely be-cause it was "a big Baja event."

In preparation for the eclipse we gathered under the parachute, or in the shade with the mist machine, to listen to six resident lecturers, including a cosmologist, an infrared astronomer and an astronaut in waiting. "It's best to know all you can ahead," said a U.S. Navy astronomer just back from the Gulf War, "because an eclipse is delicious terror, a rollercoaster, and you'll miss too much by being overwhelmed." As he explained the sun's chromos-phere, however, it was difficult not to let one's gaze drift from the parachute silk out to the sun's photons pouring on date palms full of orioles, the thorny brush of the dunes, the blues of the Sierra de la Laguna dancing inland. At either end of the dune sat telescopes like an orchestral brass section, with owners who invited passersby to peer at phenomena visible by day: sunspots, Venus going through phases like the moon. The least morning mist, con-densation or alto-cumulus wisp was read like a hurricane warning: what if the eclipse were happening *now*? Was Baja California the wrong choice? As the cosmologist lectured on dark matter, his listeners looked up and gasped: a flock of pelicans shadowed the parachute in a primeval wedge. At day's end, campers hauled their folding chairs to the dune's edge to learn how to watch sunsets. Reddening is really the elimination of blue; rays diverge to rejoin behind you like railroad tracks; the earth's rotation creates the daily solar eclipse we call night. Our spinning globe kept people riveted to their seats, scouring the sunset for the green flash, naming the first planets. By dark people clustered to learn the stars along the ecliptic while others, their tents near telescopes, fell asleep to such phrases as "You're looking back thirty mil-lion years in time. . . ."

We were also riveted to our seats because we were afraid of losing them.

Each person had been issued a folding aluminum chair on arrival, but we were unused to hauling seats from tent to lecture to feeding area and many of us conscripted the nearest empty. Victims began personalizing chairs with luggage tags, then with binoculars and cameras, and it was a tribute either to trust or to inverted values that people used thousand-dollar optics to claim ten-dollar furniture. Musical chairs became a comic subplot and some suspected the staff of subtracting chairs for sport. One man made the mistake of boasting to Walter that he was sitting in a heisted chair. "I brought these chairs here," snapped Walter, glaring, "and you're sitting in *mine.*"

In our diversity we seemed a more balanced, less erratic group than I'd imagined, and I asked Robert Fadal, one of the two resident doctors, whether we were as healthy as we seemed. We were. There was concern over small things: people got suntan lotion in their eyes; they complained of jellyfish stings with no welts to show for it. "I brought medicine for heart attacks but no tweezers for pulling cactus spines." Despite the vigor of his charges, Dr. Fadal was the most traumatized member of the Centerline staff. Five minutes after his arrival a fifty-five-year-old man from Rancho Leonero showed up trembling, sweating and saying, "Doctor, I don't feel good." Fadal took him to the infirmary that Walter had slapped together, ruled out heart attack, stroke and other life threateners, and concluded it was only panic at being far from medical care. Walking him back to Rancho Leonero, Fadal encountered a hulking man with fuzzy eyes and slurred speech that emanated from the back of his mouth. Fadal was reminded of Frankenstein's monster and learned from an employee that the man had beaten up another guest the previous day. There had also been an unidentified streaker in the night. How, wondered Fadal, had so many borderline cases wound up at the same resort? Eventually he learned that the ranch had been struck by a group of rich psychiatric patients who routinely traveled together, apparently unattended. Into this turmoil arrived a young man who had recently been diagnosed with lymphoma, had spent all his money beating it, had hitched to the eclipse, wound up at Leonero, and spent most of his time cornering other guests and telling them how good it was to be alive. Dr. Fadal described him as obtrusive, hypersexual, and right at home.

Long braced for, nearly dreaded, July 11 dawned free of the least blemish. At breakfast all were handed postcard-sized cardboards with insets of an aluminum-coated plastic called Mylar through which we could safely stare at the sun. Hesitantly, watching neighbors for signs of blindness, we put them to our eyes. The sun was a pale bulb. Many began pacing the dune, calculating the optimum viewing spot. Those with telescopes that ran on electricity triple-checked the cord from the dune to the generator, as well as the generator. A man who had set up in the cactus for an unobstructed view could be heard cursing his tripods, along with the country that made them. In the midst of scrambling and fussing there was a cheer like the stroke of New Year's. The moon had bitten the sun, on time to the nanosecond.

What followed seemed like bits of a tribal dream. People laid the spread fingers of one hand over the other, creating a mesh through which light fell onto bedsheets in a lattice of crescents. Shadows crispened, cast by a shrinking sun. Three men in blue uniforms, with semiautomatic rifles over their shoulders, suddenly materialized on the dune and strode through the darkening sky watchers. Refusing at first to identify themselves, they admitted under pressure that they were from the Mexican navy. I asked one why they had come. "To protect you," he said. "From what?" I asked. He didn't answer. "From theft?" I persisted. "Yes, from theft during the eclipse." Given that any serious thief would come in the night rather than during the six-minute dusk of the eclipse, and that all of us had been using expensive equipment to nail down cheap seats, the military guard added the traditional spice of the irrational—missing from the Centerline Camp if not from Rancho Leonero—and if I had thought of it in time, I would have asked one of the patrol to guard my folding chair. Invited to peer through lenses and to pose with the more glamorous staff members, they lightened up. All had been warned against taking flash photos that would disrupt night vision, but I neither realized how dark it had become nor remembered my cheap camera's automatic flash, and my blast was answered by a volley of threats. The mountains to the north darkened swiftly, as if under thunderclouds, but without the blackness and screams I had read about in Annie Dillard.

Another cheer went up, followed by a hush: totality had begun. It was now safe to look directly at the sun, yet out of instinct I still hesitated. Soon every naked eye saw the whole moon, opaque as a manhole cover, blot the whole sun, which flared in blond streamers. After the slow, relentless advance toward darkness, motion stopped. The horizon in all directions glowed melon-pale. However anticipated, it was suddenly stunning that the sun and moon, each a mere 360th of the visible sky, had achieved a cosmic bull's eye, giving a sense of the clock stopped at a high noon that was midnight. Orion, an impossible sight in July, wobbled behind the sun.

A man stood back from his telescope and cried, "Look at the prominences. Line up and look, but look *quickly*." Through flares like angels' wings a filament of purple tungsten shot out and halfway back like a varicose vein— or so people afterward, trying to describe it, compounded their metaphors. The coastal resort of Buena Vista sparkled to the north, its light sensors tricked by the dark, and during the middle of totality two dune buggies roared down the beach with their headlights on. While some chattered compulsively and others scurried between instruments, some lay hushed on their backs. A dozen people shouted at once, "Don't look!" Dilated, about to be struck, this was the eyes' one moment of peril. Time ceased stopping, a third cheer went up, and light thin as neon brought back the desert.

After the slow dimming into the eclipse, the equally slow, symmetrical return to full sunlight seemed swift. The gangly pianist danced through the gazers like a crane, blurting impressions from one person to another regardless of who heard what and without slowing his gait. Exhilaration became relief, and crying, "It's Corona time!" many raced to the bar at the parachute silk. At the university in La Paz the researchers were still at their posts, but before the moon had freed the sun, the dune was nearly abandoned and the postmortems had begun.

"I had to go to the bathroom during the partial," said one woman, "and light through the straw roof made hundreds of little crescent suns on the toilet seat." A man with a thermometer reported a seventeen-degree drop in temperature. Another couldn't handle his camera, felt his hand paralyze on the shutter, and compared the effect to the rapture of the deep. Replied another, "I had so many straps around my neck, I think my rapture was oxygen deprivation." Someone had heard on the radio that Hawaii was socked in, and I pictured the *Times* reporters in La Paz, giddy with schadenfreude. I asked one of the cosmologists why Dillard's shadow had been more dramatic than ours. "Her eclipse was at daybreak to the north," he said, "while we saw it at noon on the Tropic of Cancer. We got more light from the corona." Unknown to the dune people, a foal was born that afternoon at the ranch behind us. It had a crescent moon—or perhaps a crescent sun—on its forehead and was named, inevitably, Eclipse.

The beach camp unwound through days of snorkeling and sunburn, and I stayed for a day of it. I hiked the beach south toward the little town of La Ribera, past the lagoon where horses were still feeding on underwater weeds as I had first seen them in 1968. Noticing a crowd of people at a large building and thinking it might be a public establishment where I could get a beer, I walked up to find a group of Americans and Mexicans standing around in a sour mood. I slipped away without asking questions and later learned from Dr. Fadal that a retired American man had just died of a massive heart attack while trying to move furniture at noon into his new beach house. Knowing there were doctors at the Centerline Camp, a family member picked them up in a dune buggy and raced them to the house, where they pronounced the man dead. It would take two or three days of paperwork before the body could be flown to the States, with nothing to do but to lay him in the shade under a tarp.

Dr. Fadal also had a curious post-eclipse visit from the senior astronomer, who had signaled when it was safe to watch and when danger returned. He had crescent burns, as if from tiny branding irons, on both retinas and had lost some vision. "Isn't that a particularly dumb thing for an *astronomer* to do?" I asked.

"No, I admire him for it," said Dr. Fadal. "Those are honorable battle scars."

When I returned to La Paz, one story overwhelmed all others: the visit of the Japanese. The 360 visitors consisted of hobbyists and semiprofessionals of an astronomy club led by a tour company that had contracted with Baja Expeditions. All the amenities were ready, and when the nuns refused to allow alcohol in the convent, Tim had backed a truck to their refrigeration room in the middle of the night and stashed the beer behind the soft drinks. The Japanese arrived in an anxious mood because their charter flight had been delayed by a cracked windshield. Baja Expeditions guide Andrew Davidson, fluent from living three years in Japan, accompanied the group from the moment they landed at the airport and heard one of their own guides apologize for the bad road into town. When a visitor remarked that the road, which is paved and smooth, wasn't so bad, the guide said, "But the rest of the streets are *terrible.*"

Although two-thirds of the group had beds in other hotels, all spent the night awake at the convent, determining which among them deserved the view from the roof. They convened in the chapel. Everything in Japan, said Andrew, even an astronomy club, was a hierarchy, and the most important people, by cosmic necessity, would see more of the eclipse. Most club members had brought telescopes with trackers plus still cameras and video equipment, and they determined that each person needed two square meters. The most important people picked what they deemed the prime spots, then voices rose in contention over how to allocate roof sites among the rest. For a moment Tim couldn't place where he had heard that shouting before, then realized it was at a cock fight. At one point the nuns asked a staff person to remind them that they were in a house of God and to please pipe down. Tim was called in to arbitrate, and as soon as he began to speak the voices dropped to an eerie silence as his advice emerged from the interpreter. Tim suggested a lottery. It was held. Winners selected spots next to the elite and losers wound up on an adjacent basketball court. Andrew, because he wasn't Japanese, was not welcome on the roof. Choice vantage points were so important that those who didn't get them were suddenly failures in life. The irony, said Andrew, was that all views were equally good and the Japanese were imposing a rigid power structure on an egalitarian event. Losers on the basketball court, for that matter, would see changes in the colors of the leaves that the elite on the roof would miss.

In the midst of the tension over where to watch fell the long-planned evening meal. The touring company had asked for a barbecue and the nuns didn't want burning fat splattering the garden and the cloister. In an exchange of faxes, Tim realized that the Japanese wanted a fantasy Mexican meal, which appeared to be meat revolving on a spit over leaping flames. He borrowed a rotisserie motor from a street stand, rigged it to his grill, precooked the meat and skewered it over wood doused in diesel fuel. As the meat spun, fat fell to the flames, spurring them higher, and smoke floated into the chapel, where the Japanese were still bickering over how to split up the roof. When the lottery was over, all got a taste of the beef, but the Japanese had expected—or the tour company had led them to expect—that each of the 360 visitors would enjoy a steak-sized cut, not bites to roll in tortillas. Said Andrew, they wanted traditional Mexican food, wanted a cow on a spit, and had Mexico confused with Texas. A woman with the tour company told him, "Your word is your word, it's a matter of honor. Either you provide us with beef or you get us a private beach with shade and drinks for viewing the eclipse."

Tim was summoned to the convent and presented with the ultimatum: a shady beach or beef for 360. He tugged on his moustache, hemmed for time, then promised beef. The eve of the eclipse was a poor night for shopping, but he returned with five kilos of taco meat and presented it to the directors.

"No," they said, "we want to *see beef cooking*."

Tim said to Maria Eugenia, "Where can we find three hundred kilos of meat tonight?"

Maria Eugenia said, "Tim, it's three in the morning. I hope you're joking."

"They're not," said Tim, "so I'm not."

Tim, Maria Eugenia and another Baja Expeditions employee beat on the doors of butchers, roused them out of their sleep, and begged them to sell their entire stock. Tim was determined to hold a grand barbecue for the Japanese after the eclipse. Said Tim, "I want them to eat beef until they pop."

No staff slept that night. They didn't find three hundred kilos of beef, but they did find sixty, in large chunks, which various employees—including Maria Eugenia, who is vegetarian—partially precooked in their homes to lessen the impact on the nuns. In the morning the nuns held a mass that was, in Andrew's words, "very loud, very stagy," and handed out computer print-outs saying that the meeting of the sun and moon was the work of God. One female tour guide kept hounding Andrew with questions while blowing cigarette smoke in his face until he threw her out of the kitchen. A few of the Japanese women said to him privately, "I'm so embarrassed, I can't believe people are acting this way." Three of the nuns sneaked up quietly and asked for beer. In their black and grey habits and their Mylar glasses for viewing before totality, said Andrew, they looked like tipplers from Star Trek.

Shortly before the eclipse one of the cooks wanted more *machaca* for the impending hors d'oeuvres. Maria Eugenia, seeing an escape from the convent, volunteered, headed to the waterfront, and watched the eclipse in the peace of the crowds. Andrew invaded the convent roof and found the Japanese too preoccupied with their equipment to object to his presence. Once the eclipse began, he says, they wholly ignored the square meters they had fought for, melded together, shared equipment, and the whole hierarchical structure dissolved in fraternity.

After the eclipse every previous problem ceased to exist. The Japanese drank margaritas, laughed, danced, put their arms around each other, loved everyone, and hardly noticed they were eating a mere sixty kilos of beef. Nuns joined them in downing margaritas. Group pictures were snapped. When they were finally bused back to the plane, everyone who had served them was so exhausted that it seemed barely credible that the Japanese had spent only twenty-two hours in La Paz.

Maria Eugenia's immediate reaction was to quit taking Japanese lessons from Andrew: she didn't want to learn another word. The Japanese, she concluded, were anti-American and she, though Mexican, had been treated as an American. Japanese don't hate Americans, countered Andrew; a foreigner is a foreigner and they dismiss them all equally. Looking back on the event, both concluded that the tour guides, wanting to turn the eclipse into a production starring themselves, were the actual villains, while members of the astronomy club were mostly decent people, merely wound up. When a few of them sent Maria Eugenia souvenir photos of their visit, she resumed her study of Japanese.

As for La Paz itself, one of its more clever preparations had been to declare the eclipse the theme of the preceding Carnaval, enabling the town to save the floats and run them through again on the three nights before the event, with Miss Eclipse waving in a white gown from her pyramid of solar flames. On the great day a fair crowd gathered at the waterfront, with a mob in front of the Hotel La Perla cheering and applauding, and it was said that as the temperature plunged during totality, there was a quick and pungent smell of the sea. A woman in back of town reported that during the eclipse all dogs, children and roosters fell silent; then when the sun emerged, the roosters began to crow. One family watched their neighbors stand outside during the partial eclipse, then pile into the house and bolt the door during totality, when it was safe to look. Several people reported neighbors who tied red ribbons around their trees to keep the fruit from rotting and the trees themselves from dying, including a woman who proceeded to kill the same trees next month with an overdose of fertilizer. Tim, who climbed above the most elite of the Japanese to watch from the convent bell tower, described the eclipse as a compressed sunset. Doves returned to the tower to roost, spotted him and swerved back to the penumbra. His attention was torn between strange sights in the sky and strange sounds from the roof, where the Japanese were saying *whoa* and *ooh* and emitting low guttural rumblings that he took for darker versions of *wow*. The Sheik watched with friends in his backyard menagerie, where his rabbits ate more furiously and his doves went to sleep. He also said that he created a cocktail called The Eclipse, compounded of brandy and his damiana liqueur, producing a private eclipse in whoever drank it. "Downing those," I asked, "how could you tell *what* your animals were doing?"

"We saved them for after the eclipse," he said, fluttering his eyebrows. "One blackout at a time."

The last minute held a last surprise, a chartered DC-10 from Salt Lake City that landed at the La Paz airport at three in the morning before the event, disgorging two hundred people with sleeping bags, lawn chairs, scopes, cameras, and no plans at all. When they headed with their gear over the nearest barbed-wire fence in the dark, airport officials became alarmed that they would impale themselves on the cholla and directed them to a nearby soccer field. The Utahns calmly set up, watched the eclipse unobstructed, and boarded their plane back to Salt Lake at four the next afternoon.

As for the dreaded Woodstock of astronomy, it never happened. There was actually less traffic than during Carnaval, a purely local event. A tour of the gift shops showed little dent in the ashtrays and T-shirts, and indeed I bought my own souvenir eclipse mug the following winter. A man who had invested his savings in Mylar to sell during the eclipse lost all when the Mexican government, without advance notice, passed out free Mylar to protect the eyes of its citizens. Of the businesses named for the eclipse that I encountered, the Palapa Eclipse in San Ignacio lasted only a season but the Eclipse Disco in Ciudad Constitución, Eclipse Purified Water in La Paz and '91 Eclipse Honey became lingering concerns. Almost no one patronized the government tent cities at sixty dollars a night, and no one who rented a house to eclipse watchers is known to have paid a tax or offered it for government inspection. An official visitor count was never published, but the braced-for half million is thought to have been somewhere between thirty thousand and fifty thousand. The millennial tradition of anticipating calamities was thus maintained. Instead of earthquakes and invasion, people projected the more contemporary fears of roadblocks, running out of gas and not finding a motel room for the night.

As for the eclipse itself, a year and a half after the event I asked Dr. Fadal how it struck him. "I frankly wasn't interested in the actual eclipse," he said, "and couldn't see what the fuss was about. I came because it was something different to do as a doctor. Then totality began and here was the most pure, penetrating, all-encompassing, magnanimous, black, engulfing, sucking thing, which was surrounded by"—and here he began to hiss—"this sssearing, sssilver ssstrip, with these little chartreuse daggers sticking into it and this—whauw!—wispy aurora on either side six hundred million miles, and you're looking at this thing and thinking that it has absolutely nothing to do with you. It doesn't care if there's a perception to perceive it, it's just a phenomenon, but it gives you faith that there's beauty in the world."

That same winter I asked Andrew, who defied the Japanese on the convent roof, how it affected him. "It was like, like . . ." He groped for a sufficient metaphor. "It was like intravenous poetry."

THE SEARCH FOR MATA HARI

8

In the winter of 1973, as the rain pounded and Brandy and I burned iron-wood to stay warm, more than bright weather I craved a consoling piano. I had played since I was eight, had ingested the classical repertoire and could fake the popular styles. My three-year nightclub career in Andalucía taught me that the piano was a good passport to a country's interior. In 1973 I was more interested in soothing my own interior than in penetrating La Paz, but I had gazed with curiosity at a one-story building of rough-hewn *cantera* on one corner of the plaza. Labeled *Escuela de Música,* it could hardly be a music school without a piano.

One morning I stepped though the open door and found myself in a room of cool bare walls, utterly silent. Perhaps their day had not yet begun. Through the shadows gloomed an original painting of Schumann, his eye-brows like scrolls over a deep mad gaze, lost in the manic phase of his schiz-ophrenia. From another room came a sound of sweeping. Open doorways gave in two directions and I advanced toward the broom. It was wielded by a boy in his teens. *"Buenos dias,"* I said.

He jumped. *"Buenos dias."*

I explained that I was a visitor in search of a piano: was there one in the school I might practice on? There were two, he said, but I would have to ask the *profesora,* who wouldn't arrive until later.

I returned at eleven. The front room was still empty but sounds of a key-board and voices rose from the interior. I passed through a small room con-taining a single glass cabinet with a few stringed instruments and reached a third room with a middle-aged woman, a Yamaha console piano, and two girls of about eleven. I excused myself for interrupting and explained my presence. The woman introduced herself as Consuelo Amador de Ribera. She did not seem startled by my request and explained that she was teaching a piece she particularly liked. Would I like to hear it?

I would indeed.

She played a mid-nineteenth-century salon piece, a little stiffly but with strong left-hand octaves I envied. I squinted at the score and didn't recognize the composer. When she finished, I told her I admired her octaves.

"Really?" She seemed genuinely pleased. "But now you play something."

There is an intermezzo by Schumann with a singing melody and a rolling bass that falls easily under the fingers, which I have trained myself to discharge amid most states of panic, inebriation or absence of practice, and I discharged it. I turned around to apologize for the wooden fingers and found the *profesora* staring wide-eyed. "But this is wasted on just the three of us," she said. "I'm trying to teach a history of music course in the afternoon but I don't have any examples. You must come back tomorrow and let me tape some music."

It was clear that I was not going to sit down and practice, but flushed with the idea of recording, I promised to return tomorrow at the same time.

The next morning I was greeted by Consuelo, two colleagues on the faculty, and some forty children ranging in age from six to late teens. Consuelo introduced me to the other two adults, then asked me to play. Not to repeat the Schumann, I played a couple of pieces by Brahms. During the applause I looked in vain for a tape recorder.

"Our problem here," said Consuelo, "is that the government gives us this large building and our small salaries but no equipment. As you see, we have almost no furniture. We have this console, an upright in another room, and what the students can provide themselves. Do you think it might be possible to play a benefit concert for us, so we could raise some money?"

To be an international concert pianist was a lifetime dream whose possibility suddenly struck terror. Yet when would I be asked again? If I came apart, no one I knew would find out. Even Brandy couldn't attend. "I don't know how long I'll be here," I said. "I could be leaving as soon as next week."

"Then we'd better try for this weekend. How's Saturday?"

It was Tuesday. That would mean only five days of preparation, five days of dread. "Saturday would be fine."

"And what are you going to play?"

Now I was truly off guard. "I'd need a day to figure that out." At this point anyone who mistook me for a concert pianist should have wondered at my not having a choice of programs at my fingertips, but Consuelo merely answered, "We don't have a day. If we're going to put this on by Saturday, we should get the program to the printer this afternoon."

"Then let me think about it and come back in a couple of hours. By the way, who is your favorite composer?"

"Mozart. But I really think any recital should begin with Bach."

I made my escape before I received further instruction.

I stopped by the house to check on Brandy, changed into swimming trunks, grabbed a pencil and notebook, and headed to the beach. The sun poured on my back while my mind raced. I was safest with romantics like Schumann, whom I could blur with overpedaling if I got in trouble, and with moderns that could absorb mistakes in the general dissonance. The delicacy and precision of Mozart was treacherous: Mozart was out. I could pass off Bach with a couple of selections from the French suites, then recover with the Schumann. Next I listed Chopin's *Ballade in g,* two pieces by Brahms, four preludes by Rachmaninoff, Debussy's *Reflets dans l'eau,* a movement from a Hindemith sonata, the *Sevilla* of Albéniz to touch base with the Spanish repertoire, and concluded with Gershwin's *Rhapsody in Blue,* which I could grandstand to the point of annihilating whatever had preceded it. I added the estimated times: it came to an hour and a half. Nine composers was unprecedented variety, but constant shifts would obscure the deficiencies of any particular style, and with a generous intermission and perhaps a late start it should see me through the evening.

I returned to Consuelo with the line-up. "*Estupendo,*" she proclaimed, ignoring the absence of Mozart.

"Before you take it to the printer," I said, "I'd like to run through it to make sure the length is all right." My actual motive was to assure myself I could get through it at all. We put a stopwatch on the piano, and while children gathered and the temperature spiraled, I plugged away to the end. It was just an hour and a half.

Consuelo was grinning. "Now," she said, "I need to know something of your training and career so I can get going on the publicity."

I told her that I had studied at Yale, that I had performed for three years in Spain as well as variously in the United States, that I had played for a theater company and for Ballet West. I did not tell her that I merely took lessons on the side while pursuing a degree in English, that in Spain I had played only restaurants and nightclubs, that the theater company was performing a melodrama called *The Drunkard,* that for Ballet West I ground out exercise classes, that my American career consisted of private parties, silent films and one counterculture funeral. I never directly lied but was judicious with the truth.

"There is another problem," I said, "which is that I didn't expect to be performing and don't have anything formal to wear." My wardrobe, in fact, consisted of plaid shirts and jeans, with a choice of hiking boots, sandals or sneakers.

"No problem," she said, "we should be able to borrow a suit and shoes. We have several students your size."

"Since this is a benefit, if you get anything from a store, make them donate it. Don't spend any money. . . ."

"You do the music," she said, "and I'll handle the rest."

"One more thing. I can't remember some of the opus numbers for the program."

"We'll look up what we can."

Next morning I bought the papers to see if the publicity had started. I found myself on the front page of one and the third page of another, an international concert star with an extensive career in the United States and Europe, possessed of golden hands, magic fingers, the kind of paraphernalia thought to have been buried with Liszt. I proceeded to the music school to start practicing. The energetic Consuelo met me with a suit jacket from a tailor down the street who rented clothes, primarily to ranchers who attended city weddings. It was a small and hideous black-and-white checked affair that bound me like a cobra. The first cross-hand passage would surely split the back. "No," recoiled Consuelo, to my relief, "that will never do."

"Can't you borrow something from a student?"

"Leave it to me."

Next was the matter of the piano. The concert was to be held at the back end of town, in La Casa de la Juventud, a primary-school auditorium supposedly equipped with a baby grand. I drove us out there to test it. The action veered from the shrill to the nonfunctional and the instrument was, in concert parlance, a piano-shaped object. "What else is there?"

"The two at the school." That meant the dysfunctional upright or the Japanese console, a model that was halfway between an upright and a spinet.

"Then it's the console."

On Thursday morning I found that Consuelo had assembled a full suit of clothes, including a well-fitted blue blazer, trousers, tie, and a white shirt and loafers in boxes from a store. "I hope you didn't *buy* the shirt and shoes," I said.

"Will you leave those details to me?" She then told me that the concert had been plugged constantly on radio and TV and was now nearly sold out.

The government had reserved the first three rows in a block. "And you have a live interview on television tomorrow, just after the evening news."

"Incidentally," I suddenly asked, "have any other visiting pianists played in La Paz?"

"No, you're the first."

The next day I got in some practice and studied the press clippings so as not to say anything that might conflict with my official career. In the evening I got into my blue blazer and drove out to the TV station, a small building on a hill over the bay. The sensations came so fast I had little time to panic. A pair of announcers under punishingly bright lights traded dispatches, international politics followed by local crimes. One of them then informed the viewers that they were in for a special privilege, an interview with an internationally known concert pianist. He got up and gave me his seat.

To sit in someone else's clothes, blinded by lights, and account for a fictional self in another language gave me a burst of confidence. I was asked where I was trained and where I had played, and replied with the information I had given Consuelo. When I mentioned what I was going to play, the announcer said, "Well, that sounds like a very melodic, very popular program," suggesting a suspicious knowledge of music. The interview, which I'm told lasted five minutes, seemed over the instant it began.

The morning of the concert I woke at dawn and faced a long day of anxiety. Midmorning I drove to the plaza, parked and walked toward the post office. A pickup with the piano pulled up to the light as I waited to cross. It was the perfect diversion. I hailed the students riding with the piano and jumped into the truck just as the light changed. As the truck pulled away, I tumbled toward the street, the students grabbed me, and but for split-second timing I might have ended my apprehension with a broken arm.

We parked at the back of the auditorium and were supervised by a woman who seemed baffled by my presence. "Do you have a ticket to tonight's performance?" she asked.

"Well, no," I said, taken aback.

"Then I'm afraid you can't come," she shrugged. "It's sold out."

Inside I found Consuelo attending to the decoration of the stage. The piano was to sit on one side, balanced on the other by the manic portrait of Schumann propped on an easel between sprays of white gladiolas, glaring as if to say, you will enjoy this concert or else. Until now I had greeted every detail like a rapt spectator, but now that I was a *concertista internacional,* surely I could indulge my moment of temperament. Schumann, I informed Consuelo, had to go.

"*¿Pero porqué?*"

"Because," I said, hardly knowing where to begin, "he just isn't right."

I arrived well before concert time, to find most of the audience already seated. From the wings I could see that the stage itself was lined with folding chairs, several deep, and the air was already dense and steamy. I glanced at the program. The Chopin *Ballade in g* was listed as opus 4. "I looked it up," said Consuelo. I knew that the *Ballade* had been written in Paris, that Chopin didn't get out of Poland until well after opus 10, and that the number couldn't be right. Admission, I noted, was ten pesos, about seventy cents. It was 8:30. "Shouldn't we begin?" I asked Consuelo. She ignored the suggestion. I kept thinking that in a couple of hours I would be on my way to the banquet they were throwing afterward. However I played, I was soon headed toward food and drink. My heart hammered, but with a fatalistic calm.

At five minutes of nine the house lights flashed. I handed Consuelo my glasses, less for cosmetic reasons than to blur the audience, and like a first-time parachuter I walked out of the wings, through the folding chairs, past gladiolas bereft of Schumann, and bowed toward a mist of applause. The first few measures would determine it all. I raised my hands over a G major chord and began. I was answered by Bach, inexpressive but without a hitch. When I reached the end of the first piece there was applause, which I hadn't expected until I finished the Bach selection. There was nothing to do but stand up and acknowledge it. I got through the rest of the Bach, bowed again, and dove into the Schumann with a flourish. From here to the end it was a matter of sheer perseverance and remembering what I was supposed to play next.

As I got used to the occasion, the playing loosened and I began to take in my surroundings. It was hot and getting hotter; it was easily eighty-five degrees. The entire audience seemed to be coughing. The flu had been sweeping La Paz—I was to come down with it the following week—and the more I listened, the more the hall sounded like a hospital. There were, in addition, children of all ages, many of them with me on stage, many of them whispering and playing furtive games. The distraction might have ruffled a career performer, but I have always played better when someone was running the vacuum or arguing in another room and the clatter had a tonic effect.

In practicing the music, however, I had forgotten the nakedest moment of all: the bow. Scheduling so many short pieces for an audience inclined to applaud every cadence, there were many, many bows. When the piece ended I would stand up with my left hand on the piano, as I was once taught, make a forward nod from the waist, hold the position a moment, and do it again if the noise didn't stop. After the first three or four of those maneuvers I could hear a snickering, slightly more public each time. Why hadn't I practiced in front of a mirror? Did I dare experiment with it now?

I bowed for intermission and escaped backstage. Consuelo was jubilant. I talked little and tried to sustain an inner momentum. Drinks were an hour away. The four Rachmaninoff preludes were next. To avoid bowing for each I extended my palm like a traffic cop, glared at the blur over the piano and recommenced. Soon I was through the Albéniz, through the Hindemith, and ready to plunge into the *Rhapsody in Blue.* I gunned the pedal, flung my arms, and gave a rendition my more candid friends refer to as "The Killing of Sister George." I made a last wooden bow into sustained applause and fled backstage. It was over.

The applause continued. "They want an encore," whispered Consuelo, prodding my arm. Was this never to end? After the *Rhapsody* it would have to be something quiet and simple. I played the first section of Chopin's *Etude in E.* The audience collectively sighed. I stopped where it comes to a cadence, before the pyrotechnic middle, stood up and bowed once more.

When I was backstage and the audience was at last filing out, Consuelo asked, "Why didn't you play the rest of the étude?"

"It's not under my fingers at the moment."

"Anyway they all knew the melody, since they used it on TV for a tissue commercial."

But not all the audience left. A fair crowd had gathered around stage to have their programs signed, mostly children, with a couple of middle-aged women who gushed and raved. When their demands were met, we piled into cars and headed to the banquet.

El Yate was the most exclusive restaurant in La Paz, but my dreams of eating there had only gone as far as fresh lobster and hadn't imagined a dinner in my honor. A U-shaped table awaited, glittering with silver and white napery. Consuelo and I presided at the center, flanked by people Consuelo identified as local officials, parents of students, financial contributors and assorted relatives. I ate copiously, drank all that appeared in my glass, and was gnawed by a lingering doubt. What if some reporter knew the difference between overpedaling and clean playing? What if I were unmasked in the morning papers? I asked Consuelo whether any critics might be reviewing the event.

"Oh, yes," she said brightly, "they're here with us tonight."

"Which are they?" I asked in fright. When she pointed to the two gushy ladies who had asked for autographs, I knew I was home free.

In the morning I stopped by the music school to return the suit and find out how much they had made from the concert. At ten pesos a head they had netted around four hundred dollars, indicating an audience of about three hundred. "We had to buy the shirt and shoes," admitted Consuelo, handing them back, "so please keep them as a gift." I assumed that the spotlight had passed, but for days afterward people came up to me on the street, or detained me as I cashed a traveler's check, or collared me as I bought potatoes, to tell me they especially liked the Brahms or the Debussy. I still felt I had acted out a fantasy, but if people took me for the real thing, was I the deceived? La Paz struck me as unturned soil where anything artistic, or at least musical, might grow.

I watched for the reviews. I never found anything by either of the ladies, but I did discover one of some length by a man whose name was unfamiliar. He praised the precision of the Bach, the delicacy of the Debussy, the vigor of the Gershwin, then denounced the hair in the musical soup—the wretched behavior of the children and the failure of parents to control them. I bought the last copy on the stand, then ran from store to store looking for more. I ran into an acquaintance who asked why I was dashing about with so little dignity. When I explained, he told me the reviewer was a close friend and he would conduct me to him. I found myself in a newspaper office talking to a man in his mid-thirties from Mexico City, a veteran of many concerts who was stuck in the provinces and sincerely liked the performance.

And there the episode would have ended but for a strange coda. A few days later I received a call from a woman named Quichu Isaïs. She belonged to a faction that had split from Consuelo and had rallied around an old and distinguished composer who had written, among other things, the official Baja California Sur state song, "Costa Azul." Luis Pelaez had been the music school's first director and had taught there until Consuelo, they claimed, kicked him out. They couldn't be seen at any function arranged by Consuelo, but neither did they want to miss the visiting pianist. Quichu would be *so* grateful if I would go some morning to the composer's house and repeat the performance for him and a few friends. . . . Was this a musical tar baby from which I would never be free? I couldn't imagine anyone not liking the gracious and lively Consuelo, but what did I know about La Paz intrigue?

I met Quichu at her home near the waterfront and rode with her to the composer's house. I asked about the rift between the composer and Consuelo. It was a scandal, she said. He had taught Consuelo music, hired her to teach at the school, then he put her in charge and she fired him.

A silver-haired ruddy-faced man in his sixties met us at the door. Instead of shaking my hand he took them both in his, inspected them as if estimating karats and pronounced, "We must take advantage of genius when it comes along." I nearly broke out in a cold sweat.

In the room were a half dozen people, including two nuns with a tape recorder. I accepted coffee, then asked the composer about his music. Was any of it recorded? Could I hear some? He said that he had never gotten around to copyrighting it, was afraid someone would steal it, and therefore kept it to himself. He would, however, play some for me. He played a couple of fast character pieces, of mild syncopation and dissonance, then announced he would play his personal favorite, called "Mata Hari, or the Bird of Morning."

"Mata Hari, the spy?" I asked.

"There is the delusion. People think she was a spy, but I have read all the books and sifted the evidence. She was innocent and she was martyred. I have written her music." He turned around, and over a bass of sevenths, with a melody colored by grace notes a fifth above, he picked out an obsessively reharmonized phrase that called up some ravishing slow movement from Villa-Lobos.

"Could I hear it again?" I asked. He obliged.

I knew that my moment was fast approaching. The composer excused himself and went to the kitchen. Under a clock that now read 10:30 I saw him pour a stiff splash of what looked like Kentucky bourbon into a tumbler, toss it off, steady himself a moment, then return. Might that have been a factor in his dismissal? The composer resettled in his armchair, one of the nuns punched on the recorder and I lit into the trusty Schumann. I played a few more pieces without trying to repeat the entire program. As a gesture toward the composer's own heritage I concluded with the *Sevilla*, which trails off in diminishing chords and ends with a final chord that should blaze like a gong. I have learned since to place my hands over the keys and snap my wrists so that the chord rings true as the hands fly up, but at the time I knew only to swoop upon it like a hawk. I missed.

I was the only one to laugh. The rest applauded politely and the nuns switched off the recorder. I asked the composer if I could have a copy of "Mata Hari." No, he said sadly, he couldn't risk having it pirated. I rose to go, urging him to get his work copyrighted so it could be heard. He urged me to keep playing and, in the episode's most truthful moment, to find more time to practice.

On the way back Quichu said she had been trying for years to get the composer even to write down his work so that *she* could copyright it but, she sighed, he was basically lazy. I left La Paz with an image of a public hungry for music and a small musical community at each other's throats.

Over the next seventeen years I kept marginally in touch with music in La Paz. I too was haunted by Mata Hari—the music, not the spy—and in 1975 I knocked on the composer's door. He greeted me warmly and asked me in. I told him how much I had admired "Mata Hari." Would he play it for me? When he finished, I asked again for a copy of the score. He was so afraid it would be plagiarized, he said, that he hadn't even committed it to staff paper. In that case, would he play it again? He did, and I asked to hear it one more time. Pleased, he repeated it as I ran my mental recording system. If I could hear it a few more times, I thought, I could capture it, but to ask for it again was awkward. The music itself was elusive, and when I left the house it vanished like a dream that melts as one reaches for it.

When I returned to La Paz in 1977 after the cave painting trip, myopic from the theft of my glasses, a friend drove me to the music school's new location on a street off the plaza. Consuelo was bustlingly in charge but the quarters were cramped and no better equipped. Consuelo asked me to play, and in front of a dozen students I attempted Chopin's *Ballade no. 3,* which had been well under control before I left home. Half blind and stiff after weeks without playing, I slaughtered it. When I inquired after Luis Pelaez, the composer, I learned he had died, presumably taking "Mata Hari" with him.

In the early eighties I learned that the music school had acquired its own campus, and I pulled up to the orange iron fence endemic to state-run schools. I walked dumbstruck into a complex of long elegant buildings landscaped with hibiscus, oleander, almond and rubber trees. I found the office and asked for Consuelo. A secretary told me she was in conference; would I please be seated. Consuelo, ten minutes later, was friendly but harried and offered me a quick tour. There were rows of practice rooms, classrooms, and a small auditorium, all surrounded by immaculate foliage. I recognized the Yamaha console and saw that the mad portrait of Schumann was part of a series that included Beethoven and Bach. How had all this sprung into being?

It was, said Consuelo, a conjunction of luck. A man who had studied eight years with the music school became governor and allocated funds for the campus. When the buildings were up but empty, Carmen de López Portillo, wife of Mexican president José López Portillo, came through La Paz and Consuelo staged a concert in her honor. Señora López Portillo was so impressed that a month later the necessary instruments arrived—pianos, guitars, violins, violas and cellos. Meanwhile the school had snared a Brazilian pianist who had studied for five years in Vienna and was the new star of the faculty. Consuelo's five minutes for me were up and I left awed by the music school's turn of fortune.

When I returned to spend entire winters in La Paz in the early nineties, I approached the new music school as I had once approached the old one off the plaza, a bit intimidated, suffering piano withdrawal and craving practice. Consuelo had retired, but the new director told me I was welcome to play weekday mornings—quiet time before schools let out and children poured in for lessons. The school became a daily routine during which I drilled under the gaze of Schumann or Bach and rested my eyes out the window, where a woman cleaned and a man hosed and gardened, gossiping excitedly, and another man, idle and silent, paraded through the courtyard making sure nothing was amiss.

Since the morning students were all adults with their own pianos, I was the only regular who used the rooms strictly for practice. Iberê, the Brazilian teacher, was bearded, detached, humorous, a virtuoso with an eye for irony. Among his students were Alejandrina the veterinarian, full of well-focused enthusiasm; Fernando, a young man who owned a shoe store; Lupe, who sought refuge in the piano from her socially prominent family; Iliana, a university student; Maricela, who had an aquarium concession at Alejandrina's clinic; and assorted housewives. The stringed instruments that Consuelo had received from Señora López Portillo were in storage and I never saw one. Aside from an occasional drummer through the wall, a couple of guitarists and a brass band on Fridays, the school was purely a piano school. Classical concerts by the school were piano solos, piano duets or duo piano. During my first winter at the school I was invited to participate in a duo piano recital with Iberê and his students.

The occasion was the school's fiftieth anniversary, for it had been founded in 1942, in a location previous to the one on the plaza. I was keen on the piece—a Busoni transcription of Mozart's overture to *The Magic Flute*—and still more eager for the social events that surrounded the concert. The first of these, whose object was to make plans, was convened at Alejandrina's veterinary clinic.

It surprised me that the music school and the venues around town, all staffed by ample bureaucracies, left the performers to design programs, make and distribute posters, print and sell tickets. I had attended the inauguration of the city's landmark hall, the Teatro de la Ciudad, in 1986. Notables included the president of Mexico, Miguel de la Madrid, and I had been struck by the casualness with which his small entourage passed while people stood in silence. A young man in our party gave a yip like a bored coyote, saying afterward that it was, after all, the president and somebody should do *something*. The hall was large and architecturally impressive, but the grand piano that accompanied the popular program thudded without resonance, hadn't been tuned, and was periodically drowned out by a gale-force air conditioner behind us. The air conditioner had since been tempered but the instrument was the same piano-shaped object. Local performers could only rent this imposing hall at exorbitant rates and do all the publicity themselves. Jeni Bergold, La Paz's other Brazilian pianist, played a recital there when she first arrived, but despite a respectable house she lost money. To avoid the theater's pitfalls we would be playing the municipal art gallery next door, where the audience would writhe on folding chairs but the musicians would stay in the black.

We met in the back room of the veterinary clinic, a cavernous chamber with a spinet. The adult pianists had become a social group with a name—*La Tecla Perpetua* or The Eternal Key—and the standard drink was the *cubano,* a mix of brandy, Pepsi, club soda and ice, nursed while packs of cigarettes were consumed. We spent a couple of hours over a statement for the program. How, for instance, were we to refer to our audience? The first suggestion, Paceños and Baja Californians, was discarded when we realized that most concertgoers came from elsewhere. The majority were from Mexico City and other urban areas of the interior, with a sprinkling of foreigners that included Americans from the marina. Someone mentioned that a teachers' event conflicted with ours and perhaps we should reschedule. No, came the objection, teachers were paid too little to attend concerts and weren't our target. Alejandrina said she would get the governor to attend because she was veterinarian to his pets. By midnight we had knocked out our three sentences, and each of us then played our half of the duo piano pieces amid enthusiastic comment though, musically, they made only half-sense.

The evening before the performance we gathered at the gallery to see to the placement of the pianos and to run through the program on site. Two consoles from the school, one of them the Yamaha I had played seventeen years before, waited next to planking for a stage. We constructed a small platform and angled the pianos just so. As we ran through the pieces we had spent months perfecting, they suddenly sounded hollow and deficient. The echo of our practice room at the school, where the pianos spanned an entire wall, had redoubled the sonority and deceived us. Here the pianos were naked, ill-matched, untuned by the move, and lost in the reaches of the gallery. We lacked even a tuner to turn to. All were let down, and Iberê, for whom the concert was a momentary focus of his career, railed against incompetence and appeared to be facing the abyss. We opened the piano tops, to no avail. Alejandrina suggested removing the boards under the keys to expose the harplike entrails, and suddenly we felt the vibrations and heard the sonority. All of us played better, and though the pianos were still ill-matched and untuned, at least we could make noise for the audience.

At midnight Alejandrina invited us to her clinic, which was just across the street, for *cubas*. Before she could attend us she had to check on two sick animals. She returned five minutes later to report that the monkey was hanging on but the dog had died. As she was reaching into the ice chest to fill our glasses, she suddenly looked up and said, "I just wanted you to know that I washed my hands after I disposed of the dead dog." That moment, more than any other, still evokes for me the flavor of classical music in La Paz.

The day of the concert I was again scrambling for suitable clothes. Fernando had lent me a white shirt and black pants, but the waist was too small and at the last minute he had to substitute a pair of his father's, which Alejandrina ironed an hour before starting time. Word of mouth and our few posters had filled the chairs, with more attendants lining the walls, menacing the lithographs, and we cut off ticket sales at 150. The governor didn't show and was rumored to have gone to a boxing match instead. Iberê uncorked a bottle of rosé backstage and each of us had a belt before going on to perform. The preconcert crises must have relaxed us, for we all played our best, drank at the waterfront afterward with fans, then repaired to the veterinary clinic for a celebratory session of *La Tecla Perpetua*. Deep into the night Iberê disclosed that he was a grand-nephew of the soprano Renate Tebaldi. Consuelo's son admitted that as a nine-year-old, what he remembered from my concert in 1973 wasn't the music but my Hush Puppies, cool new shoes that had not yet reached La Paz. I wanted to see the evening's revelations to a close but was facing a radio interview the next morning and left at three. I later learned that Iberê, Alejandrina and Fernando philosophized until eight, then went out to breakfast and were spotted, with much amusement, by a doctor who had attended the concert and recognized that the bleary-eyed musicians were still dressed for performance.

In subsequent years of practicing at the school, participating in concerts and socializing with *La Tecla Perpetua,* I was constantly reminded that Baja California remained a frontier for the arts. The indigenous population had been wiped out and the peninsula resettled by ranchers, fishermen, miners and traders whose concerns were necessarily practical. When they expressed themselves artistically, it was in crafts—in tooled leatherwork for saddles, in intricately strung beds of wood and rawhide. They appropriated the ranch music of Northern Mexico, sometimes adding new tunes and local verses. Even the most popular presentation at El Teatro de La Paz, *Los Huizapoles*— roughly, The Burrs—was a pair of comics who glorified ranching culture by taking it to its extremes in parody. Artistically, La Paz was said to be "behind the Cholla Curtain." Iberê, who eventually left La Paz because of better per- forming opportunities elsewhere, felt exhilarated by the idea of inscribing classical music on a blank slate. In La Paz one could sell shoes or inoculate cats by day and perform classical music by night. Because Baja California was a cultural desert, those of modest ability—as I had learned sometime be- fore—could participate at a higher level than they could where culture was deep-rooted.

But I noticed that older members of the La Paz musical community didn't think of themselves as pioneers but of having fallen from a golden age. In the thirties and early forties, went their version, La Paz had more grand pianos than cars. Quichu Isaïs, who had summoned me to the old composer's home in 1973 and had since moved to Vienna, told a radio interviewer that pianism in Baja California had started in the small silver mining town of El Triunfo, south of La Paz, toward the end of the last century. The leading families were European, with little indigenous blood, and every ranch had two grand pianos, some even three. Playing piano was as natural as breathing and little girls who stumbled over their Beethoven were admonished, what do you want to do when you grow up, *cook?* Pianists kept up with new European music and the latest scores by Debussy were better known in El Triunfo than they were in Mexico City. With the close of the El Triunfo silver mines, the leading families moved to La Paz and perpetuated the tradition in the form of salons and *tertulias,* weekly get-togethers whose members would recite, stage dramatic works and make music. The founding of the La Paz Music School actually predated Bellas Artes, the famous school in Mexico City. The music school extended the public grade and high school curricula, requiring knowledge of solfeggio, mastery of scales and the performance of difficult music from memory. In a flourish of genealogy, Quichu said that Luis Pelaez, founding director of the music school, had studied with Gomez Anda, who studied with Krauze, who studied with Liszt, who studied with Czerny, who studied with Beethoven. Classical music in Baja California came straight from the source.

Iberê was agnostic about La Paz's golden age of music. To hear them talk, he said, you would think El Triunfo and La Paz were Paris and Berlin. Nobody throws away a grand piano, and if there were more of them than cars, where are they now? We don't lack for old cars. Why didn't the old guard perpetuate the golden age instead of waxing nostalgic and blaming the present? Why, for instance, did Quichu move to Vienna—where she met Iberê and dispatched *him* to rescue music in La Paz? Elma Vidaurri, the deodorizer distributor who visited La Paz in the fifties and moved there in the early seventies, confirmed the vitality of the *tertulias*. The weekly gatherings were anticipated, were exciting, were the heart of La Paz. Most gathering places had pianos, though most of the pianos, she added, were uprights. She ascribed the death of the *tertulias* to the coming of TV, videos and discos, as well as the swamping of tight-knit groups by new arrivals—a point also made by Quichu in her interview. The older generation felt that La Paz was losing culture rather than gaining it as it grew. Newcomers felt left out.

An instance of cultural decline was made vivid to me one morning by Lupe, descendant of the family that was said to have had the best salon in La Paz. She was desperate to play the piano, even though she had one in her own living room. When she played at home, her husband and even her grown live-in children verbally abused her: why did she have to play that horrible music, that Mozart, that Chopin? Sometimes they went so far as to drown her out with rock radio. She taught at the music school in the afternoon, in a room with her name on the door, and I usually practiced in that room in the morning because it had the best piano. Occasionally she dropped by herself to play and would ask if I would be so kind as to switch to some other room in the few minutes when she could have some peace. I knew through *La Tecla Perpetua* that her husband's life was a nonstop cabaret, but I was newly shocked that this patriarchal family's insensitivity should reduce this lovely woman to apologizing for her rights. Never did I more eagerly surrender a piano.

If La Paz had fallen from a golden age, what was the evidence in the other arts? The best-known painter in town was Francisco Merino, who had arrived from Mexico City in the early eighties, had created such public art as murals for city hall, modernized cave paintings for the Hotel La Perla, and even the blue shell behind the altar of the Adorers, along with his own easel paintings. For him the only conceivable golden age in the visual arts would be the era of the original cave paintings, whenever that was. But there had been two minor waves of art, the first, between 1950 and 1965, centered around the Escuela Normal, the teachers' college. La Paz was still physically isolated, and its art, reflecting a ranching and fishing culture, tended toward naive landscape painting. In the early seventies, when Baja California Sur became a state, the road was finished, ferry service was in place, and the university was founded, the arts received a larger, state-funded impulse. Fishing was already in decline and the government thought that tourism might be boosted by an infusion of art that looked folkloric and indigenous. A group of artists trekked by mule to the midpeninsula cave paintings, though only Francisco actually incorporated the motifs in his work. Literary magazines surfaced and succumbed at the university. Francisco opened a *peña*—a café where customers could perform verbally and musically, a kind of public *tertulia*—and kept it open for a couple of years. The university now and then brought out books of scholarship and original poetry. With the election in 1986 of the governor who had chosen boxing over our concert, state funding for the arts came to an end. La Paz lacked even a commercial gallery and anyone who wanted to live by the brush had to go to Cabo San Lucas, with its hotels full of rich foreigners. Perhaps there had been a golden age of the piano, but even pianists were back to being pioneers.

As a foreigner in La Paz I enjoyed the pioneering: a request to play for an oceanography class graduation, the offer of a formal recital in the small auditorium of the music school. This latter was a chance, twenty years later, to improve on the concert of 1973, and I scheduled largely the same program. This time I was armed with my own white shirt and black pants and I knew the correct opus numbers of all the pieces. The piano was a new Chinese grand donated to the school by Consuelo, and the hall, with extra chairs, probably held a hundred people. Over my head, instead of the manic portrait of Schumann, was a reproduction of Delacroix's Chopin, my favorite painting of any composer. The ambient temperature was normal, there was little coughing, the children didn't squirm, and I had learned how to bow. I did notice an inordinate amount of whispering between pieces. During intermission I learned that the programs, with their impeccable information and meticulously worded tribute to the music school faculty, had been inadvertently locked in the office, no one had the key, and the audience was trying to figure out what I was playing. I was still pioneering after all, and I announced the rest of the program from the stage.

In 1993 came an unexpected addition to La Paz culture, a café that Nora opened on the waterfront. To my private delight, it was the very space that had been occupied by El Yate, where the banquet had been held after my concert in 1973. A more elaborate version of the *peña* that Francisco Merino had tried earlier, the Café Chanate offered beer and wine, cappucino and light food, views in three directions, and an upright piano. Nora encouraged locals and visitors to try their acts, often sight unseen. I worked up nights of tangos, of Brazilian music and, closest to my heart, an all-Gershwin concert to take place during the Fiestas de La Paz—ten days each May when La Paz celebrates Cortés's disastrous attempt to found it in 1534. La Paz is casual about time, but the Gershwin concert had to be punctual because the Café Chanate shared a plaza where rock bands played every night during the fiesta, and there was no way a piano could compete. Nora had the manager of the sound system drop a mike into the piano and connect it to the outdoor speakers. Eight o'clock was far too early for Paceños and we started with no one in the cafe, but the tables soon filled with people who had followed the music through the speakers from blocks away. Young rockers hovered at the window by the piano, unexpectedly immersed in the music. After days of being tormented by plug-in guitars, it was sheer joy to retaliate on a creaking upright with the *Rhapsody in Blue*.

Concerns were misplaced that the American-owned Chanate would not be patronized by locals, and it even became the site of *La Tecla Perpetua*'s greatest social debacle. I had just participated in Iberê's duo-piano concert of short pieces, some involving two players at each piano, for a grand total of nineteen pianists. There were so many guests for the celebration afterward that rather than overwhelm someone's house we invaded the Chanate. We joined the tables in a grand U and sat as if at a banquet. As I ordered my beer, I noticed several carafes of what appeared to be water. Wine glasses were distributed, the carafes were poured, toasts were made, and the clear liquid proved to be tequila. When I had nearly finished my glass, someone tipped it over, apologized, refilled it, and I downed it during the next round of toasts. The seat next to Lupe the socialite was vacant and she gestured for me to join her. She filled the empty wine glass in front of me with tequila. The tequila was her contribution to the evening, she said; it was a special brew that wasn't sold commercially and that her husband obtained from the interior. Wasn't it delicious? I felt compelled to sip and appreciate while Lupe told me she had actually gotten her disco-crazed husband to the concert, though he refused to come backstage afterward and greet her friends. Suddenly the two beers and the three tequilas collided in my brain. I felt socially incapacitated and I slipped away, grateful to have arrived on foot.

I learned next day that the party had lasted three hours after my midnight departure. By that time Lupe had passed out. One of the women took her home, tucked her into a guest bed, then called Lupe's husband to assure him that she was in good hands and would be home in the morning. Rather than thanking the Samaritan and apologizing for any inconvenience, he and Lupe's brother charged over to the house, seized her, told her that she was never again to talk to any members of *La Tecla Perpetua,* threatened to confiscate her piano and declared the music school off-limits when she wasn't teaching. Furthermore, she would no longer be corrupted by classical music at home, for the house was henceforth to be free of all but the sensible strains of disco and rock. Knowing the men's mindset, said Lupe's friend, if any of the males of the group—Iberê or Fernando or I—had been on the premises, merely having a drink in the parlor while Lupe was sleeping it off, there would have been further hell to pay.

"Lupe's family treats her like a servant," I said to Lupe's friend.

"No," she replied, "people like that already have servants, who are people to the extent that they are useful. When a woman is more lovely and giving than they deserve, she turns into a piece of furniture."

To use the piano as a passport to a locale's interior does not always lead to views of joy, but the paths are revelatory and I still hoped that one might lead to "Mata Hari." In 1992, two nights before I left La Paz, I learned that the composer's nephew, Pichu Pelaez, was playing piano in an Italian restaurant called Ciao. I listened until his break, then asked if he could play "Mata Hari," by Luis Pelaez.

"I don't play it," Pichu calmly replied, "but I do have a tape of it." I implored him for a copy and he promised to bring one the following night. When I returned on the eve of my departure, I was told it was Pichu's night off.

Maddeningly, the music had slipped away one more time. When I returned to La Paz, Ciao had closed and Pichu was spending time on the mainland. Just before I left La Paz in 1993, I learned that Pichu was managing the gallery where Iberê held his duo-piano concerts. I showed up with a blank cassette and asked for "Mata Hari." The next day Pichu returned the cassette with the music and told me the circumstance of the recording. Quichu, who had pestered the old composer for his music and also realized it was going to die with him, arranged to meet him one day at the music school and arrived with a tape recorder running in her purse. She asked if he would play his compositions in one of the practice rooms, purely for her enjoyment. He played his trademark "Costa Azul," a march of his devising, then "Mata Hari." I took the tape triumphantly back to Aspen and worked it out in my house.

The piece was still elusive and I realized I was naive to think I could have caught it if the composer had run through it a few more times. He played it three times on the tape. Half of the piece—the part I nearly remembered—remained fixed between playings, but the second half wandered over a loose pattern and was clearly part improvisation. A second reason for his not writing it down might have been that it hadn't quite jelled, even for him—and, furthermore, that indeterminacy was part of "Mata Hari's" very character. In this lone survival of the music, the notes were muffled by the folds of Quichu's purse, with extraneous notes added by a child practicing scales in the next room. Aside from Quichu's exclamation, "¡Qué bonita!" at the conclusion of "Mata Hari," her voice and the composer's are too blurred to decipher. Overheard as if through a series of veils, the music remained as fugitive as the figure who inspired it, and anyone who tried it would have to extemporize. I played it over and over, experimenting with the free part, and came up with my own slightly unstable version of "Mata Hari."

I had the music at last and wanted to make it public, but in 1994 there were no recitals in the offing. That left the Chanate. When Nora asked for an event during the Fiestas de La Paz, I proposed a night of Mexican and La Paz music, with photocopied lyrics so the audience could sing along, all to conclude with the reintroduction of "Mata Hari." Nora got the event listed on the official calendar of events, and I told the story of the music in full during a radio interview two weeks before. Nora set the time with the manager of the sound system. We were to commence at 7:30 sharp, for the first band would begin at nine.

When I arrived at 7:30, the Chanate was empty. No matter, said Nora; they've changed the schedule and we can't have the mike now anyway. Gradually those who came for the event filtered in, including the strong voices I had asked to lead the singing. But the plaza emcee introduced one band after another and wouldn't tell Nora when we could start. By nine, when our program was supposed to be over, those who had come for it had left, including the booming voices. It wasn't until 10:30 — three hours after the time listed on the calendar and plugged on the radio — that the host in the plaza announced that a program of Mexican music was about to begin in the Café Chanate. A crowd of total strangers surged in and filled the tables. Nora passed out song lyrics, a mike was dropped in the piano and I plunged in.

Without the strong voices to lead, people sang quietly, but the mood was more of nostalgia than self-consciousness. As I got to the last song, "Costa Azul"—the official state song by Luis Pelaez that was to precede "Mata Hari"—I heard another band cranking up in the plaza. The rockers had found a way to shortcut the mike, but I was not going to be stopped from playing "Mata Hari." I stood up and shouted a single sentence in Spanish that I was about to play a lost piece of music called "Mata Hari," by La Paz's own composer, Luis Pelaez Manríquez, and played it as loudly as the piece's impressionism would tolerate. When I finished, someone shouted back, "That was beautiful! Would you play it again?" I did. Then the roar from the plaza overcame all and the event was over. When I got over my exasperation at the interference, I realized that "Mata Hari"—sought by my failing memory, pursued in failed appointments, finally caught through the fabric of a purse and against a child's scales—had once more been glimpsed, as was now tradition, behind an updated veil.

The next morning a tiny ill-dressed man came up to me on the street and tapped my arm. Winter carnival and the Fiestas de La Paz are the only times that the city is afflicted with beggars and I was prepared to be asked for money. "I just wanted to thank you for the Mexican music last night," he said, "especially that last thing you played, that 'Mata Hari.' That was extraordinary. I hope I can hear it again."

9

SALT ON THEIR TALES

Guerrero Negro, a town I had long treated as a beer and gas stop midway down the peninsula, always struck me as small but monotonous. Here the word "salary," literally "salt money," returned to its roots, for nearly every citizen worked for the world's largest evaporative salt operation or its support businesses. City blocks in unvarying rectangles democratically apportioned the potholes and dust. Pacific fogs broke midmorning or shrouded the town all day. Interest was briefly sparked by fences made from a yucca called *datilillo,* whose posts had taken root and seasonally sprouted and bloomed—and, while it lasted, the curiously named Bermuda Triangle Billiard Parlor. Salt company officials lived in a small but trim suburban area distanced from ramshackle plebeian housing by a well-tended park; more indicative of the town's status was a quonset hut post office that retained a permanently transient quality even as the company became a world player in the salt market. An artist from La Paz told me that oxidation from the briny air gave an interestingly rusty cast to the litter. Once, waiting in line for unleaded, I counted an even hundred turkey vultures on the microwave tower over town.

Guerrero Negro blossomed into an unlikely spur to adventure when I chanced to meet a biologist from Mexico City who had moved there to work for the federal interior department. Fernando Heredia had taken a better paying job with the salt operation but remained a volunteer in a program to protect the Peninsular pronghorn, an endangered subspecies of the animal most Americans refer to, inaccurately, as the antelope. I had once seen the Sonoran pronghorn, another endangered subspecies, in the Cabeza Prieta Wildlife Refuge in Arizona, and had been struck by its size, delicacy and speed. The pronghorn was the swiftest sustained runner in the world and had been clocked up to ninety-five kilometers per hour for several minutes at a time. Its eyes were like eight-power binoculars. The Baja California population, which had diverged in isolation, once numbered in the thousands and roamed an area eight hundred kilometers in length, from San Felipe and San Quentín in the north to the latitude of Bahía Magdalena in the south. Despite a risky curiosity, pronghorn don't tolerate much human presence. Hunting and the disruption of habitat had so decimated the population that Mexico made the killing of pronghorn illegal in 1922. A census of the peninsula in 1925, conducted by unknown means, found roughly five hundred animals. When censuses resumed in 1977, the Peninsular pronghorn was confined to a single area within the Vizcaíno Desert of the midpeninsula, a stretch of lowlands projecting into the Pacific between the whale-breeding waters of Scammon's Lagoon and Laguna San Ignacio. Census figures had since hovered around one hundred, dropping in December 1990 to as few as twenty-two animals.

When SEDUE—then the Mexican environmental department's acronym—first undertook to protect the remaining animals, they began with a ploy also popular in the United States, the poisoning of coyotes. Coyotes, and in rare cases mountain lions, did take occasional young, but the three species had long led lives in balance and poisoning was soon seen to be futile. SEDUE then turned its attention to educating ranchers and townspeople, particularly inhabitants in the coastal villages between the two lagoons, who made their living harvesting wildlife of the sea. Signs warned that penalties for shooting pronghorn included fines and up to three years in jail. The Peninsular subspecies looked enough like other pronghorn that outside trophy hunters weren't considered a threat, but the small gene pool left the population vulnerable to inbreeding and disease. The best insurance seemed a second, captive population.

Unexpectedly, an opportunity opened up. In 1986, Exportadora de Sal, the salt company, enlarged its complex of evaporation ponds so as to wholly surround an area of former pronghorn habitat fifty thousand hectares in extent, known as La Mesa de la Cholla. The sprawling hill was covered with native vegetation, moated by basins of seawater and an impassable canal, and all points of access were controlled by Exportadora. A few fawns could be captured shortly after birth and transferred to the island, where they could be bottle-fed in an enclosure for three months, then raised on vegetation grown on-site. Predators would be banished, and adult pronghorn could later be introduced so as to have a diverse breeding population. If the captive

animals flourished, some could be transferred to current habitat and eventually—once human beings had been persuaded not to shoot them—
returned to areas in which they had been exterminated. Experts in animal
capture from the United States, the country with the most pronghorn, had
been down to investigate, and Mexican biologists had conferred with them
in Minnesota. The grand plan would be formulated by the Center for Biological Investigations in La Paz, coordinated by SEDUE, and financed by Exportadora. The first capture was set for February 1991, three months after I
heard about it. I asked Fernando, the biologist I had met, whether I could
watch if I kept out of the way. I didn't have to stand aside; I could help.

In the three months between Fernando's invitation and the proposed capture, SEDUE reconsidered its resources and knowledge, knew they couldn't
afford to jeopardize a single animal, and opted for another year of study. Fernando told me I was still welcome to visit the habitat, but when the head of
SEDUE in La Paz heard about an expedition he hadn't authorized, he summoned me to his office. After a crisp exchange he allowed me to enter the
area with SEDUE officials and conduct an unofficial census if I paid all expenses. I enlisted a friend in La Paz and, unsure what to expect, we arrived
in Guerrero Negro on February 28, 1991.

We certainly didn't expect that SEDUE's three Guerrero Negro employees—charged with overseeing midpeninsula resources that included
cave paintings, whale-breeding lagoons, and the Vizcaíno Desert with its
rare plants and endangered pronghorn—had no vehicle they trusted out of
town. Once they had numbered up to nine people, with dependable wheels,
but bureaucratic support fluctuated wildly. At the moment they were down
to two former Exportadora pickups rusted out from years of driving between salt ponds, and until we arrived they couldn't even get out to where
their duties lay. But by a stroke of timing we arrived at sundown on the last
day of the month, just when they piled into the pickups to count the town's
osprey population in the brief time between the birds' return to the nest and
nightfall.

Upon the system of wires that distributed electricity from the diesel gen-
erating plant, ospreys had assembled their vast, shaggy nests. Wherever a post
formed a corner, sprouted a branch, or supported a couple of crosspieces
with insulators, these fish-eating eagles had tossed their salads of sticks and
trash. Fernando said that bird electrocutions were rare, but over the years so

many damp sticks had been dropped across the wires, shorting the current and blackening parts of town, that enraged citizens once pressured the electric company into dismantling all the nests. To the delight of SEDUE officials, the birds immediately rebuilt. SEDUE talked the electric company into building platforms for nests above its wires and convinced the public that the privilege of hosting osprey was worth the occasional blackout. Our count turned up thirty-three osprey, which particularly pleased the officials in that a recent French visitor reported that there were only three nesting pairs in all of France.

Fascinated by the huge nests in the dusk, I revisited them on foot the next morning. The stick piles had been colonized by sparrows that swarmed in and out of their nests within nests, and cries of ospreys that stayed home to raise their young shrilled through Guerrero Negro's clamor of radios and combustion. Fewer than half of the ospreys had taken advantage of the pallets nailed up by the electric company. By osprey standards it seemed more chic to rig the nest on the electrical system and to innovate with burlap and plastic bags. The prize, I decided on my house tour, went to a creation that shaded an oversized tire where women with small children rested while making the social rounds. Engulfing its few sticks were palm fronds, strips of canvas, turquoise fishnet, torn clothing, pieces of rope, a garland of plastic ivy, a hem of blue tarp, blanket shreds, the brush end of a broom, a fan belt, a hanger, pantyhose and shredded Visqueen—an entire airborne landfill— upon which the architect glared at me through the pinhole of his yellow eye as if daring me to dispute his taste.

With a census already under our belts, we bought three days' worth of food, signed the papers that let the two of us from La Paz plus Fernando and a SEDUE official through the gates of Exportadora, and roared off in the jeep toward the salt flats. After years of peering toward the mists of Scammon's Lagoon and reading about the salt harvest, I thought I knew what to expect. I knew the company was 51 percent national and 49 percent owned by Mitsubishi of Japan and that, beginning in 1957, a system of dikes and canals had converted the broad tidal flats of the lagoon into evaporation ponds that now occupied 250 square kilometers. Water entered a gate and made a three-year pilgrimage through thirteen enormous ponds, each more saline than the one before, as seawater evaporated and rendered its salt. Pacific winds and steady noonday sun speeded the process. Each pond was precisely one meter deep, so closely calculated that aside from ten pumps at the entrance and two along the way, the entire system was kept imperceptibly in motion by a tiny drop in elevation. Exportadora boasted that its products were pure and "the only chemicals are wind and sun." Actually the process was not so simple. Seawater contains algae and other organic materials, as well as sulphur and various minerals, and all need to be removed or condensed out. In ponds 4 through 6, microorganisms were introduced to decrease the reflection of light and increase its absorption. Table salt precipitated out first, then salts of magnesium and potassium. Harvesting machines collected 2,000 tons of salt per hour from the last pond and dispatched it to a washing plant, where it was pelted with a brine spray that brought its purity to 99.7 percent. A conveyor loaded the salt onto barges that floated it in elongated pyramids to nearby Isla Cedros. Ships that could stash up to 7,500 tons of salt hauled it to other ports in Mexico, the United States and Asia—coarse-grained for water softeners, de-icing and industrial use; fine-grained for table use. Japan, whose national palate is commonly identified with soy sauce, got half its salt from Guerrero Negro.

As we drove onto the dikes between the ponds, my image of saline mechanics was overwhelmed by billowing color and light. The air was dense with moisture, radiant, cool and fishy. Rectangular ponds suggesting snow-fields stretched on either side of causeways of packed sand as we skimmed on a single track. Some basins were so mistily blue that only a white line of salt divided water from sky; others were pink with algae or tinged a corrosive green. Because different salinities bred different insects and marine life, certain ponds were favored by curlews or yellow-legged sandpipers or avocets, so that each pond took on different geometric patterns from the forms and markings of its birds. We paused to watch more than two hundred waders making an angular design with the spindly legs that give them their English name, stilt, and the white bellies and black backs that give them the Spanish *monjita,* little nun. Eared grebes skimmed the surface by the hundreds in lines of smoke; northern shovelers and lesser scaups gathered in separate flotillas; flocks of sandpipers turned in flight like filings of a single mind— dark and striped backs that pivoted en masse, nearly disappearing, to reform as clouds of pale breasts. Certain areas featured a preponderance of white: white pelicans with their black wingtips hidden in folds, great and snowy egrets, blue herons in the white phase, as if they had all been dipped in salt. Marbled godwits suddenly burst from the surface with perfect spacing between each bird, forming an elongated cloud that swelled, shrank and drew itself out like a single sky serpent in a shifting lens. Some rectangles of water were so wide, their horizons so low, that they seemed the sea itself, and their spume blew onto our tracks like meringue. Occasionally we were jolted by having to make room for yellow trucks whose tires were as big as our jeep and whose gondolas were blinding with salt. Over subsequent censuses this skimming of the salt ponds became my favorite driving anywhere, and Fernando remarked that he had a colleague who drove the 30 kilometers of causeways for sport, attaining nonbirdwatching speeds of up to 120 kilometers per hour.

The last causeway ushered us onto La Mesa de la Cholla. After the evaporation ponds, this imagined haven for baby pronghorn was spectacularly nondescript, a wide elevation of scrubby plants. At its far end ten small yellow pumps straddled seawater, initiating its three-year drifting separation toward commerce and sky.

Seabirds, human geometry and screaming pumps dropped behind when we crossed the canal, and the silent dunes that ring Scammon's Lagoon received us with the earthy, medicinal smell of a weed called *manzanilla de coyote*. We had arrived at the bleakest, westernmost extension of the Vizcaíno Desert. The strange trees and endemic plants for which the Vizcaíno is known faded here to isolated shrubs and low vegetation. It was hard to believe that the pronghorn could get all the moisture they needed from these leathery leaves and the dew on their surface, but with no open water in their habitat, these greens were their drink as well as their food. There was no mistaking the plants' toughness, visible in the way their talonlike roots built cones of sand that held in the wind. Normally such shrubs provided a mere dusting of green over gritty sand, but 1991 was gloriously abnormal. Recent rains had broken six years of drought, and wildflowers awaiting this grace had burst into stabs and sweeps of color. Horned larks darted and swooped from our wheels as we followed, lost, and refound tracks made by Pemex, the national oil company, which prospected here in the 1970s, found three wells of natural gas, capped them without revealing which of their many wells they were, and had so far held them in reserve. It was these roads, ruled in straight lines over the pitch of terrain and now nearly lost in vegetation and blowing sand, that we frequently took in search of pronghorn.

We shifted into four-wheel and crawled several kilometers down a rocky arroyo. Abandoning the car, we climbed a rust-colored hill where "you can always see pronghorn." We scanned the circumference for the animals' white rump patches, fur they can actually flare outward, using special muscles, to signal danger to each other. Fernando set up the SEDUE telescope. Through the grainy enlargement it was possible to make out a moving Pleiades that melted as soon as it wobbled into focus. We walked for an hour toward the far specks. The pronghorn vanished, but as we trudged back to the car against the sun, my eyes, driven downward, were dazzled by small yellow flowers called *airito,* or little airs, blue starbursts of wild onion, and magenta clouds of sand verbena, called *alfombrilla,* or little rugs.

We drove back up the arroyo, mashed flowered-over tracks until dark and camped for the night. Distant rains lingered and under a full moon we could see a downpour in the mountains to the east. Clouds circled the horizon, climbed a third of the way into the sky, and hemmed us like a broken bowl. Suddenly Fernando exclaimed and pointed opposite the moon, where an arc of rain and moonlight stood unbroken. It was a moonlit rainbow. I had seen the effect once before, more dimly, in Nevada, but hadn't otherwise heard or read about it and didn't know its name. Binoculars vaporized rather than focused it, but to the naked eye it appeared to shade from orange above to green within. As we sat for more than an hour watching the phenomenon, I asked what distinguished the Peninsular pronghorn from other subspecies. Fernando said that the differences in markings were slight, the most significant being a darker coloration. The important variation was behavioral, a life cycle that diverged several months from that of other subspecies, with mating in June and July instead of September and October, and parturition in late January and early February instead of April to June. Because this displaced biological clock had evolved on the peninsula, it was unlikely that another subspecies could be introduced into Baja California and survive. It would be the Peninsular pronghorn or none.

As we broke camp in the morning, a truck with three ranchers pulled up. Had we seen any cattle? No, said Fernando; had they seen any pronghorn? Adding up sightings, they had recently seen twenty-three, assuming no animals were counted twice. When they left, I asked Fernando whether cows didn't compete with pronghorn for precious forage. "Ranchers claim that cows and pronghorn eat the same thing during wet years when there's plenty of vegetation, like now, but during drought they specialize in different plants."

"Isn't that just the kind of answer you'd expect from ranchers?" I asked.

"Sure, but we don't have to take their word for it. A biologist in La Paz is studying the impact of cattle. We should know soon."

We had driven no more than a half hour beyond our campsite when Fernando spotted a pair of sticks pointing from a far bush. We bailed out, confirmed them as horns through binoculars, then moved noiselessly forward as they stayed put. I was suddenly aware that the others were drably dressed while I was flagrant in a red sweatshirt, but it was too late to change. After we had covered half the distance we began to walk with deeply bent knees to obscure ourselves, remaining upright to keep track of the horned bush, advancing in the Groucho Marx slide until my back cried for relief. We stopped behind a bush of our own, and through the binoculars I could see the spurs on the front of the horns that give the pronghorn its name. We also spotted a female behind the bush and two recently born pronghorns sprawling in the foliage in front of it. A newborn sprang to its feet and collapsed back in the weeds. "Do you have anything red?" whispered Fernando. I laughed and indicated my whole sweatshirt. "Are you wearing an undershirt?" he asked, apparently concerned for my warmth. I peeled to it and handed him the sweatshirt. "Pronghorns are attracted to red," he whispered, flipping the shirt on top of our bush and prodding it with a stick. There was no reaction from the other bush.

Fernando handed me my sweatshirt on the end of his stick, then advanced on all fours. I tied the red sleeves around my neck and crawled behind him. We stopped at another bush, twice as close as the previous one. Fernando took my shirt again and poked it provocatively on top of the bush. A mockingbird chattered like an informant on a tree behind us. The female pronghorn stepped from behind her bush and peered with interest. Hesitantly she made her way forward, starting, stopping, as if conscious that curiosity was mastering sense. She halted some twenty-five meters away, stared a moment, then retreated to her bush. The male then took his turn, ambling steadily until he was huge to the naked eye, fully detailed through binoculars.

I had never been so close to any variety of pronghorn and was struck by the long firm jaw. The horns especially had an assertive flourish, thrusting forward with the prongs, then curling back at the tip. The fur of this darker subspecies shone burnished cinnamon in the sun. Most winning up close were the eyes—huge, dark and moist, with long upwardly turned lashes one would term, by human standards, glamorous. After both sides had satisfied their mutual curiosity, the family of four took off with a delicate bounce.

Relieved of our crouch, we went to see what they had been eating. Their bush, *frutilla*, is known to be pronghorn forage, but they had been cropping flowers. Tracks swarmed all over, the adults' the length of my thumb, the fawns' a bit larger than my thumbnail, angled forward in the form of two-chambered hearts. I reminded Fernando that he had told me the male takes off after birth, leaving the young to be tended by the female. "This was an exception," he explained.

Over the next day and a half we spotted many more pronghorn, none so close as the shirt inspectors, but occasionally in larger groups. We worked toward the Pacific, scanning the flats with binoculars, setting up the scope, trying to fix for each other where a group of white dots stood out from the fawn-colored earth by aligning them with distant peaks of the Sierra Santa Clara, or mid-distance brush and cactus. The distinguishing white of the pronghorns' backs winked on and off like lighthouses. We also saw, singly, four coyotes, all fat and healthy—from gulping a wet year's bounty of rodents, we hoped, not baby pronghorn. At a crossroads near the Pacific, by a road to the fishing villages, we came upon a SEDUE sign warning of fines and jail terms for killing pronghorn.

Unexpectedly we ran into three men sinking a new well. We peered into the hole: surrounded by cement and doubled by a reflection at the bottom, it looked far deeper than its three meters. No, they informed us, they had not struck water, they had merely poured in enough to soften the earth and make digging easier. They lowered themselves to the bottom by rope, loosened the earth with a pick and hauled it up in a bucket. The actual water table, they figured, was at least double that depth.

Was this a new ranch? I asked as we left. No, said the SEDUE official with us, it was part of the *ejido,* the communal farm that ran cattle and owned a vast part of the desert through which we had passed. The three men were professional well diggers the *ejido* had hired, and as men in an unfamiliar location, far from a source of food, they were just the sort to pick off a pronghorn.

"Does the *ejido* have permission to put in the well?" I asked.

"Not from us," said the SEDUE official, "and we'll be looking into it. But they need three permissions in all, one from us, one from Recursos Hidraulicos, which manages the water, and one from the county government in Santa Rosalía. Any one of them can deny permission."

"And if the agencies disagree about the well, who wins?"

"You mustn't think of this system as a hierarchy, with one agency over another. They are all separate."

"So if there is a disagreement among agencies, the matter winds up in court?"

"That's the American system. We don't have courts that decide such matters. We appeal to higher authorities, and the party with the most pull wins. The *ejido,* for instance, is politically powerful and might appeal to the governor's office, or the governor himself, even though SEDUE denied permission to put in the well. *Ejidos* are older and have more pull than SEDUE. I personally doubt whether this well is going to strike water, but just by being here people drive away the pronghorn and the habitat shrinks. That's why the captive breeding program is so important."

By the end of three days our unofficial census, which covered most of the known habitat, had found sixty-seven animals. I also had glimpsed the human complication that protecting pronghorn could breed.

The dramatic live capture that first lured me to the pronghorn program was further postponed, pending more censuses and study, but having seen the creature in its habitat I became a chronic volunteer. SEDUE had lost the aerial support that had once helped with the census, and I recruited a friend who piloted for Project LightHawk, an American nonprofit that flew light planes for environmental projects. The pilot arrived in February 1992, with only two available days. We were unable to muster a ground crew to coordinate with him, and two SEDUE officials and I joined him in the four-seater, flying transects at one hundred feet over likely terrain.

Having learned the area through immersion, I was curious to see how it was laid out. Salt ponds almost wholly encrusted bladder-shaped Scammon's Lagoon. Currents of the bay, driven by seven-foot tides, made pinwheels of turquoise, aquamarine and cobalt through which grey whales—enormous even from the air—swam in pairs, single file, at random. The collage of light and dark splotches on their skin, caused by barnacles and amphipods that colonize them from birth, showed even more strikingly than from a boat. As we droned to and from the Vizcaíno Desert, I realized that whalewatching by plane would be still more intrusive than by skiff, even as I tasted its forbidden clarity. And we saw, alas, more whales than pronghorn, for our hours of transects roused only twelve animals. We trusted they were beyond the confines of our search rather than wiped out, and the pilot remarked how strong and vibrant were the few we spotted compared with the ratty specimens he had flown over in Wyoming. I noted how the wide grid of one-lane tracks put in by Pemex in the seventies, at times nearly invisible on the ground, was still clear from the sky. The SEDUE officials noted how fresh ranching activity had generated new, upgraded roads that were exerting more human pressure.

Now that I had participated in censuses by land and by air, I was eager to experience the modes in combination. SEDUE and the Center for Biological

Investigation in La Paz made plans to count the animals three times a year—in April, to document the newborn; in June, to see how many young had survived the first months; and in early December, when the animals gathered in herds and were most easily counted. If the pronghorn consistently numbered over one hundred, the capture could be reconsidered. Meanwhile, the very fact of our being seen in the field five days at a time, with a plane overhead, strengthened the notion that people who bothered the animals might wind up in jail.

Another LightHawk pilot volunteered for the next census, then the job was taken over on a regular basis by Sandy Lanham, a woman from Tucson who ran a one-person environmental aviation program specializing in Mexico. In theory, the plane was to spot the animals, the ground forces were to verify the sightings, and each was to advise the other on where to look. In practice, radio contact consistently broke down. We could only communicate when the plane was nearly overhead, and whatever ground radio we mustered for a given census faithfully crackled dead by the third morning. Such censuses must have looked strange to its rare witnesses. Once we arrived at a new illegal ranch at the end of a suspiciously traveled spur. As we grilled the inhabitants and learned that they had been sent there by a cooperative in Bahía Tortugas, the plane appeared after a two-day absence. I whipped out the radio and as the plane circled our party screamed in two languages into its tiny microphone. The plane sped off, one of our officials informed the ranchers that the cooperative would be receiving an official complaint about their ranch, and we roared away in a government pickup and a jeep with Colorado plates. As soon as we had left, our second pickup showed up looking for us, and on learning which way we went, took off in pursuit. As the dust settled, I wondered what the ranchers, who claimed to know nothing of endangered pronghorn, made of such madness. The result of this scrambled procedure was two simultaneous surveys, one from the air and one from the ground. Combining them was only possible because, for the duration of the census, the pronghorn generally maintained their groupings—say, one male, three females and one newborn—and by eliminating similar groups we calculated the population.

Unforeseen was the degree to which endangered pronghorns pursued me to La Paz. I had befriended a biologist who was studying pronghorn habits, nutrition and the impact of cows, and who was the leading proponent of the live capture. He represented the Center for Biological Investigations in La Paz. His opposite number at SEDUE, a biologist turned bureaucrat, felt that the capture was dangerous and that the animals were better off dying of natural causes than by human interference. Both sides had defensible positions, analogous to a recent debate about whether the last California condors should be left in the wild or bred in captivity. The underlying problem was that the two men despised each other personally and refused to communicate. Their institutions were locked into the program as partners, but the bureaucrat convened meetings without the biologist and the biologist wouldn't telephone the bureaucrat. I went back and forth with messages and positions, and finally took the biologist in person to SEDUE headquarters and explained his position for him to the bureaucrat. When the bureaucrat suddenly committed to all the support we requested, I felt that my own role in the program had eerily switched from jeep driver to shuttle diplomat and facilitator.

Prickliness and animosities even followed us to the eve of departure in Guerrero Negro, where a biologist once complained that SEDUE officials had unfairly pulled rank on him over seats in the aerial census and that the salt company hadn't bought enough food for the ground contingent. When I replied that there were numerous boxes of food, that this wasn't the moment for perfectionism and it was time to count pronghorn, he countered that perfectionism was obligatory when dealing with endangered animals and he boarded the bus back to La Paz before we started. Just as communications were improving in La Paz, the difficult bureaucrat quit because his programs weren't being funded, President Salinas reorganized SEDUE itself—replacing higher officials and changing its acronym to SEDESOL—and a new bureaucrat had to be educated about the pronghorn program. The newcomer asked me if I realized that La Mesa de la Cholla, the intended refuge for baby pronghorn, had only one of the three vegetational types that pronghorn eat in their yearly cycle. The biologist studying pronghorn forage told me he had never heard of such a fact and why was I, a nonbiologist volunteer, even being asked such a question? At that point I realized that I would rather help pronghorn in the desert than in La Paz, and I withdrew from the fray.

Mercifully, once we pulled through the Exportadora gates and headed toward the pronghorn counts, tensions dropped away and all worked professionally together. The itinerary became familiar: across the salt basins to the dunes, through the arroyos, over the inland flats and mesas, south to the coast, then out five days later on bone-rattling washboard, completing a grand loop. In the absence of rain, tiny plants made a ratty carpet between freestanding tangles of barbs. The expanses were silent, with often no sound but the wheeze of a gnatcatcher or the gurgling of a black-throated sparrow until we turned our ignitions. On side trips when we didn't need my jeep, I sat on a drum of gas in the back of a pickup and watched the mottled desert floor with its sweeps of *vidrillo*, a plant as rusty as the cinders it thrived on. The first couple of days we were routinely alarmed at the scarcity of prong-horn, and the first sightings were always an event. On one nervous count we climbed out of an arroyo and caught our first pronghorn in a mound of green-ery, then another and another until a group of seven had opened like a fan. On the next count we saw only loners until the third day, when we drove up a mesa behind our camp. There, to our disbelief, were herds—thirteen here, twenty-four over there—tearing across the brush radiant with well-being.

Censuses took character from changing personnel. Besides being joined by rotating government officials, we were once accompanied by a biologist who came to study burrowing owls. Along the clay banks of the arroyos lay small holes with dripping white entrances, and occasionally a small pale face that withdrew as we approached. While a SEDUE official carped at this deviation from our mission, the biologist gathered regurgitated pellets and wrapped them in foil for later analysis. On a far different census, four SEDUE officials were replaced at the last minute by four workers from Exportadora. They had no knowledge of pronghorns and did not even possess binoculars, but their truck was well stocked and their leader was an excellent chef.

Also distinguishing various trips were inevitable car problems. The rusted trucks that couldn't leave town in 1991 were patched and back in the field two years later, but at the beginning of that census I had to haul both out of the dunes. Many of the flat tires were caused by the tough needles of the *frutilla*, and I realized that in addition to providing food and cover, this ally of the pronghorn also stabbed the wheels of their main predator. On the trip with the saltworkers, my jeep mysteriously stopped. One found that the carbon had fallen out of the distributor so that it didn't pass current and announced that we needed to find the old kind of flashlight battery with a carbon core. Another almost instantly picked one out of the sand, cut out the core, popped a piece of it into the distributor, and in five minutes we were off. Everywhere we camped for the duration of that trip, the saltworkers found and clipped old batteries until I amassed an envelope full of carbon. Their improvisa-tions weren't confined to mechanics, for when we camped in a spot with no firewood because their truck had two flats at once, they stuck two dead yuccas in an abandoned tire, torched it, and we gathered around a glow that was steady and pleasant if you didn't get downwind.

Driving back to La Paz—once with the original piece of flashlight battery still passing current at eighty kilometers per hour—I would savor the census's oddities. One April the Vizcaíno was alive with thousands of migrating Monarch butterflies glistening orange in the air and splashing yellow on the windshield. In an empty valley I spotted a surreal burst of color that resolved through binoculars into a bouquet of lilac and cream party balloons, from who knows what far birthday, that had snagged on a *frutilla* without puncturing. Somewhat later, a larger cream-colored globe on a similar bush turned out to be a ferruginous hawk. There was the woman in the coastal village whose husband had been struck at by a rattler. The snake had missed his skin, but the woman was so traumatized by the fang holes when she washed his pants that she no longer ventured outdoors during the hot half of the year. Most satisfyingly, we ventured beyond pronghorn habitat to the scavenger beach of Malarrimo, where objects carried by the Kiro Siwi current from the north are snagged by a spur that protrudes into the Pacific. We allowed ourselves fifteen minutes to look for objects other than pronghorn at this Lourdes of debris. I found an empty flask of mink oil from the Pacific Cruise Line, a KFC bucket hundreds of miles from the nearest franchise and a serviceable mauve plastic hanger, which I kept. As government agents we reminded a handful of campers not to litter and, surprisingly, were not laughed at on this beach treasured for its trash. We arrived at the April 1994 census to find that one of the Guerrero Negro biologists had festooned SEDUE headquarters' mango trees with red bows so the fruit wouldn't be rotted by an upcoming anular eclipse. The week before, four pronghorn had been seen parading past the Guerrero Negro shooting range. Perhaps this was not an animal we could help. . . .

The greatest anomaly was that the live capture, reportedly three months off when I first heard about it, seemed to recede as we labored toward it. The biologist who most favored it was encouraged when the November 1993 census turned up a record 175 animals, then disheartened that the subsequent April count was down to 45. We attributed these fluctuations to our inability at times to find the animals rather than to population bursts and die-offs, but radio collaring the animals to track their movements would entail the same risks as a live capture. Another biologist, equally knowledgeable and serious about the program, opposed the capture because he didn't trust the salt company not to abandon the animals once they were on La Mesa de la Cholla. He pointed out that the whole midpeninsula was, on paper, a biological reserve in which firearms were illegal, but nobody did anything about it. Given the authority, he would disarm the populace, put wardens in the field, enforce the penalties, and leave the pronghorn right where they were. I began to see La Mesa de la Cholla—biologists' dream, bureaucratic concoction, secret garden for baby pronghorn—receding like a mythic golden age rather than advancing like salvation.

Thinking of Guerrero Negro itself, I saw radiating species: ospreys in the center, embraced by salt ponds with their spectrum of seabirds, followed by Scammon's Lagoon with its whales, then the Vizcaíno Desert with its scrub and its pronghorn. One February I was alarmed for the center when I read in a La Paz paper that hurricane-force winds had battered Guerrero Negro. I called Fernando Heredia, the salt company biologist, to learn the consequences. The blast had knocked over his satellite dish, the principal relief from life by the salt ponds. More ominously, osprey nests had been swept to the ground, killing at least one mature osprey and chick, full damage unknown.

When I next arrived in Guerrero Negro, I was relieved to see so much rubbish still poised on the electrical system, and I learned that only three nests had failed to hang tight. I sped to my favorite. Most of its sticks had blown away, leaving pure trash. As I admired a newly revealed paintbrush, a huge form glided into sight. There was a shriek from the nest, a small head craned from the fan belts and pantyhose, and fish fresh from the brine passed parent to child in sheer defiance against the sky.

UNDER THE CYPRESS

10

Citizens of San Ignacio work, beget children, pay taxes, even die, but so relaxed is their oasis that jokes about them have swept the peninsula. It is said that the cows wear sneakers so they won't waken their owners. Ignacianos are alleged to have altered their phones so that instead of ringing, they go *pssst*. They cut the vocal cords of roosters that crow them awake. To frighten away their ghosts, Ignacianos set out hammers, hatchets, rakes—tools of work. It is said that Ignacianos grease the palm leaves to soften the rustling and that they have replaced the bronze clapper of the mission bell with a duplicate of rubber. A 100,000 peso note is said to have floated toward an Ignaciano drowsing against a palm. As he reached for it the wind shifted, the note settled several meters away, the Ignaciano muttered *Damn!* and sank back to sleep. One Ignaciano made it to the American border, where all Mexicans were asked where they were from and whether they had work permits. "Your permit," demanded the border guard.

"I don't have one."

"Where are you from?"

"San Ignacio."

"You're not going to work anyway," said the guard. "Go on through."

For many of the reasons implied by the jokes, San Ignacio had been my favorite town in Baja California since I first saw it in 1968. Its palms beckoned like deliverance when it could only be reached on a one-lane track through hundreds of miles of volcanic rubble. I was afraid the highway would run roughshod through the middle, but pavement kept a thoughtful distance, respecting the two-kilometer approach to its plaza across the lagoon and through its greased palms.

I stopped whenever I could over the years, still taking one of the six rooms of Oscar Fischer's motel in back of town, and discovered my own palm to lean against. It swooped over the lagoon, inviting me to clamber backward along its trunk, libation in hand and binoculars around my neck, to settle where it curved in perfect lumbar support and extended a headrest. My gaze, cradled upward, met the top of a fan palm where finches and orioles nested. Coots, egrets and pied-billed grebes paddled the lagoon around me; night herons flapped past, complaining *gwork;* least grebes, sleek as rodents, dove beneath me; and if a 100,000 peso note had floated toward me, a reach for it would have landed me in the drink. I wasn't the only outsider working on his indolence, for at Oscar Fischer's I met a Chicano who drove down from a Los Angeles barrio whenever he could to unwind. He reported knocking on the unmarked door of a haircutter, to be told she was asleep and didn't appreciate being roused. When he went out for his evening jog, an old man stopped him and asked what was the matter. On learning nothing was the matter, the old man suggested the Chicano slow down and stop setting a bad example. San Ignacio, lacking aerobics, is known for its centenarians. When I first arrived the oldest Ignaciano was 114, though by 1992 the quickening pace had dropped that figure to 105. It was said that Ignacianos who stayed home far outlived relatives who moved to the coast to fish or to Isla Cedros to work the salt company's fishing port.

I got to know a number of Ignacianos during early stays at Becky's *pensión,* and though there were stretches during the seventies and eighties when I didn't drop by for years, the familiars hadn't budged. Foremost of these was Héctor, who in 1969 had led me and Katie Lee to a cave where manos and metates lay undisturbed on the bedrock. He had also given me a mail-order catalog in Spanish for a company in Brooklyn, a compendium of switchblade knives, Virgin Marys that glowed in the dark, pornographic playing cards and spray cans of frankincense and myrrh. He once counted out money to send for a paint sprayer, asking me to bring it in person the following year so it wouldn't disappear in the mail. Twenty years later, our friendship secure, he admitted that the sprayer worked on 220 volts and only dribbled paint on the 110 volts locally available, and I confessed that I had done better by the catalog, making quite a hit the Christmas I gave out spray cans of myrrh.

Héctor lived on several acres of agricultural land that had belonged to the family for generations. An alley off the plaza led to a slatted gate where the tiny dogs known in San Ignacio as "doorbells" announced visitors in yips that convulsed their frames. A scattering of small buildings shaped a courtyard of packed earth, shaded by citrus, a cedar and three sprawling pepper trees of a sort I had not seen elsewhere. Their low branches were propped by stakes and suspended from them, singing and shrieking, were caged orioles, cardinals, assorted canaries and a large magpie jay from southern Mexico, along with a clear Japanese fishing ball that bolts of sun turned opalescent. On folding metal chairs, Héctor and I sipped coffee and discussed international politics, paranormal phenomena, a new way of fertilizing grapes— whatever occupied Héctor at the moment. Angling a chair just right, you could glimpse whoever was leaving the plaza or case who was headed toward the gate. Often we were joined by Héctor's father, who followed the conversation keenly and sometimes took part. When Héctor once marveled in his father's presence how at ninety he could still hear perfectly and read without glasses, I added, "And his brain is still intact."

His father looked at me sharply and snapped, "No, I'm not crazy yet."

Héctor was all the more rooted in his property for having sampled life away from it. During the long hiatus in our friendship, Héctor worked at many of the projects that had changed the central part of the peninsula. He joined the road crew that paved the *Cuesta del Infiernillo,* the Descent of the Little Hell, with its scenic, pan-banging drop-offs. As a landscaper at Hotel El Presidente, where Nora and Beth consumed their fateful margaritas, he acquired the pepper tree saplings whose shade we now enjoyed, and which were the only such trees in San Ignacio. When the mission underwent an extensive restoration, Héctor was enlisted as a stonemason. He endured several wind-blasted months at a fish-packing plant on Isla Cedros, the island from which Exportadora de Sal dispatched salt to the world. Most adventurous of all, Héctor had helped lay the grid of single-track roads over the Vizcaíno Desert when Pemex prospected for oil in the seventies, tracks whose endurance I had witnessed by air. Groups of five or six men had worked as teams, were paid by the kilometer and averaged a kilometer a day. Over dunes, through arroyos, maintaining straight lines whether nature flourished or languished, rose or sank, they macheted shrubbery, felled trees and scraped the leavings from their path with a bulldozer. A Pemex functionary showed up every three days to check up; otherwise they were responsible for buying and preparing their own food and for packing medicines to cope with accidents, illnesses and snakebites. Héctor thrived on camping out, loved exploring hidden parts of the peninsula and despised the work. During those years it was considered a feat for off-roaders to reach Malarrimo, the scavenger beach I finally saw, after years of anticipation, on a pronghorn count. Of all the fabled treasures—ships' wheels, World War II cans of Spam, cases of scotch—the pièces de résistance were the glass floats for fishnets, clear or turquoise, known as Japanese fishing balls. While Pemex found treasure in its secret wells of natural gas, Héctor scored a Japanese fishing ball, and instead of maneuvering a four-wheeler over rocks and through loose sand, he rode to Malarrimo by tractor.

When I got back in touch with Héctor in the late eighties, I found someone who had seen enough of life beyond his property to be consumed by his land. He married late, to a woman past the age of childbearing, and his paternal feelings were sluiced onto the growing things around him. He referred to his land as a *huerta,* a word narrowly translated as "orchard," and Héctor's *huerta* was a compound of fruit trees, vegetable and flower garden, and vineyard. After we finished our coffee and caught up on the world and each other's lives, we always eddied slowly through the *huerta,* commenting on what was new or seeing how the old was coming along. I never ceased marveling at the sheer abundance. In the vegetable garden were onions, garlic, chiles, hops, potatoes, celery, peppers, cabbage, parsley, cilantro and a variety of greens for spice, salads, medicines and herbal teas whose English names I didn't know. Overhead hung bananas, papayas, pomegranates, dates and citrus crosses of Héctor's devising. Spiking the greenery were zinnias, marigolds, roses, hollyhocks and cosmos, and the balance of the property drifted in grapevines. When I asked what three tubs of dirt were for, Héctor explained that two contained soil from different arroyos, the third held loam from a hillside, and he was testing various combinations for ornamental flowers. He sliced off leaves from two aloe vera plants, one the commercial strain, one the wild original, and had me smell their gelatinous cross-sections: the wild was odorless and the commercial one stank. "Wouldn't you think they could improve on a plant without ruining the smell?" he asked. We would stop to inspect a giant four-clove garlic from a plant brought in from Tijuana, or a tangerine-mandarin cross from Héctor's endless grafting experiments. One year I noted an unlikely number of tomato seedlings and asked if he planned to market tomatoes.

"No," he sighed, "people will only pay for tomatoes that arrive in boxes from the north."

"But surely you can't eat so many."

"Of course not, I'll be lucky even to give them away. I just started planting tomatoes and couldn't stop."

As we paused by a mulch pile, Héctor would reflect on his attitude toward plants. Like most Ignacianos, he refused to use chemical fertilizers or insecticides, believing their avoidance was one reason for local longevity. "When you raise poison for other people," he says, "you wind up eating it yourself." It was important to factor in phases of the moon, and anything planted between the dark of the moon and the first quarter would come out weak. We moved on to the bird trap. With the passion for variety common to birders, but without their binoculars, Héctor reversed the process by bringing the birds to him. He had contrived a box of wire screens whose lid was propped open with a small stick. He rested a date on the stick, and when a bird landed to eat, the stick gave way and the lid collapsed on the bird. After Héctor had reached in for the cardinal or thrasher, looked it in the eye and turned it to the light, he let it go. It frustrated Héctor that he knew only the local names of birds, which he didn't trust, and I understood the problem when year after year he referred to his magpie jay as a lark. At last I found him a Peterson guide in Spanish. The next year I asked him what happened to his lark. "That wasn't a lark," he said, "it was a magpie jay and it didn't belong here. I gave it to my brother in Ensenada."

On one of our strolls through the *huerta* I noted that the doorbell trotting after us sported a collar of corklike projections between bits of metal. "An ornament for the dog?" I asked.

"It's to keep her from getting pregnant," said Héctor.

"How does it work?"

"The collar is made of sections of copper tubing for natural gas, alternating with slices of corn cob. Male dogs can't stand the smell of it and stay away."

During early winter months Héctor spent his days at long waist-high tables covered with woven reeds, spread with dates drying in the sun. Beginning in November, five Ignacianos adept at tree climbing knocked down date branches for the whole town, batting them with extensions of the ropes that held them to the trunks. The golden branches were arrayed on the matted tables to bake for three or four days. The dates were then raked from the branches with a device like a giant wooden comb and sun-dried for another three or four days while the bad ones were weeded out. Cured but still moist, they were stuffed into polystyrene sacks advertising such products as "Wyoming Grown Cowboy Brand Twice-Washed Pinto Beans." What wasn't fit for human consumption got fed to the animals.

Every several days, all year long, came Héctor's turn to irrigate from a communally owned tank at one corner of the property. Some ten meters across, it dated to the time of the padres and received water from the spring that fed the lagoons, two kilometers away, by a system of *acequias,* or irrigation canals, also pioneered by the padres. Héctor opened the hole to his irrigation system by shoveling muck away from the tank's underwater hole, freeing the flow. Carp kept the tank clean and their droppings added to the water's nutrients. When I asked if the carp were also good eating, Héctor replied that they were but that Ignacianos had no tradition of eating them and so seldom did. The carp's most curious aspect, he added, was that every quarter moon they thrashed and roiled the water so violently that all the water outlets had to be cleaned the next day.

Life on the few acres, varied by invented fruits and new birds in the trap, was further livened by visitors at the gate. Neighbors showed up to buy dates, mostly in small bags for home use, or to buy small quantities of the two wines Héctor distilled from his grapes. Héctor was usually out of bottles, so people brought their own, or just a glass for washing down the next meal. Called *semiseco* and *dulce,* semidry and sweet, to my palate they were sweet and saccharine, and Héctor himself, otherwise a nondrinker, had only an occasional glass "after breakfast to settle my stomach." For a time the priest bought Héctor's wine to use for communion, then switched to another brand. Héctor also sold ornamental plants, along with citrus, mangos, melons, papaya and bananas from his *huerta.*

Little money switched hands in these transactions, and Héctor often exchanged his products for whatever people showed up with. The versatility that enabled him to pave roads, landscape hotels and pack fish also gave him trading potential for skills at carpentry, plumbing, even repairing tvs. A dentist from Tijuana, traveling with his instruments, got paid in fruit and wine. Ranchers traded meat and milk for produce and dates. There was no public newsstand and a La Paz daily offering home delivery, insisting on cash, got no business from Héctor. One day when I arrived from the south, passing up the chance to patronize the El Boleo Bakery in Santa Rosalía in my eagerness to reach San Ignacio, a young salesman from El Boleo arrived at Héctor's gate. He was from Veracruz, knew little about his wares, and I had the privilege of telling him he was peddling the best bread on the peninsula, made from recipes brought in by the French who started the copper mines. Héctor continued his education by advising him to handle the bread with tongs instead of his hands.

One morning a man in an ironed shirt and polyester pants was shrilled at by the doorbells and passed through the gate with five plastic bags of small packages. Héctor asked him to sit down, relatives gathered from the compound and a couple of women followed him from the street. The stranger pulled out packets of herbs and spices—cilantro, cinnamon, bay leaves, tea of *manzanilla* and *cardón* cactus—as well as various creams and unguents. Health and flavor were temptingly fused in his pitch. One woman raved how one of his teas "cleansed the grease from my blood" and helped her lose weight, and she bought more to finish the job. When I bought an ointment for an aching finger joint, the salesman pulled out another product for the same ailment, *aceite de víbora,* or snake oil. Never having seen the product so honestly labeled, I snapped it up. When the transactions were finished and the customers left, Héctor, the salesman and I discussed global problems for nearly an hour. The salesman worried that Russia's economic weakness might tempt it to sell the bomb to countries like Iran and Iraq, though it seemed in general that the world was getting safer and governments were converging. Overpopulation was the world's great threat and religions shouldn't be permitted to undermine birth-control programs. When I remarked on the power of the church, he replied that Mexico, though deeply religious, practiced a strict and sensible division between church and state, and as far as he was concerned, the only god worth respecting was reason. If this was snake oil, I was still buying.

Over the years I realized that I had become part of the view from Héctor's courtyard. Héctor asked for enlargements of my first photographs of San Ignacio to show how extensive the family vineyards had been, and he had me take new shots from the vantage of historic photos for before-and-after sequences. No one asked for tidings from the States, but I always stopped to and from the pronghorn census and was pressed for the latest numbers. San Ignacio had never been pronghorn habitat, but most older Ignacianos had seen them toward the coast and wanted to be assured of their well-being. Oscar Fischer, who had hunted them with his father as a young man, described migration patterns that were only theories to biologists. I left brochures at the little restaurant where I ate and one of the regulars, a doctor who traveled the coastal fishing villages we suspected of poaching, promised to dispense pronghorn lectures with his medicine. Most avid of all was Héctor's father, who rhapsodized over each of the markings on the folder—the horns, the face pattern, the little tufts of hair over the hooves—concluding, "They're so adorable and so delicious."

As a visitor, alas, I was as drab as the bread boy and the snake oil salesman. A man on a plateau over town saw a bright orange ball rise straight up, then shoot sideways out of sight. A woman saw an odd turquoise glimmer through the palms, thought it was an odd place for an American to park a trailer, then watched it soar through the fronds and vanish. The sightings were duly mulled in Héctor's courtyard and I had the impression that when local gossip ran thin, UFOs took pity.

The future was an occasional drop-in but it was the past, embodied in the mission, that dominated the town. In his vineyard Héctor spaded up a coin with the same schematic castle and lions rampant that appeared on the shield of the mission's facade, a tangible link with the founding Spaniards. Knowing the mission well from having worked as a stonecutter on the restoration, he began a tiny replica from similar lava, completing a tower with a raisin-sized wooden bell, and vowed to complete it when the *huerta* gave him time. The priest summoned him back to shoot a pair of doves that were nesting inside the church, strewing sticks, defecating on the pews and frightening people as they swooped in and out of the door. Héctor questioned the propriety of shooting in church, but the priest insisted. Héctor's air rifle reported like a cannon in the old stone vault but it did the job.

"Héctor," I said, pausing for drama, "you shot doves in church? You shot the Holy Ghost?"

He shrugged, expecting it. "It's what the priest asked for."

As a traveler Héctor had only gotten as far from San Ignacio as Tijuana and La Paz, and on the first trip he was so tormented by San Ignacio jokes that subsequently he said he was from Santa Rosalía. He had two younger brothers, one a store manager in a coastal village, the other a traveling salesman who lived in Ensenada, bought cheap and often used merchandise in Northern Mexico and San Diego, and sold it out of his car in isolated towns like San Ignacio. Both of them urged Héctor to travel more, to see something of the world, and they seized the opportunity when Héctor needed to spend ten days in Ensenada because of a stomach ailment. He stayed with his salesman brother, had only to report to the hospital for tests, and the rest of his time was free. The brothers wanted to show him the sights, and they arranged phone calls in which Héctor's wife assured him she was feeding the birds and Héctor's nephew swore he was watering the plants. The only sight in Ensenada Héctor wanted to see was one they hadn't thought of, the bird market, and he demanded to be taken immediately back to the *huerta*. When I asked Héctor what he had seen in Ensenada, he replied excitedly that he had counted two hundred house finches on a single phone line and seventy starlings on another.

What Héctor's brothers took for terminal incuriosity was simply that cities effaced what he found of interest. He hadn't possessed a car in years, and when I suggested excursions, he hesitated, claiming duties in the *huerta* while overcoming a certain shyness about occupying my time and vehicle. That barrier crossed, he became the eager explorer, alert to the faintest shifts in plants and rocks, a connoisseur of remote ranches. We pored over a limestone shelf where fossilized mollusks, clam shells and sea snails lay embedded in blinding white rock. We scrambled through some scree where Héctor thought the Jesuits had quarried the stone for the mission. We bought cheese from an embittered man from Tamaulipas who had fled to an abandoned ranch where he would only have to deal with goats. We visited a geothermal project where the government hoped to tap underground steam near the still active volcanoes of Las Tres Virgenes. We followed a thirteen-kilometer graded road to a clearing with scattered machinery and I pulled up to the nearest idle man. He was the foreman and told me they had not reached the steam they expected; for now they were tending equipment while someone in Mexico City decided whether to send a bigger drill or give up. At the end of the exchange the foreman looked past me to Héctor in the passenger seat, rigid with his high-crowned hat and his distinctive features of the Arce family that dominated the midpeninsula, and said, "Don't you speak Spanish?" Remarked Héctor as we pulled away, "It must be my pink complexion."

One year I suggested a jaunt to Rancho Santa Martha, where I had begun the mule trip to the cave paintings eighteen years before: I had heard they had opened a museum and couldn't imagine it. Héctor lit up. Thirty years ago he had ridden there by mule with his father, a journey they had lingered over six days, and they arrived to be feasted royally by distant relatives. The people were wonderful and also they might buy some dates. Ten kilometers of highway and thirty more of bad ruts shrank the trip to three hours. A couple of men greeted us cordially while assorted people on porches glanced up and continued what they were doing. Nobody bought dates, though we bought goat cheese. At my request they showed us the small museum, a spread of arrows, metates, dried plants, kids' drawings, rocks and animal skins, a hobbyist's heap lit through the door, discernible when our eyes dilated. Héctor told them of his visit thirty years before and they replied that all the people he mentioned were gone. As we left, Héctor remarked that they didn't even offer us coffee. I pointed out that Santa Martha was the lesser of two jumping-off points for the cave paintings and that if they served every stranger they'd be running a free café, but I could see that the visit left a sour taste. I told Héctor I knew of a ranch that hadn't been spoiled by visitation.

On a pronghorn count we had ventured up a strange valley surrounded by enormous free-standing rhyolite domes. We didn't encounter human habitation until we reached a small ranch at the end, where a man in a hand-tooled leather hat explained to us pronghorn experts that the rocks and dense vegetation in a valley like this wouldn't allow speed-dependent animals to get away from their enemies. He had last seen pronghorn where we had, out on the flats. I swore to return without a mission.

Héctor was thrilled by the great formations glittering bronze in the sun, their drainage choked with cactus and *datilillo* half again their normal size. It had rained the month before and the desert was in riotous bloom. We stopped frequently and Héctor wrapped flowering plants in wet newspapers. As we neared the ranch, I glanced in the rearview mirror and saw it filled with a large blue pickup. Another truck preceded us as we pulled in. It turned out that the ranch had been unoccupied and that three vehicles unaware of each other converged as if for a party. "Watch for snakes," called the first man on the porch as we started through the mallow. "This ranch is full of them, the whole valley is full of them." Two men had come to look for lost cattle, two were storing things for a cousin who owned the ranch, and we were the excursionists. The men pulled up chairs, one brewed coffee and we talked through the midday. One told of a criminal who became teacher of a one-man school because police couldn't enter school grounds without permission, and another recounted a journey so rough that the car came back "bleeding like Cleopatra." This, said Héctor as we left, was what ranches were supposed to be like, and the next morning he showed me his new wildflower garden. Twenty species of plants from the volcanic valley stood in brilliant rows, to bring the desert to people from San Ignacio who were "too old to go to the desert themselves, or too lazy."

As committed birders I thought we should visit Estero Coyote, an anvil-shaped, mangrove-encrusted inlet on the Pacific coast that I had never quite reached. As we walked along the inlet's mouth with the binoculars and bird book, we gazed across to a concentration of blue herons in the white phase flanked by white seagulls, a far spill of salt. In another direction, hundreds of brown pelicans stood with their toes just short of water. Suddenly a seagull at our feet rose over our heads, hovered, dropped a small object, then lit on the ground to devour a clam in the shell it had just cracked. Héctor gaped, stupefied. "I saw that on a nature show on TV and thought maybe they made it up. I can't believe the birds are that clever and that I saw it with my own eyes." We returned our gaze to the distance. "What are those birds over there going *quar quar*?" asked Héctor excitedly.

I fixed the binoculars on some dark birds with white streaks on their necks. "Those are brants," I said, "a kind of sea-going goose."

"Those are the birds I hear over the house at night!" said Héctor, astonished to have come so far to learn something new about the *huerta*. When we left the estuary I told him it was only a little farther to the town of Punta Abreojos, if he wanted to take a spin. "No," he said, "it's not worth seeing and the people are unpleasant." Abreojos was apparently a miniature Ensenada.

Our most inspired pretext for an excursion came from Héctor's nephew, who had been taken on a school outing to a fumarole spouting sulfur. Héctor had tried a commercial insecticide on his chile plants, found it turned the chiles to mush, and heard that mixing sulfur in the soil made the leaves oily, fending off bugs while sparing the plant. He prepared for the trip by fashioning wooden strap-on soles so his shoes wouldn't melt near the vents, and beating a sardine can into a scoop. We drove a side road from the highway, hiked a maze of elephant trees and cholla, climbed a ridge and gasped: on the facing slope, framed in a maroon outcrop, was a clay cutaway of fluorescent mustard and lime fissured with hissing steam. As we picked our way to the raw hillside we were assaulted by a breath of putrified eggs. Steam thickened over the vents, obscuring them and clamming our faces with hot gauze, then dispersed in a gust of wind. Around the vents and in cracks between rocks were small deposits of the sulfur we had come for. I crouched to see one closer, resting my knee against a rock, and nearly singed my jeans. My sneakers were vulnerable but my glasses fogged well before the ground got hot enough to melt rubber. Héctor strapped on his soles and advanced with the scoop, only to find it too large for the tiny piles. "I should have brought a teaspoon," he sighed, scrambling below for a cool rock to beat the sardine can to a blunted point. As I watched, wiping my glasses, he zeroed in on the fumaroles, looking like a prospector in hell, and filled the jar with a soft marigold powder. "A little sulfur goes a long way," he said, and in less than an hour he had a lifetime supply.

So pleasant was it to stay in Oscar Fischer's motel and roam with Héctor that I was shocked, at the beginning of a stay, when Oscar asked me to leave the motel: an incoming group was going whalewatching in Laguna San Ignacio, then to the cave paintings, and had booked all six rooms. I asked Héctor where to camp. "In the *huerta*," he replied. Now I was the shy one, with a barrier about intrusion to overcome. More practically, I wondered how to set up my typewriter to write up the latest pronghorn census. He led me through the vineyard, past an abandoned trailer, to a cypress tree with a cleared space beneath it. To my disbelief, a masonite table projected from the cypress trunk as if engineered for a typewriter. Scaly branches drooped shade over the site and I angled the tent so that from the inside I could see the mission over the vineyard. Héctor opened a gate on the far side of the property and I pulled in my jeep to a spot hidden by foliage. This tiny move gave me a sense of arrival. San Ignacio itself was situated in the middle of the peninsula, north and south, east and west, and Héctor's property was in the middle of San Ignacio. Under the cypress tree I was at the center of Héctor's property and, in my own mythology, I had reached the heart of the peninsula.

I got out my butane burner, made coffee, set up the typewriter, faced it on a folding chair Héctor had provided, and sat. Beyond me the vines stretched leafily toward the date palms, then the laurels of the plaza and the mission, and white and lavender mallow stood waist-high in a field to one side. A vermilion flycatcher sparked to and from its nest in the cypress, and in a citrus tree behind me a bulbous nest with a hole near the bottom slurped up a verdin—a small yellow-capped desert bird—like a strand of spaghetti. The trailer was the only discordant note, but I discovered its use when Héctor's father ambled toward me. I thought he was coming to visit, but he reached a blistered chaise longue in the trailer's shade, knocked off his hat, kicked off his boots, lay on his side and went to sleep. San Ignacio had the wrong namesake in Ignatius Loyola, the fanatic disciplinarian who founded the Jesuits. Surely here was a perfect patron saint in this vigorous ninety-year-old, surrounded by the bounteous earth, asleep in the blaze of day.

Late afternoon I roused myself to get some beer for sunset. As I crossed the plaza to Manuel Meza's store, Oscar Fischer hailed me from a park bench. His incoming group had car trouble in Guerrero Negro. They were cutting their trip short, skipping the caves and spending their remaining night camped by the whales. The motel was empty. I could have any room I wanted! "Thanks," I replied, a little maliciously, "I'm content in Héctor's *huerta*."

My new days began before daylight with the silky chitter of the vermilion flycatcher overhead in the cypress. I made coffee inside the tent and gazed at the mission, rose with auburn trim in the first light. As my pulse quickened, my eyes played over the inventively balanced pilasters, sawtooth cornices, round windows, diamond-shaped adornments, niches for four saints (one of them headless), a single tower with three bronze bells and two speakers. By the second coffee I progressed to the folding chair and listened to San Ignacio waking up: roosters, dogs, coughing pickups, the mocking laughter of school-bound teenagers, mourning doves, the chucking of an unseen spade. Hearing and glimpsing, invisible, I was in a blind for observing humanity even as orioles, woodpeckers, cardinals and kinglets darted about, oblivious of my presence. By the third coffee I made myself type notes. Héctor showed up now and then with things to eat, not meals but treats: manta-ray *machaca,* corn soup, a dessert called *dulce de papaya* to be eaten hot, homemade tortillas, the latest citrus crosses. Occasionally I ventured into town for a full meal at the little restaurant but mostly I stayed by the tent, steeping in where I was. At night, bits of disintegrating cypress cones pelted the tent like fat raindrops. In the words of a La Paz friend, it was so idyllic I was jealous of myself.

At dusk Héctor would come to chat. The first evening he pulled up the blistered chaise longue his father had napped on, insisting I take it over, and spent his nightfalls on the folding chair. He declined my beer, saying that "cold things are bad for the stomach," and let his thoughts wander over times I hadn't heard about. The Arce family traced itself back to the soldiers who had accompanied the Jesuits, but it was his grandfather Lucas who consolidated the family holdings in the last century. Among Lucas's many children was an unmarried daughter named Anastasia who was credited with prophetic powers. When Héctor was a little boy "still trailing a blanket," Anastasia singled him out as "someone who would spend his life with plants."

Perhaps Anastasia needed only sharp observation to distinguish the young Héctor from the brother who would become an Ensenada-based trader and the one who would become a store manager on the coast. It was the traveling salesman who had deposited the trailer with its useful shade. Héctor's father had preferred ranching to gardening and ran cattle in the desert above town until one year he had to sell off the entire herd, instead of just the calves, because of a drought. Héctor said that the fate of his father's cattle proved the superiority of horticulture, for if you tended plants, they never let you down. The others gardened but didn't have a feel for it; they planted, watered and walked away. Héctor inspected his plants daily, sifted their roots, checked their leaves for parasites and disease, trimmed their dead matter and kept in touch with them as fellow beings. Reaching for some dirt under the cypress tree, he let it fall through his fingers and spoke a litany so familiar that he must have said it often to himself, if not out loud. "Look

what plants are. They're our food, peace, the beauty around us, homes for
the birds and animals. They're the very air we breathe. They're the cradles
we're born in and the coffins of our graves."

From the vantage of Héctor's *huerta,* San Ignacio seemed like an idyllic
plant kingdom, but it was clear from talking around town and to Héctor
himself that productivity had fallen drastically and the social fabric was
shearing. With its tens of thousands of palms, San Ignacio had not gotten
rich off its dates. The market was once at the mercy of a single powerful
buyer who paid just enough that Ignacianos sold to him rather than let the
fruit rot. Completion of the highway in 1973 allowed traders from Tijuana to
arrive by truck and by bus, and a few enterprising Ignacianos even transported dates to Tijuana. But there was still no organized market, nothing so
crass as promotion, and most growers were content to let the market find
them. The trees, meanwhile, were less and less well-tended and San Ignacio
dates were losing their cachet. There were those who whispered the unutter-
able: that the dates of Ejido Bonfil, a communal farm off the highway where
dates were grown on midget clones that could be stripped without ladders,
were the firm, succulent sweets that San Ignacio no longer produced.

As with everywhere else on the peninsula, when traditional business
failed, people looked to tourism. The Hotel El Presidente, built shortly after
the highway opened, succumbed so fast that I saw weeds growing through its
abandoned concrete three years after it was built; patched and refurbished,
it became part of a small motel chain that catered to overnighters off the
highway, generally at a fraction of capacity. Day trips from San Ignacio to the
whales and cave paintings required so much travel time that people serious
about either preferred to camp on-site, leaving barely enough business for
Oscar Fischer's six-room motel. The unlucrative truth was that tourism—
Mexican or foreign, active or passive—was water oriented. People came to
Baja California to be on the gulf, the cape or the Pacific, and tourism was
profitable only along the coasts. Once visitors had walked around the San
Ignacio plaza, inspected the mission and snapped pictures of the lagoon,
they drove on. Said Hercilia, a pharmacist I knew from my first stays at
Becky's *pensión,* there was actually more tourism before the highway, when
the diehards who fought their way down the old jeep track laid over a few
days to lick their wounds and fix their cars.

The chief social problem since the highway was that the young left town as soon as they left high school, to pursue higher education or higher pay. There was little money in the date business and less in tourism. And as Hercilia's husband, Carlos, the town's leading doctor, pointed out, because everyone in San Ignacio was related to everyone else, or was a lifelong neighbor, Ignacianos expected free goods and service and little money changed hands. The main destinations for San Ignacio's youth were the fishing towns of the Pacific coast, which were primarily founded and replenished by Ignacianos who could not find work at home. "San Ignacio is a kind of incubator," says Carlos, "raising humanity and sending it forth." Ignacianos worked elsewhere, then came home to visit and relax. And here lay the local explanation for San Ignacio's reputation for laziness, the source of the jokes: Ignacianos worked elsewhere seasonally and returned to recuperate in the homes of their parents. Strangers who drove into town and saw working-age people lying around were actually seeing vacationers in reverse, people who traveled to their hard work and came home to relax.

Though San Ignacio was one of the most insular towns on the peninsula, it had—along with visitors and offspring who returned to it from their working lives—television, with its news of disasters. Tapping a clean aquifer, with weather that blew fresh from the open Pacific, and with a bias against the chemicals of agribusiness, the town seemed shielded from natural devastations occurring elsewhere, but the one threat Ignacianos took seriously was environmental collapse. Héctor, his father and others found the palms paler than they had been, deciduous leaves more ashen, and said all the vegetation was looking burned. It wasn't a matter of trees and plants being old, for the new ones were similarly afflicted. Fruit trees were susceptible to parasites and diseases previously unknown, didn't bear as they once did, and those who tended them were getting sunburned more quickly.

Héctor's brother in the coastal village had more alarming news. The abalone had gone soft and weightless. Certain fish now had strange spots on them. Children were coming down with mysterious ailments, including stomachaches that couldn't be diagnosed. The natural support system, even in the seeming isolation of the midpeninsula, was becoming less dependable, all the more threatening because the danger was so amorphous, so unfocused. It was in the sky and it was on TV. Héctor's brother speculated that the deterioration of marine life resulted from accumulated oil spills along with the mysterious warm-water phenomenon known as El Niño and—in a locally flavored touch—that the damage to plants was a combination of ozone depletion and too many eclipses.

The tangible changes in San Ignacio, meanwhile, were slow, subtle, and resembled gestures in a Noh play. In the winter of 1992 the main occurrence was construction of a cutoff from the plaza to a few stranded residential blocks. Héctor was conflicted, pleased to gain vehicular access to the farthest corner of the vineyard, dismayed that a cluster of date palms near the mission would be felled. In his mania to document everything, he asked me to take pictures of the palm trees before they went. We stood in the area being cleared, watching ranchers unload a truckful of *palo blanco* trunks to be used for fencing along the new road. Supervising them was a large, dark, smooth-faced man in sunglasses, expressionless among gesturers in the manner of provincial bureaucrats. Héctor identified him as the *delegado*—the non-elected mayor, appointed from the regional seat in Santa Rosalía. As Héctor left the scene, I paused by the *delegado*. He was declaiming to the ranchers about the future of San Ignacio, drawing building lots with his machete in the dust.

In 1993 the road was in and a new structure appeared beside it on Héctor's property—a thatched roof on posts, with obscure objects underneath. Héctor identified it as a small second-hand store put up by his salesman brother from Ensenada. He boasted how it could be left unattended for days without anyone ever taking anything. As we approached, the contents resolved themselves into old chairs, ironing boards, car parts, stoves and washing machines, in the middle of which, on a cracked pad, lay Héctor's father, asleep. New shade to conquer. . . .

In 1994 half of Héctor's grapevines had been torn out, leaving pure dirt stretching behind the second-hand store. In what seemed a violation, I was able to drive from a new gate off the new road all the way to the cypress tree. Was this the beginning of development? I asked Héctor. Was this the property the *delegado* had drawn with his machete in the dust? No, he explained, the vines were eighty years old, had stopped producing, and were overdue for tearing out. Even the half that were left, forty years old, were well past their prime, and to prove the point Héctor snapped off a branch that cracked like dead wood. His father thought he should switch to melons and beans, but Héctor intended to plant new vines.

That dusk, as I sat by the tent with my jeep next to the trailer, still screened from the outside world but more precariously so, Héctor came and settled on the folding chair. "Are you really happy with these changes?" I asked.

"No," he admitted. "This *huerta* is where I grew up. I'm as much its product as the fruit of these trees. This orchard made me whatever I am. I felt so much at peace when I could go out in the fields and do whatever I wanted and work unseen. Now I feel like I'm on display for everyone. People watch everything I do. I'm not just going to plant more vines. I'm going to plant trees along the fence—pomegranates and bananas so the fence will produce, with thick mulberries in between. I'm going to make this place private again."

A return to privacy, a turning inward, was what might revive San Ignacio as a community, but the town instead seemed to be unraveling. On Sundays families had stopped migrating in groups from one house to another, affirming bonds by exchanging minutiae. People had lost patience, a loss particularly hard on Héctor's father, whose contemporaries were gone and who expected to be sustained by those that followed him. Too few people of intermediate age linked the very young with the very old, and all seemed cut loose. For a while weekend ballgames and picnics were organized near the lagoon so that Ignacianos could socialize, gossip, even get drunk together, but as a replacement tradition it didn't take. Television briefly united people when they gathered to watch the first satellite pickup, but then they communed with their home sets. It seemed inconceivable that only a generation back, boys and girls at dances sat in separate rows, with parents and chaperons acting as coaches and each youngster dancing with several partners. Now a dating couple was glued for the evening. The male paid admittance to a metal barn blasted by a bad rock band from Santa Rosalía or Guerrero Negro, paid again for a table, paid for each drink—paid in a town without money. Because the barn loomed just a block from the cypress, making dance nights unbearable, I once ventured as far in as I could without paying. Several dozen youths crowded the door with no thought of entering either. Around two tables of speechless customers pounded the reverberations of amped guitars from sheet metal, surely one of the most desolate sounds of advancing global culture. It was no wonder that, instead, the kids piled into cars, six-packs in hand, and headed to the lagoon or the highway beyond.

As for the physical surroundings, Ignacianos also saw decline around them. Héctor told me how a *delegado* had introduced a new fish into the lagoon, thinking to provide another food source. No one would eat the fish because it was too spiny, but the fish ate seaweed, algae and smaller fish that sustained a water snake, a species of frog and various bird species. My own photographs proved the town less meticulously tended than when I first arrived, the vineyards less extensive. It shamed Ignacianos that a field that had once borne grapes had been taken over by white and lavender mallow. Where I still saw splendor in every direction, they saw an oasis going to seed.

But it was difficult to keep perspective when the generations had lost their continuity. It was too much like regretting the pond below the lagoon, where Héctor and his brothers had learned to swim by hanging onto the roots of palms, lost to a flood that was a fact of nature, innocent of decline. Was the vegetation really bleached through the thinning ozone or had color itself lost the intensity that fired one's youth? Was San Ignacio showing signs of a globe in peril or merely human exhaustion and natural succession?

Under the cypress tree, surrounded by birds and flowering weeds, it was hard to think apocalyptically. My own hopes, modest if selfish, were that Héctor would plant his new vines, surround them with trees that bore fruit as they fended off prying stares, and that in the center remained a refuge I could count on. I wanted Héctor to resume tending his plants unseen while I vanished into a nearby quiet, a recording eye or just a cow with sneakers.

EARTH DAY WITH THE GOVERNOR

11

On my return south down the peninsular highway in December 1994 I stopped, as always, at a heroic abstract sculpture raised to commemorate completion of the pavement in December 1973. Straddling the line between the states of Baja California and Baja California Sur was a vast cement amphitheater complete with stage, tiered benches with seat numbers, and a perimeter of flagpoles. It had been built for a dedication ceremony attended by President Luis Echeverría and had been cracking with disuse ever since. Behind the stage towered a confabulation of black trusses with projections and angular supports said to represent a pair of bald eagles, one for each state. The profile of Benito Juárez on a plaque beneath it had been carefully spray-painted so that his hair, brows, moustache and beard were sagely white; other graffiti ("I love Marco") wasn't site specific. As I contemplated this melange from seat no. 245, an osprey screamed toward the sculpture and lit on a welded wing. Overwhelmed by this abstraction of its cousin, it was still a large bird. Sensing no danger from no. 245, it continued to a nest it had jury-rigged on a half-fallen road sign that identified the site.

This daft ruin was a good place to contemplate the highway stretching in either direction. As I watched asphalt being laid in the late sixties, I had been sure that its completion would bring instant devastation. It did end our two-month peninsula crawls down the sand and rock thread of the MTH. As if released by a floodgate, Winnebagos from Southern California forged their way to the cape. Accessible beaches like those in Bahía Concepción became barricaded with campers and privies that turned, in time, to ramparts of shacks and rental units. Trucks could now haul merchandise to La Paz in twenty-four hours.

It was ironic to remember our anxiety when we first set off on the MTH. You couldn't have much of a collision at twelve miles per hour and if you had a breakdown, you merely needed to survive until someone arrived to help.

Speeding past, decades later, I caught glimpses of the old MTH, eroded and clinging to drop-offs, and was impressed that we had once negotiated that precarious catwalk. But fatalities, rare on the MTH, were weekly news on the paved highway. Trucks and campers hurled from opposite directions so close you were sure they would click mirrors. Hard-edged potholes delivered instant blowouts. Cows strolled freely onto the pavement, and even if you avoided driving by night, bovine perils lurked around curves and over hills in broad daylight. Diabolically, cows were drawn to the highway because exhaust functioned as an insecticide, giving them relief from bugs that plagued them. In the early nineties exasperated truckers took to shooting them and pushing them off the road, cursing the ranchers. The ranchers retorted that the land had been theirs since the last century, that no one asked them if they wanted pavement rammed through it and if highway types wanted hundreds of kilometers of fencing, they could string it themselves.

After twenty-one years, crumbling like its dedication monument, the highway remained a slender causeway where to pull off was probably to roll. When arroyos flooded, travelers could be stranded for days. The worst stretch lay in the north, and it was said that the town of Ensenada prevailed upon the highway department not to patch it so tourists would be discouraged from venturing farther south. It seemed apt that the occasional white guideposts were known as *fantasmas,* or ghosts, and that the English word *cows* sounded eerily like the Spanish *caos,* chaos. Recklessly, I hoped that pavement would continue to crumble, that cactus would reclaim the bulldozed roadside and that we would ultimately be back on the MTH.

I had begun combing Baja California with the notion that because it was a single shaft of desert, finite, framed by the sea, after sufficient exploration it could finally be amassed inside and held in one vast, composite, visionary thought—much as it was caught in the old Telstar postcard, the tintype from space. But every focus of my attention—San Ignacio, cave paintings, pronghorn, whales, the Sierra de la Giganta, the La Paz where I now spent nearly half of each year—lay south of the eagle monument. I had become a specialist in the state of Baja California Sur. Further dooming the conceit of collecting the peninsula into one thought was my failure to consider time and change. Since the arrival of pavement, of instant communication and packaged tourism, to know the peninsula wasn't just to see whales and cave paintings and hike and explore back roads; it was also to learn how Baja Californians handled the crowds who had seen documentaries on TV and wanted to do the same thing. With the steel eagles for witnesses, in December 1994 I reduced and updated my goal. I resolved to learn as much as I could about the state of affairs in the peninsula's lower half in 1995. I had no illusions about grasping it all, let alone making predictions. I merely wanted to snapshot a year of rapid change.

Even to this diminished project the monument spoke, for beneath seat no. 245 and all the other seats stretched a subterranean hollow that once held a museum, installed when the complex went up. Gaping like a pedestrian underpass, it moldered in such darkness that even in dry seasons it puddled with water from the last deluge. When I asked people in nearby Guerrero Negro about the museum's contents and where they went, I was told vaguely contradictory stories about "a bunch of Indian stuff that someone made off with." An anthropologist in La Paz finally told me what had happened. Fossils, artifacts of Baja California tribes and examples of leatherwork had been assembled from both states and put on display. But no museum direc-tor or staff were appointed, nor was the museum awarded funding. It closed after a week and the northern state spirited away the entire contents. A few of the items were still on display in northern museums but most were dis-persed and lost: "stolen" was the anthropologist's word. The crowning touch to the museum saga was that a dead whale had washed up on a beach near Guerrero Negro before the dedication and select bones were put on display before the flesh had finished decomposing. During the florid speeches about Baja California Sur's passage to statehood and this grand new link to the north, dignitaries and celebrants steeped in fumes from the museum. It was an appropriate cautionary tale as I headed south twenty-two years later to take the peninsular pulse.

I arrived in La Paz to learn that Mary Shroyer, manager of the Marina de La Paz, was organizing a private trip to the cave paintings. I hadn't been back since Mary and I had first visited the caves together eighteen years before, on the test run for Baja Expeditions that had ended disastrously when our com-panions Nora and Beth drove their Volkswagen into a palm tree. That trip had been led by Tacho Arce, whose sixty-seven years in the Sierra de San Francisco so embraced the area that we had turned all decisions over to him. Our advice to Tim had been not to do commercial trips, but for a while Baja Expeditions offered excursions to the caves every winter, using Tacho and his young relations as guides in combination with American staff. As the area received more pressure, visitation was increasingly restricted. By 1995 Tacho had died and access was controlled by the federal department of archaeology, known by the acronym INAH. Our party included a former American guide named Gail, who had loved the improvisation of the early trips, regarded the new rules with misgivings and primarily wanted to visit old friends in the mountains. It had taken Mary two months of phone calls to INAH to secure our permission and guides.

Regulations required that we check in first at a new museum INAH had installed in San Ignacio. The building had been constructed by Héctor's great-great-grandfather Buenaventura Arce to store his harvest and had later been used to show silent movies. Héctor had advised INAH on where to find matching stones to repair it, and I was pleased for him that its panels and cave painting replica had turned out so well. When we identified ourselves to the official in charge, he asked Mary for her permit to enter the mountains. Mary exploded. "I have been on the phone weekly to you people for two months and no one ever mentioned such a paper. Twelve of us have arrived with five days' worth of food. And you have the temerity . . ." Gail, the official and I all grinned and he backed off. After Mary walked out in triumph, Gail and I informed the smiling official that Mary's nickname in La Paz was "La Pitahaya," after a cactus known for its barbs.

We caravanned on a dirt road to a camping spot outside the principal mountain village. Gail joyfully greeted our head guide, an older man with a Tacho-like generosity of spirit. They reminisced about the days when they picked the camps they wanted and explored the caves they chose. It wasn't like that anymore, he sighed. The new system had been in place just over a year. Some forty men from the ranches led visitors by strict rotation. Every man got work, but guides and visitors were both frustrated because visitors who came every year had formed friendships with specific guides and resented being forced to travel with strangers, while those best at guiding sat it out as the less competent took their customers. Most of the roughly two hundred caves were now off-limits unless one got permission six months in advance and traveled with a representative from INAH. Visitors were restricted to designated trails and campsites. Flash pictures were forbidden in the caves because of possible damage to pigment. Fires and liquor were both prohibited, meaning that we wouldn't be sharing our rum with the guides. When I asked what would happen if we built a fire, Gail's friend replied with a layered response that combined lifting his shoulders, displaying his palms, and saying, "Bury the evidence and leave everything clean."

To demonstrate the new dispensation he took us to Cueva Ratón, the closest mural to town. A freshly laid stone stairway led to a locked gate, for which he produced the key. A wooden platform extended along the over-hang, and large signs told us what was known about the mural, with equal space for rules of behavior and the importance of protection. The actual painting, with its fading figures, seemed overwhelmed by its new packaging: what did people here think of it? Most residents, he said, found it intrusive, overdone and destructive of their character. "This is our heritage," he said, "and we protect it ourselves without all this." I knew, however, from read-ing *La Pintura Rupestre de Baja California* by Enrique Hambleton, a man from La Paz who had been exploring the caves since the seventies, that when he and the American writer Harry Crosby first arrived, the ranchers felt no connection to the paintings and occasionally even shot at them. At first they couldn't believe that Hambleton and Crosby weren't using the paintings as a pretext for looking for gold, and they didn't take the murals seriously until more visitors showed up. Ranchers who had become guides now protected the caves with pride, but the paintings were nonetheless threatened. Fires in the caves had damaged the figures and there were reports that people had actually chipped off pieces and hauled them away. Every nationality took from the area, said Gail's friend, but the worst were fellow Mexicans. Be-cause it was their own country, they did not consider it theft—merely the transfer of a bit of their patrimony from one place to another. With so many strangers showing up unannounced, sometimes abusing the area, clearly the old freedom had to be curtailed if the murals were to survive. The question was how to proceed.

In the morning we continued to a smaller village where mules and burros were being gathered. After an eighteen-year absence from these mountains I found that the buildings, still slat walls with thatch roofs, were trimmed with satellite dishes and solar panels. A short-wave radio linked the two villages with chatter of kids and kitchens. As gear was being loaded I asked assorted bystanders what supported life there. Tourism brought in more money than traditional ranching, they said. A recent drought had killed hundreds of cattle, and people in towns now preferred factory cheese to their own. Ranchers had turned to raising goats, selling them in bulk to a buyer who showed up with a large truck from Tijuana. Their greatest frus-tration was the number of animals they lost to mountain lions—goats, calves, even burros and mules. Remembering the skins of slaughtered lions I had seen the last time, I asked how they could be increasing. "They just breed and multiply and kill and eat," a man answered.

I had forgotten the scale of these mountains, whose canyons drop from five thousand feet almost to sea level, and I was impressed that we descended the same steep crumbling trail for hours. I had anticipated having to prod our mounts into motion, but instead of burros we were issued mules as responsive as well-trained horses. As we plunged down the trail, talk centered on INAH's representative in the mountains, a woman referred to simply as "The Archaeologist." The Archaeologist was a nag and we would have to watch ourselves. The Archaeologist lectured against littering but tossed things away herself, either thoughtlessly or expecting others to pick up. She took things from the caves—knives, hatchets, animal skins—"just like Mr. Gardner," a reference to the mystery writer Erle Stanley Gardner, who had promoted his 1962 expedition into a cover story in *Life* magazine. Mr. Gardner had arrived from Santa Rosalía by helicopter, a trip that then took eight days by mule, bringing steaks and cigars and swiping knives and hatchets. The Archaeologist was the new Mr. Gardner. She wanted to kick everyone out of the ranches and declare the mountains an archaeological zone. She wanted to move everyone from the village so she could put up her own hotel and restaurant. One guide didn't even know whether she was affiliated with INAH or just working alone. In the midst of this abuse, headed up the trail and accompanied by a rancher was The Archaeologist herself. I heard her ask one of the guides what caves we were going to visit, then suggest a different order. As she passed our party I said hello, hoping to detain her in conversation. She was brushy-haired, fortyish, dignified, returned a polite hello and kept going. I asked the guide why she changed the order of our trip.

"No special reason. She just likes to wield power for its own sake."

It occurred to me that as a woman from Mexico City, she already had two strikes against her. For a female outsider to initiate a new system in a male-dominated culture that had been isolated for two hundred years must have taken immense courage, and the notion that she could order people around without governmental backing was ludicrous. Whether she did her job well or ill, she had clearly become a lightning rod for every dissatisfaction and had been demonized. As I mulled her fate we were attacked by an overpowering stench. A dead mule lay bloated in the trail. Some of the pack animals bolted and we had to dismount and lead our mules around. We were within smelling distance of our campsite, particularly if the wind blew downhill. "Can't we do something about it?" asked Mary.

"The best," said one of our guides, "would be to douse it with gasoline and burn it, but The Archaeologist might see the smoke, think it was a campfire and complain."

The campsite lay on a flat stretch of canyon bottom under palms cleared of brush, with little signs that told us where to cook and where to sleep. Taking these as suggestions rather than commands, Gail, one of the guides and I camped around the bend, far from the group and each other. Gripes about the new system continued. Visitors usually arrived with food but no cooking equipment, the government forbade fires but didn't supply stoves, and the guides were stuck with what new American jargon was calling an "unfunded mandate." The nearby Cueva Pintada, most extensive and spectacular of all the painted caves, had been issued a varnished wooden walkway with cables and silver bolts. It brought some figures closer but prevented stepping back for the larger sweep. The guides were bothered that we no longer saw from the vantage of the mural's creators. For us the mural had been labeled and distanced, as if it were a museum reproduction.

Yet quibbles about systems seemed petty beneath these towering volcanic slopes. It was more than enough just to sit still in a vein of these mountains, to hear the wind seethe through palms racketing with orioles. I watched Xantus hummingbirds, one of the peninsula's two endemic bird species, gather one by one to bathe under a lip of water until seventeen tiny birds were all chattering and splashing in a row. What I thought was the drone of a plane turned out to be a swarm of bees looking for a new place to hive. The ranch that had most impressed me before was still heaped in flowers, though my favorite detail—its palm log irrigation system—had been replaced with black hose that was easier to maintain and more flexible in floods. As we packed to move campsites I watched our animals being driven across a canyon wall on a ledge hardly wider than themselves, their bells clanging like a carillon, a fresco come to life. The paintings, a goal for some, remained for me a mere accent in this range of ceaseless small miracles.

During our climb out, conversation reverted to The Archaeologist. A meeting between the guides and INAH was to take place the following month in San Ignacio and the guides were preparing a formal complaint that would clean—they used the verb *limpiar*—the mountains of The Archaeologist. Mary, who had visited various times since our first trip, declared in English that this was her last visit because the spontaneity had been lost, and Gail said she would return only to see friends. When our cars parted company at the highway and others returned to La Paz, I continued north to Guerrero Negro to talk with one of the government biologists who supervised the midpeninsula. When I told him of the ranchers' discontent, he replied that it had taken several years to get control over whalewatching in Laguna San Ignacio, least visited of the breeding lagoons, and he supposed it would take a similar time to smooth out a visitation system for the caves. In any case, as a naturalist he was far more concerned with damage to vegetation from all the goats being raised to ship to Tijuana. The only plant left in abundance was *estafiate,* a ferny shrub poisonous to goats. If he were king of the sierra, he would phase out cows and goats.

Back in La Paz I called Enrique Hambleton, who had remained involved with the caves since the publication of his book and was uniformly revered by our guides despite his hand in formulating the new system. I enumerated the charges against The Archaeologist and when I got to the part about her wanting to replace the village with a hotel and restaurant, he retorted that she would be sacked and sent to jail if she attempted anything of the sort. To the contrary, she was doing a superb job in a tough situation. Whatever the ranchers' complaints, they had agreed in full knowledge to the rotation, it was the first consensus plan for an archaeological site in Mexico and it was on its way to success. He planned to attend the meeting in San Ignacio and would tell me how it went.

A month later Enrique reported that as the session opened, The Archaeologist cut through the rumors swirling about her by stating, unequivocally, that she had no intention of displacing ranchers or of interfering with their lives other than to protect the caves. Visitors would be allowed to camp where they liked and more trails would be open. A few guides much in demand were placed in a special category that allowed them to go more often and, as Enrique pointed out, visitors who went frequently enough to make friends could also afford to hire those friends as extra hands or invite them as guests. We had merely experienced, it seemed, an awkward period of transition, but I could see that the evolution from improvised trips to a tight system duplicated in miniature the paving of the highway. Those who knew the old freedom would stop coming, or would suffer a diminished experience while pestering newcomers with tales of how much better it used to be.

Demands on the caves were nothing like the explosion in whalewatching. The two northernmost breeding lagoons were under control but the situation at Bahía Magdalena, four hours by highway from La Paz, had become anarchic. Two towns, each with several thousand inhabitants, sat on the bay and channel complex itself. Tim, the first foreign outfitter, had always hired local guides and secured proper permits. Now fishing cooperatives with whalewatching concessions complained of foreign competition while Tim countered that his trips, which lasted days instead of hours, played to a different clientele. He, in turn, complained of other foreign outfitters who showed up without paperwork and didn't get caught. Noncommercial boats put in undetected from shore and entered freely from the Pacific. Kayaks were officially illegal because currents were considered too swift and whales too large for their safety, but kayakers paddled undeterred and camped where they liked, sometimes leaving messes. It might be possible for a single person like The Archaeologist to control the Sierra de San Francisco because there were only two points of entry, a village and a ranch, but whale season at Bahía Magdalena, with its hundreds of miles of shoreline, was a free-for-all.

Whalewatching had turned to whalemania by the early 1980s, when visitors, mainly foreign, showed up at Puerto López Mateos and Puerto San Carlos asking to see whales. For López Mateos it was a windfall. The town had been founded in the 1950s when the government installed a fish cannery. Fishing declined, the cannery was privatized and collapsed, and suddenly whalewatchers came to the rescue. The season only lasted a couple of months and competition among destitute fishermen was fierce. Whale tourism grew 300 percent between 1993 and 1994, when there were up to fifty-four boats in the channel at once and as many as a dozen circling a "friendly" whale. Petting and even kissing whales had become chic. Defenders of whales pressured the government to take charge.

In 1995 the interior department announced it was reducing the permitted number of skiffs to eight at a time. The five fishing cooperatives protested that they had floated multiples of that number the previous year "without problems" and they appealed to regional politicians. The authorities crumpled and allowed a single operator as many as twenty boats at once, setting a speed limit of five kilometers per hour. A pair of fishermen hit the headlines for staging boat races, scaring both whales and tourists, and were headed toward punishment. Six inspectors were hired to supervise an area that received fourteen thousand visitors in the first three months of 1995. Sometimes the inspectors quit when their paychecks failed to arrive and the head of one cooperative suggested that if environmental officials couldn't handle the job, the government should send in the navy. Amid this melee three towns initiated a phenomenon called the Grey Whale Festival. The first had erupted two years before in Guerrero Negro. Pianist friends from La Paz had been dispatched to play a classical concert and judge a beauty contest. The next year San Carlos and López Mateos sported their own whale festivals with parades, arts, crafts and music. Having experienced the hush of whalewatching in the seventies, when we simply sat in skiffs and let whales surface around us, I decided to join the nineties by attending whale festivals.

Neither the La Paz papers nor the Office of Tourism seemed to know when the festivals were to take place, so I drove to López Mateos on the first Saturday of whale season hoping that Miss Grey Whale would be vast, pale and spotted. I passed the failed packing plant, crossed the dusty landing strip and parked. A compound of stands offered whale keychains, whale T-shirts, ironwood whale sculptures, fresh coconuts and watermelon. A man demonstrated how to burn designs into leather, his two subjects being contours of the peninsula and female nudes. Another stand peddled seashell sports cars and religious grottos, along with starfish that had been turned into elephants by bending four legs down and the fifth into a braying trunk. Behind a freshly carpentered stage stood a mural of an underwater calf whose mother was breaching overhead. A painter was finishing lettering that read A GIANT THAT NEEDS OUR PROTECTION and I asked him when the show was to begin. "Who knows?" he replied. "They just hired me to paint." No one else in the compound knew either.

I walked to shore, where several hundred people were milling about. At the booth of the fishing cooperative I asked the price of an hour's whale-watch. "It's one price per boat, by yourself or with a group." I didn't have a group; could he put me with one? "No," said the man with a dismissive gesture, turning to the next customer. An hour was so little time to go out in the lagoon, see whales and return that the whole circuit could be followed through binoculars, and I settled among the gawkers. Initiated by foreigners, day trips had become popular with Baja Californians, and skiffs of families and school groups made tight circles around the visible humps of whales. Lycra-clad Americans pulled kayaks ashore. Isla Magdalena, across the channel, glittered with lime and fuschia nylon tents of more kayakers. A motorized two-person parasail proclaiming TECATE on the underwing flew back and forth to the whales, combusting through the snarl of outboards like a mutant wasp. My binoculars, trained on the lagoon, were suddenly filled with a three-deck cabin cruiser with bikini-clad sunbathers and an American flag on the stern, an outtake from Fellini. I retreated to the landing strip, where I learned that a small airline was making whale flights from Los Cabos on the cape, and that the TECATE parasail was hawking fifteen-minute whale rides.

If there was a show that night, I couldn't stand the wait. I floored it back to La Paz.

Now that I had given up, the paper announced that there would be a whale festival show at 8 P.M. in San Carlos the following Saturday, and I drove back north. A stage like the one at López Mateos had been set up on the plaza's basketball court, with souvenir booths around the perimeter. The show opened with a gyrating Elvis clone singing about an office romance. In lengthy succession appeared folk dancers from López Mateos, a men's chorus from Ciudad Constitución and assorted ranchera singers. An hour and a half into the show came the first mention of whales when a biologist and bureaucrat, whom I knew slightly from La Paz, described how American whalers had nearly exterminated the species while Mexico had been the first country to protect their breeding lagoons, a speech longer on patriotism than biology. A group of schoolchildren called *Los Niños Ecologistas* then sang about whale protection to the tune of Beethoven's "Ode to Joy." The show culminated with the arrival of Miss Grey Whale Festival—neither vast, pale nor spotted—surrounded by a pod of beauties representing the Lions' Club, the Rotary, Puerto López Mateos and a local motel. Flashbulbs popped. The emcee announced that similar shows would be held every Saturday during whale season, and the event was over. The crowd had been almost purely Mexican, perhaps wholly local, and by the end I was the only foreigner I could detect. Whalewatching had reached such a pitch, I concluded, that local towns could afford entertainments purely for their own amusement.

Mary Shroyer did go on a day trip in 1995. As her party chugged toward the bay, another boat tore across their bow at full throttle and scared off the whales they were approaching. She had gone annually for the last twenty years but, as with the cave paintings, she would not go again.

The great controversy over the threat to whales in 1995 centered, ironically, on the most remote of the breeding waters. Laguna San Ignacio could only be reached over a braiding, often flooded sixty-eight-kilometer track from the town of San Ignacio or from a landing strip usually too eroded to use. The few concessionaires included the local fishing cooperative, the two San Ignacio motels and one or two outfitters, one of whom was always Tim. Tim had perfected the timing of his yearly petition to fix the road so that it would be ready by whale season but wouldn't wash out again until he no longer needed it.

In 1991, after a pronghorn count to the north, I threaded the road's many detours to Tim's operation. I was secretly impressed that the government, for environmental reasons, had denied him the island camp he preferred and directed him to a beach where he had to haul away cans, old stoves and a junked car left by a fishing camp. What remained was a minimalist landscape, a shore of ground shells and fine sand colonized by salt-tolerant plants such as pickleweed and the sticky *meado de sapo,* toad piss. Baja Expeditions' old canvas tents that looked like houses on the Monopoly board had been replaced by nylon bats that whapped in the breeze. Water and land melted in blinding mist as the lagoon deepened from a shrimplike pallor to corrosive green. On the horizon I could barely make out the peaks we used as direction markers while spotting pronghorn. Beyond earshot of the nylon one heard only the pleadings of sandpipers and the whales' explosive sighs. Out in the skiffs, whalewatching was still the trancelike encounter I had first known at Bahía Magdalena, and the government had stationed a representative among the boats to ensure that we didn't stray. The upper reaches of the lagoon, where whales gave birth in the shallowest, saltiest, most supportive water, was declared off-limits to fishermen and visitors during whale season. If the government could claim a success in handling pressures on the peninsula, it was surely at Laguna San Ignacio.

But there were rumors that Exportadora de Sal, which already possessed the world's largest evaporative salt export operation at Scammon's Lagoon, wished to duplicate the procedure at Laguna San Ignacio. Whales had returned to Scammon's Lagoon in historic numbers despite the saltworks, but questions still abounded. Could whales sustain the same pressure in a smaller, shallower lagoon? Would Exportadora pitch a town like Guerrero Negro on its banks? Would employees shuttle through the land in-between, last habitat of the Peninsular pronghorn? It was speculated that Exportadora supported the pronghorn program to appease environmentalists before pouncing on the lagoon, and I realized the project was imminent on the last night of the April 1994 census when we stayed at Exportadora's base camp for surveyors, and a fresh logo—LSI, for Laguna San Ignacio, in the company's interwound blue lettering—blazoned the mess hall door. Months later the project surfaced and in 1995 it became Baja California's major controversy.

The new plan would more than double Exportadora's harvest, enabling the company to retain its title as the world's largest evaporative salt operation. The ponds would cover twenty-one thousand hectares—seventy square miles—of sparsely vegetated salt flat on the north side of the lagoon. Pumps at the lagoon's inmost corner would propel water pondward through canals. Conveyor belts rather than trucks would shuttle the harvest to a giant pier twenty kilometers from the lagoon's mouth. Stretching two kilometers into the Pacific, the pier would receive cargo ships that made pickups twice a week. Each day's pumping would take only .005 percent of the content of a lagoon whose water was changed 40 percent daily by tides. One thousand jobs would be generated by construction, shrinking to an estimated three hundred for the permanent operation. There would be no new town. Workers would swell the fishing town of Abreojos, access would remain on existing roads and office work would stay in Guerrero Negro. The project represented an investment of $110 million and was expected to bring in $100 million a year in revenues, ensuring that Mexico, beating South America and Australia, would be the global leader in salt production in the twenty-first century.

Eighteen investigators from the biology institute in La Paz—the same institute that was formulating the pronghorn program—had prepared an environmental impact statement that endorsed the project. Now that it was public, it was open to attack. First targeted were the pumps and the pier. Whales depend upon hearing for communication and their sense of direction, and combusting pumps were located by the shallow area where they gave birth. Whale migration routes were too ill-defined to know whether a two-kilometer pier would deflect or confuse them, let alone whether incoming ships would hit them. It particularly inflamed environmentalists that grey whales—Mexico's environmental success story to the extent that a government pamphlet called grey whales "Mexican by birth"—were allotted only 23 lines of a 465-page report. The evaporation of seawater into salt, meanwhile, was less benign than it appeared. It threw off a residue of heavy metals and toxic chemicals that the company was planning to use for containment barriers and road maintenance, when the substance itself should be contained. And salt had to be picked up regularly, just as a cow needed to be milked, because there was nowhere to store the continuing product. If cargo ships couldn't reach the pier because of storms, or the pier itself were knocked out, would company barges invade the lagoon?

The final complication was that Laguna San Ignacio lay in the Vizcaíno Biosphere Reserve, recognized as a World Heritage Site by UNESCO, and was the largest area in such status in all of Latin America. Created in 1988 on the last day of the de la Madrid administration, it stretched from the state line at the eagle monument, south through Scammon's Lagoon, Laguna San Ignacio and the pronghorn habitat on the Pacific side, then swept eastward across the peninsula to encompass the Sierra San Francisco with its cave paintings, finally embracing a smaller coastline on the Gulf of California. The area was to be managed to protect its natural and cultural resources, with certain areas, called "nuclear zones," declared off-limits to development. The rest would be a buffer zone in which inhabitants could continue their traditional activities. New human settlements were not permitted. Despite the exalted plans, no signs announced that one was entering or leaving the protected area, nor had I ever met anyone who represented it. I learned of its existence years after I had been counting pronghorn in its midst, was impressed by its conceptual grandeur and concluded that it only existed as a shaded area on certain maps. But the salt proposal suddenly elevated the Biosphere Reserve to public prominence, with environmentalists claiming the project was a horrific intrusion and Exportadora retorting that it was wholly within the buffer zone and no more illegal than its thirty-year-old ponds at Scammon's Lagoon, which no one proposed to remove.

As invective flew, in late February the National Ecological Institute, a branch of the interior department that would make the final decision, vetoed the project. Voices within the government, all of the same political party, rose in contention. Exportadora was itself 51 percent owned by the federal government, and the secretary of commerce, its nominal chairman of the board, angrily protested that the Ecological Institute was ill informed. The Group of 100, an alliance of Mexico City artists and intellectuals who comprised Mexico's leading environmental organization, came out strongly anti-salt. A biologist in Guerrero Negro showed me one of the group's bulletins, which had errors of date and location and allegations that the pumps would invade an island of nesting birds and that a train would connect the lagoons. As an opponent of the project himself, it angered him that environmentalists should discredit their position with dumb mistakes. The fishing cooperatives along the coast worried that the pier and its traffic of large boats, with inevitable oil leaks and propellers churning the bottom, would inhibit their own movement and possibly kill crustacean, mollusk and fish populations that were their livelihood. The cooperative in Laguna San Ignacio pointed out that visitation at Scammon's Lagoon, site of the current salt operation, was less than 10 percent of their own despite its greater accessibility because no one wanted to watch whales in an industrial setting. Why should they give up their traditional fishing and whalewatching to work for the salt company?

Exportadora moved on several fronts, offering to win over environmentalists by showing the site and also threatening an injunction. I happened upon two articles about the project in different La Paz papers on the same day, stressing the environmental goodwill of the salt company. They were identical, word for word, and I realized that they were not the journalism they appeared but were press releases from the company. All peninsula politicians seemed to support Exportadora, the most vociferous being the governor. Environmentalists, he said, should leave their desks and see that thirty years of the salt company had not ruined Scammon's Lagoon. The baseless conclusion of the National Ecological Institute could threaten the project and scare away foreign investment, but it would be reversed "after the company presents impact studies made by proven and recognized investigators. The state government is the principal promoter of preservation and conservation of the environment. In every investment our priority will be to protect the ecology."

In visits to the midpeninsula I asked everyone I knew what they thought of the saltworks. In San Ignacio they were mildly opposed because it might harm whales, or mildly in favor because it might create jobs, and mainly found it futile to take sides among squabbling demigods. Coastal fishermen were staunchly opposed, not only because of the threat to their fisheries but also because they already made many times the average saltworker's salary. In Guerrero Negro, Exportadora's support town, opinion was mixed, with opponents saying that a company that couldn't alleviate the squalor of the town it had already spawned had no business expanding elsewhere. A biologist with Exportadora found the pier the worst aspect but explained its significance. At the present operation half the expense lay in barging salt from the evaporative ponds to Isla Cedros, where big ships could dock, whereas at Laguna San Ignacio the conveyor belt could shoot the salt straight to the deepwater pier, eliminating the barges. In his opinion, the project needed further study and approval should be contingent upon Exportadora's kicking in a percentage toward environmental protection in the Biosphere. Economists noted that the worldwide price of salt was falling because of an already glutted market and there was speculation that the project was a Japanese maneuver to ensure cheap salt into the next millennium.

After my visit to the cave paintings I called a botanist in La Paz who had asked me to report on the new visitation system. She was little interested in the trials of The Archaeologist and really wanted to know what ranchers in the sierra thought of the Biosphere. They had no opinion, I replied; they might be living in the middle of it, but they had never heard of it. What did she, meanwhile, think of the salt project?

I had no idea I'd raised a sluice gate. She was one of the eighteen people who had prepared the impact statement and she passionately favored the project because it was a nondestructive way to raise money for Mexico. She considered herself an environmentalist but was furious at other environmentalists for twisting the facts. And the pumps, I asked, and the pier? She let fly a twenty-minute oration that included, several times, rhetorical questions one through four, to which she supplied polished ripostes. Did I know that the pylons of the pier were widely spaced so that whales could pass between? If whales couldn't tolerate a pier designed for them, how did they ever manage to migrate past the tankers, bedlam and stink of, say, Long Beach, California? Mexico was a third-world country trying to go first world, with a vast population to feed. Here was a lucrative project that did little harm. And environmentalists were against it? Who was going to pay for environmental protection? Tourists? A government that was broke and put the environment at the bottom of the list? Approval could be made contingent on the company's bankrolling projects in the Biosphere. When I interjected that the project would probably be approved in any case, just because the most influential politicians were for it—intending irony—she noted their support with approval.

After the call my ears were ringing but other La Paz biologists, it turned out, concurred. The pronghorn biologist I knew best favored the project because it would help Mexico's balance of payments and he even suggested, surreally I thought, that income from the saltworks could help alleviate the poverty of indigenous rebels in Chiapas. From my experience with the American environmental movement, it surprised me that people who devoted their careers to studying and protecting the natural world put the economy first. When I expressed my own view—that economies were permanently in crises that varied only in severity while the natural world, once sacrificed, was gone for the human span—my concerns were brushed aside rather than rebutted. I spared them Tim's view that Laguna San Ignacio should be left alone because it was the last breeding lagoon that hadn't been tampered with and was so beautiful from the air. I too had gazed from a plane window at its tiers of dunes, its mazy canals through the mangroves and the swirling blue tides that mimicked the atmosphere of Earth itself, and thought it was precisely what we shouldn't violate. I also loved driving through the salt ponds with their teeming birdlife and enjoyed their own bleached quiltwork from the air, but one Scammon's Lagoon was enough. Aesthetic concerns, in any case, were irrelevant when even the biologists involved only wanted to delay the project long enough to shake money out of the salt company.

The controversy pursued me afterward to the States, where warring ads appeared in the *New York Times*. Environmentalists took out a full-pager giving a broad-brush rundown of the plan's evils under a headline screaming that Mitsubishi wanted to suck the lagoon dry—a feat that would impress even the Dutch. Exportadora retaliated with a full page touting its environmental record, along with the world's need for more salt for "food processing, product manufacturing, textiles, pharmaceuticals and de-icing." Brigitte Bardot logged in with an open letter to President Zedillo protesting the "draining" of the lagoon and calling the project "demented." Exportadora's ad committed itself to acquiring a new impact statement from "an internationally respected environmental consulting firm." Time to bargain, at least, had been bought.

In 1995 the elusive Biosphere finally materialized on the ground. A biologist from the mainland was appointed director and given a half dozen assistants. The grey whale, with a stable population of twenty thousand, was now considered "saved" and recovery of the Peninsular pronghorn was declared top priority. The new director was one of the Biosphere's creators as well as a veteran of numerous censuses, though none that I'd been on. He had spent months in the field with his crew studying and guarding pronghorn, and although it was long thought that there was no hunting of the pronghorn by outsiders, they learned that a foreign trophy hunter had recently paid local guides five thousand dollars to kill a female. They had also found baby pronghorn fur in coyote scat. Coyotes had been targets of a failed poisoning program in the seventies and had resurfaced as a serious threat. Because its shores were rich with carrion from fish to seabirds, the Vizcaíno Desert sustained one of North America's highest concentrations of coyotes; forty-five were counted at Malarrimo around one stranded whale. The director's immediate goal was to enclose five hundred hectares with electric fencing so that newborns, with their mothers, could spend their first three months coyote-free. To cope with human predation, he hoped ultimately to surround the entire pronghorn habitat with fencing that would let outsiders know they were crossing a boundary. Ranchers with cattle in the habitat would have keys to padlocked gates across access roads and would support the program because it was their own protection against rustlers. Further plans for the Biosphere included shorebird studies, survey and protection of the bighorn sheep in mountains toward the gulf, public education programs and tripling of the staff.

I only learned the foregoing when I caught up with the director months after I showed up to visit. When I arrived in Guerrero Negro, he and his staff were off with the pronghorn, and the officials I knew from my first counts were still in town, stuck without wheels, as if nothing had changed. The interior department they worked for had changed its name from SEDUE to SEDESOL since my first association with it, and now it was Something, Something and Fish—they didn't have it down yet and the new acronym, SMARNP, was unpronounceable. The new Zedillo administration—plagued by the collapse of the peso, an ongoing rebellion in Chiapas and an appalling chain of political assassinations—hadn't appointed a state director of SMARNP, and without the state director's approval nothing could go forward. The November pronghorn count had been missed. In January, without knowledge of the leading biologist in La Paz or of Sandy Lanham, the pilot who flew down regularly from Tucson to add the aerial component, an impromptu census was taken. Then the April census, most dependable of the counts, was canceled. Before I left the Biosphere I drove a stranded biologist toward his job in Laguna San Ignacio. An island of nesting birds had been invaded by coyotes swept there by the tides, as well as by cats dumped by fishermen. It was crucial for certain seagulls not to lose a year of reproduction and he was on his way to set up traps. The Biosphere coordinators, he said, had not been paid for several months and had borrowed money from friends and relatives to keep working, believing in the mission as well as eventual reimbursement.

In June, Sandy Lanham, worried about the continuity of data and finding herself in La Paz after a whale census with twelve hundred dollars of foundation money in her pocket, offered a free aerial pronghorn census. A lower SMARNP official told her he couldn't authorize flights and denied permission. As with the new system for cave visitation, the Biosphere was going through an awkward stage that its participants hoped was a transition. SMARNP, at least, was issued some vowels so that as SEMARNAP it was pronounceable.

While officialdom dithered, changes in the peninsula ranged from the high-rise to the invisible and were more than one person could assimilate. Below waterline lurked the eradication of sealife in the gulf by driftnets from Japan, the more modest stripping of the ocean bottom by shrimp boats from Guaymas and damage to the coral reef at Cabo Pulmo, the only Pacific-side reef in North America. A committed inlander, I worried more about the disappearance from the Sierra de la Giganta of ironwood trees that lined arroyos with fountains of feathery, olive-colored leaves. Their wood is the second hardest on earth and they grow slowly, living up to eight hundred years while providing direct sustenance to birds, mammals and insects. Along with mesquites they also serve as nurse trees for such large cacti as *cardóns* and the various organ-pipes, plants that need to begin their first few decades in shade. I once accompanied some biologists from La Paz in their annual count of growth under a single nurse tree: they found seventy miniature plants representing five cactus species.

Ranchers in the Sierra de la Giganta had traditionally cut only the branch tips of ironwood to feed to burros and mules, who could digest even the spines. In the latter 1970s began a ten-year drought that killed off cattle, impoverishing the tiny communities, and in 1980 a trader from Tijuana showed up and taught the ranchers to make charcoal from ironwood. At first ranchers only hacked around the base of a tree, letting it die and dry in place; then they started burning live wood. They laid the ironwood in a triangular pit with a hole at each point, placed a protective triangle of sheet metal over the wood and shoveled a meter of dirt on top. After torching the casserole at one of the holes, they sealed it, leaving the other two as vents they could regulate. By watching the color of the smoke and adjusting the holes to control the flow of air, they could make sure the wood didn't turn to ash. After three days they removed the dirt and the charcoal was cooked. Needing only tools they already possessed, ranchers made quick money, the exploding population of Tijuana received a clean, long-burning fuel and traders reaped most of the profit. Cacti beneath the nurse trees were left to shrivel in the sun.

Gradually the government realized that the key to the desert ecosystem was threatened and began requiring permits for cutting ironwood and levying fines. But inspectors were few, punishment was slight, and a highway stop was licensed to sell charcoal legally. Tables of wide-meshed screen were set up for grading chunks of coal before it was crammed into polystyrene feed bags. Bulging bags stood in a wall behind the tables, a cinder-block shed held polystyrene waiting to be stuffed and the surrounding ground was blackened for a half-acre. Slowly and legally, a key species was passing through a small, grimy operation.

The loss of ironwoods in the Sierra de la Giganta was slow compared to the state of Sonora, across the gulf, where ironwood was chucked into bags of mesquite and hauled over the border to satisfy the American taste for "mesquite-broiled" chicken and steak. I was relieved to find a normal mix of ironwoods during our trip to the cave paintings and to learn that in the

Sierra de San Francisco the making of charcoal was unknown. For a while it seemed that the burning of trees in the Sierra de la Giganta might level off because members of the older generation didn't approve and many of the young were leaving stricken ranches to find jobs in La Paz or in the north. A school superintendent told me that grade schools were closed when they had fewer than twenty students and in the Sierra de la Giganta he had fewer and fewer to supervise. Concerned about the trees, the superintendent tried to introduce the carving of ironwood into figurines, thinking that would give ranchers a stake in preserving the species. The practice had worked for Seri Indians in Sonora, but the Seris themselves were losing their trade to non-Indian Mexicans who mass-produced whales and pelicans with machines. With neither sculpting tools nor tradition, the Sierra de la Giganta ranchers turned out a few derivative figures whose appealing matte finish wasn't enough to fetch them a decent price, and they quit. An interior department official told me the ranchers had been informed how vegetation draws rain, holds topsoil, and supports other species they value, but they wouldn't give up making charcoal because they were "idiosyncratic," a word he repeated several times. When I couldn't get a more informative adjective, I asked if he meant "lazy" and he said yes. In February 1995 a rancher told me that even though the drought was over, charcoal had overtaken cattle as the leading source of income and the young had stopped leaving home. I asked what would happen when the trees were gone. He shrugged. "They take one day at a time."

The subtraction of a tree species—usually far from the highway and undetectable to the novice eye—passed without comment as hotels and condos, mostly on the cape, shot skyward. It proved impossible to live within a half day's drive of that vortex of usury without being drawn to its maw, and I joined pianist friends from *La Tecla Perpetua* for an overnight to attend a friend's concert. En route we inspected a new hotel poised on a beach between the modest, still civilized San José del Cabo and the soaring wet T-shirt ghetto of Cabo San Lucas. A cavernous lobby opened to a panorama of the hotel's own wings, cliffs of lilac and canary that swept around a spill of plants and fountains. Oxidized bedrock intruded natural accents into the terraced palms and one wing offered a cutaway to the ocean like a jumbo postcard. Exclaimed one of our party, without irony, "How great is the mind of man!" The fifty-kilometer coast between the two towns, unimproved when I had first seen it in 1968, had become a phalanx of shaved headlands with Moorish condos here, an imitation Greek village there and, in down-town Cabo San Lucas, a lurid pink knock-off of Taos Pueblo. Each building, as aggressive as its American time-share street hustlers, screamed, "Me! I'm the prize to buy into!" Residents of Cabo San Lucas found that the very ho-tels they worked for were cutting off access to beaches where they could spend their days off. Mexican tourists got bad service because they were re-puted to be stingy tippers in comparison to foreigners. As an outsider, I was grateful to the cape because, at least for now, it had siphoned the tawdriest development to a single sacrifice area and left the rest of the peninsula merely appraised.

I did keep an eye out for other signs of infection and was particularly ner-vous about a development eight kilometers south of Loreto, the original capi-tal of Baja California. After a grueling 350-kilometer drive north from La Paz over a desert plateau, across the parched farmland of the Valle de Santo Domingo and through the burnt volcanics of the Sierra de la Giganta, the highway rejoined the gulf in a roadcut V that framed a Madama Butterfly bridge over pool-felt green. The bridge dramatized a water hazard on a golf course sustained by groundwater pumped from thirty-five kilometers away. For years I had accelerated past, wondering when the course would open, glancing at the ominous buildings beyond it, tuning it out as I took it in. In this year of subjecting myself to all, I pulled in the gate.

Palm-lined boulevards led past two-story spec houses of adobe-colored concrete and red tile roofs, a neo-mission style that Frank Lloyd Wright dubbed "Realtoresque." Most streets had no houses, most houses looked unoccupied, road signs were rusting and the landscaping had been invaded by mallow. I parked at a large hotel and was assured by check-in that it was only empty because of remodeling. High season was summer, when sport fishermen braved the heat, with a little action in winter from kayakers who wanted a night of amenities after days of paddling, and whalewatchers who flew to Loreto and were bused to Bahía Magdalena. I proceeded to the club-house and asked when the golf course was slated to open. "It's been open for three years," said the manager.

"Then why don't I ever see anyone on it?"

"Because no one comes to play."

Admiring the tight logic, I drove to the promotional office. A woman with a fresh perm explained that the development was financed by FONATUR, the federal tourist ministry, in partnership with private capital, and she handed me some literature. Composed in breathless P.R. and Englished with a treacherous dictionary, its phrases were so choice that I extracted my favorites and arranged them as follows:

> Loreto was named for the Virgin who cared for the Spanish explorers. It was founded by the Jesus Company, which raised the fine edification that is the mission and which introduced cattle: bovine, equine, porcine and barnyard fowls. Project Loreto, an excellent option, is made possible by FONATUR, a development propeller. Water is supplied by well bombing. The golf course is a real challenge: hole 14, where the player must hit the ball only once and send it through the sea to put it in the green, is one of those duels. The nautical complex's natural glass of water provides a safe shelter where many boats can slip. There are even amazingly gracious grey whales (in season). It is growingly clear that the promising future is already increasingly evident.

I was relieved to have inspected Nopoló, for its increasingly evident future was clearly going nowhere and might even suggest the folly of similar developments north of the cape. More threatening because less tangible were plots from afar. The Japanese, who already owned 49 percent of the salt company through Mitsubishi, announced plans to acquire 448 square kilometers on the shore of Bahía Magdalena. A consortium called the Iwasaki Group proposed eight "resort clusters" to include hotels, restaurants, shops, tennis and golf. In the way that major developments and marginal species are drawn like star-crossed lovers, the development area comprised nearly the world's entire habitat of the *chirinola,* or creeping cactus, an organ-pipe whose spiny, dun-colored limbs sprawl on the ground, looking quite dead. Arms die on one side only to sprout and root on the other so that the cactus slowly migrates. The battle of Iwasaki versus the creeping cactus hadn't come to a head because, despite the grand plan, the company only bought 2,000 hectares and its lone Mexican guardian reported that company officials occasionally showed up, but no earth had been turned. It was comforting to remember the 1991 Japanese proposal to build a privately financed $1.3 billion toll road from Tijuana to the cape, complete with gas stations, motels and adult playgrounds, which vanished from the papers like a nightmare after the second cup of coffee.

Given that I had envisioned instant ruin for the peninsula when pavement was completed in 1973, I was grateful to find so much intact a generation later. Like old *cardón* cacti rotting to their inner shafts, unfinished buildings all over the peninsula were splintering incomplete, their rebar looping into the sky. Speculators prowled every corner, but so far the peninsula had proved rugged and extensive enough to repel most assaults. As for the cape being a useful sacrifice area, an ornithologist from the biology institute in La Paz brought home to me the poignancy of its loss. He had been making periodic observations of a vulture roost in a palm grove by the shore. A hotel was slapped up in three months and he returned to see if the birds had found a new roost. At sundown he found them circling, circling, not knowing where to put themselves, unable to leave. It reminded him, he said, of those who had lived for generations by the water—ranchers whose land I had seen foreclosed by banks as early as the late sixties—people now forced to work construction, or to make beds and clean toilets for foreigners, a population trying to find a home and earn a living now that their roost by the water was gone.

After canvassing the peninsula's new economic and recreational pressures, it was a pleasure to camp under Héctor's cypress tree and let information float to my tent. For the first time it was clear to me that the *huerta,* which I thought of as a unit, was actually divided into three strips owned by the three brothers. The fruit trees, flowers and vegetables that engulfed the buildings all flourished in Héctor's third; the grapevines still standing belonged to the brother who managed the store in Abreojos; and the salesman brother owned the weedy third where the old vines had been torn out—behind which stood the cypress. The second-hand shop had closed because the fall of the peso had made goods from north of the border too expensive, but the clearing of powder-blue disintegrating cones around the cypress had become the salesman's storage area and I found myself sharing the shade with four refrigerators and an old air-conditioning unit. Several strains of the wildflowers Héctor brought back from the valley of rhyolite domes now flourished in the garden, and snacks at the tent blossomed into full meals in the house. Surprisingly, Héctor, that committed horticulturalist, had bought a cow, a calf and a goat, intending to fatten them in the fallow area and sell them at a profit. Tossing greens to the animals gave his father something familiar to do but I found it ironic that Héctor, who scorned his father's old profession, had become a token cattleman even as his father spent his last years marooned among plants.

Global village notwithstanding, San Ignacio seemed more isolated than ever. The coastal fishing towns that San Ignacio had spawned now had more stores of their own, their population was maturing, and people returned less frequently for supplies and to visit. The Sunday dances that had kept me awake were canceled because no one could pay for them. Drivers took the new road around Héctor's property so fast that ferocious speed bumps were installed, bringing traffic to such a halt that one of the bumps had been officially removed. A friend of Héctor's told me that Mars was going to emit gases that would turn the whole peninsula green and lush at the turn of the millennium. When I asked where he read it, he stared at the ground, rifling his memory, then said, "Jules Verne." As I prepared to leave, Héctor was saddened that we wouldn't see each other for half a year. Then he brightened and said, "But time keeps passing faster and, in reality, six months is only two cylinders of gas."

La Paz, which had balked at the world's acceleration, now quickened. It distressed me that windmills, which once flourished in climax stands, had shrunk to a few bladeless skeletons or were bunched in parks for decor. Any water they could reach was contaminated and a farther aquifer had been tapped. A succession of mayors had promised to pave the streets and finally one delivered, making them one-way as well, so that within a year Paceños went from meandering through washouts to dashing through town in calculated patterns. Graffiti arrived, so novel that newspapers printed the word in quotes. It was restrained by American standards but persistent enough that Alejandrina left it on the veterinary clinic because it would just appear again and, besides, weren't the kids trying to express something? International politics had seldom penetrated La Paz but in 1995 the *mal humor*— the straw figure burned during the February carnival to dispatch ill will— was a blond gringo with a sign that said "187," a reference to the recent anti-immigration proposition passed by California. Interest in the world no longer stopped at city limits.

Such changes were obsessively discussed over brandy and Coke, and one Sunday I watched two biologists debate whether Paceños, who could once eat for nothing by scooping up crabs from the shore, were still in touch with their dazzling harbor. Contact with nature was what gave La Paz its distinction, claimed the biologist from Mexico City; even driving to the lab you could look into the water and see leaping dolphins and manta ray. You could, replied the Paceño, but you probably wouldn't. La Paz's contact with the world—mail, news, merchandise, comings and goings—once centered on the waterfront, which drew the town together at the shore. Now those functions were dispersed into planes, trucks, the postal system, phones and the media. For the contemporary Paceño, life was cars, radio, TV, business and parties, with an occasional jaunt to the beach. The proof was that most inhabitants of La Paz, port of illusion, couldn't swim. His version was corroborated by the owner of a beachfront café who told me that Americans invariably sat outside, watching the bay, following the sunset, while Paceños gathered at inside tables, more animated, more likely smoking, more focused on their social group. In a sense both biologists were right: you could remain in contact with the play of desert, mountain and sea as much as you chose, but most citizens chose not to.

Accelerating routine did not, however, rule out adventure within town. I had given my chapter on the development of La Paz to a sociology professor so she could check for errors. She seemed miffed that I had dismissed the cathedral as a patchwork of bad architecture: wouldn't readers like to know that different parts were built at different times, in different styles? I remained unconvinced until I was asked to play the organ there for a fancy wedding. The afternoon before the ceremony I was led through a padlocked door by a church guardian, up a staircase and into the choir loft—a balcony in back of the nave—where I got used to the Wagner and the Mendelssohn on a two-keyboard instrument I seldom play. On the evening of the ceremony I arrived a half hour early in a borrowed tux, tested the organ, then spotted a low arch-shaped door at the top of several stone steps. I pushed it open, ducked through, and in near darkness made my way up a continuation of the stone steps around the interior of what I knew, from the sociologist's literature, was the older of two appended towers. I reached a metal ladder with handrails and climbed until I was blocked above by a metal trapdoor. I pushed it up, it came to rest on a hidden support, and I stepped out.

The expanse was dizzying. I found myself on a small roofed platform without guardrails, its center monopolized by a large bronze bell. Last streaks of sunset were vanishing across the inner harbor. I gazed out at La Paz's miscellany of low buildings, their first lights obscured by laurel trees like cosmic dust. Shoes were still being shined in the plaza. I advanced to the edge, peered down and saw wedding guests in tuxes and smart dresses gathering by the door. Unable to resist any longer, I drew back the bell's great clapper and let go. It struck bronze. A terrifying, exhilarating tone trembled the air and passed through my viscera as if it would shove me into space. I let it die out and stepped back to the edge to see if anyone had noticed. No one looked up. Church bells rang at various hours of the day, were so much background noise, and experiments were probably safe. Could a bell so large be damped with the hand? I let the clapper bang bronze again and spread my hand against the flare. Vibrations surged up my arm, into my shoulder, and the sound rang out undimmed. Suddenly anxious, I backed down the ladder and pulled the trapdoor shut behind me.

Back in the choir I realized I had fifteen minutes left to explore the newer tower. I mounted two sets of tight metal staircases, a similar ladder with handrails and pushed open another trapdoor. I found myself surrounded by four bells of varying sizes, connected in pairs by ropes. More guests were milling below. Light fled from the sky and I felt phantomlike in my borrowed tux. I pulled a rope, sounding two great bells. Warring tones, a fourth apart, shook the air with a stirring commotion. Whatever I disliked about changing, accelerating, homogenizing La Paz, I felt immensely satisfied to be lodged in its throat and making its hoarse, primal noise. I pulled the other rope. In the lingering cacophony, as I sorted and savored overtones, I detected a new sound, that of footsteps advancing toward me on the metal steps. I pulled the trapdoor behind me and descended toward the guardian. "I'm a musician," I blurted. "I couldn't resist. I won't do it again." Wordlessly he returned down the stairs after a glare that was almost luminous in the dark. The sociologist was right: this motley building was the perfect nub for this still endearing hodgepodge of a town. I sat solemnly at the organ and struck up "Here Comes the Bride."

Looking back on my season of taking the peninsula's vital signs, I took stock of my own pathology. It had been clear for years that my original relation to Baja California had changed. I never truly believed that I could find out everything about the place, but on those first meandering trips before pavement I thought that if I could just internalize enough geology and botany and ranches and towns and fraying byways, in a blaze of neurons I could finally summon this sliver of desert into a single, sweeping vision the way it was gripped, physically, by the sea. Skeptic that I remained, this inflation of the desert pastoral was my mysticism. And as I heaped fuel for my crown fire, new facts were increasingly about asphalt and technology and tourism, about smoldering ironwood and disappearing pronghorn. Romantic, an enthusiast, I had ignored human depravity. But Baja California was staked out by human beings and, like any such place, it was also habitat for social competition, scheming, power struggles, deceit and smiling denials. It wasn't just a matter of outsiders building hotels, dragging driftnets through the gulf or turning a calving lagoon to salt. It was also the connivance of privileged Baja Californians who paid lip service to protecting their homeland while taking—under the spotlit tables of their high positions—favors and funds. To factor in this behavior was to lose the romance of discovery and become a witness, even a minor participant, in a land's betrayal. Internalize human nastiness too? It was too late in the process and too hypocritical not to. I stumbled over a paradox: that in trying to learn enough to assemble the peninsula complete in my mind, a "proxy for life itself," I had overshot the mark. Along with knowing too little, I knew too much. It is received wisdom that the beloved, won, sprouts liver spots and mean streaks, and that the mature admirer must settle for an attachment that is less ardent, less demanding, less intolerant of corruption if that spark of first infatuation is to survive.

Stepping farther back, I could see the accelerating disillusion of those who cared about places. In a few decades I had seen Glen Canyon drown, had seen the Arizona desert bulldozed for fully secured sprawl, had seen my adoptive town of Aspen, Colorado, evolve from a bohemian refuge to a rookery of egotourism. The great age of contemplative, illuminating travel, of which I was a frustrated descendant, only lasted a couple of centuries. It required a means of getting around a world that stayed put, or that evolved only slowly, so that you could mentally snag a piece of it, take it home, examine it, polish it, hold its facets to the light, and let those facets reflect your own altered self. Now, as soon as you made contact with a place, it changed in a daymare into something new, bright, nonreflective and repellent. You returned diminished, wondering if you had only imagined its former allure.

With sufficient detachment one could savor certain incongruities of change, even on the peninsula. Dignified matrons innocent of English wore T-shirts with messages like "Shit Happens" and "Born to Cruise." In Santa Rosalía I saw a hot-dog salesman neglect his stand to lean on the trunk of a sedan, on top of which a tiny TV was showing an exorcism. A doctor in San Ignacio told me he saw two Americans emerge from a trailer with a dog on a leash. When the dog defecated, they scooped up the feces with a trowel, slid them into a plastic bag and carried them back to the trailer. "At first I was dumbfounded," said the doctor. "Then I admired it."

Detachment was an easy enough stance toward the comic detail, and in its sharper formulation—nonattachment—it even constitutes the core of certain Eastern disciplines. As an incurable Westerner I found myself attaching promiscuously, bonding with every place I liked. To live without roots was not to live deeply. My first attitude toward Baja California—that it was a brilliant object of contemplation—did have overtones of non-attachment. But as changes to the landscape were increasingly revealed as threats, I felt my emotional ties: realized that in addition to visiting, admiring and reflecting on the peninsula, I had begun to feel responsible for it. Being an outsider and only mildly activist by nature, it meant, in my case, going on pronghorn counts, spouting off on the radio when asked, attending a few meetings and conferences, taking notes and using the power— it felt like the impotence—of the written word. Part of that impulse was the composition of this manuscript and I only hoped that my year of the inventory, 1995, wouldn't destroy for me the last romance of the peninsula.

As for more tangible help, it was difficult to know where to begin. Policy radiated from Mexico City, often with little knowledge of the regions it was crafted to serve. Resources for people in the field were intercepted by bureaucrats in the nearest state capital. Government agencies overlapped, contradicted each other, fought for terrain, changed their mandates, leaving confusion over which to support, and when. The only private environmental group I was in touch with in La Paz dedicated itself to influencing people from the top. The primary volunteer organization, it alerted officials to sudden threats, published specialized studies and tried to steer politicians toward enlightened policies. It was also so self-sealed that it was difficult to learn when and where it met and I kept running into people, including the professor who named it, who had quit, dismissing it as "elitist." La Paz had also become a venue for international conferences, primarily on aquatic life, with top biologists and such superstars as Jean-Michel Cousteau, but so little publicized that one generally learned about them afterward. I wanted to find them valuable, but the talk of "sustainable development" and "ecotourism" reminded me eerily of the Christian Science I was doused with as a child, when I truly wanted to believe, as adults did, in the unreality of matter. I had seen with my own eyes that ranchers were overgrazing the desert and turning ironwood to charcoal, but in my aesthetic, amoral core I still preferred cracked leather to raspberry lycra and hated to see ranchers and fishermen, impoverished as they were, become guides to gringos and other foreigners who disported while imagining they were saving the planet.

My clutch of bad attitudes often brought to mind the owner of a café in Santa Inés, in the *cirio* forest, whom Tim and I dropped in on before dawn on a trip north. The café wasn't open yet but there was a bulb on in back.

Amid heaps of dirty dishes the owner made us instant coffee in styrofoam cups and spoke nonstop. "There's no real coffee this morning because my wife is still sleeping. She's sleeping because she was up all night serving drunken truck drivers. The drivers are all from the mainland now and they drive by day and drink by night. Their trucks are half empty because people in the south grow only half the crops they used to. They don't grow crops because they steal the pumps, sell them, then can't irrigate and grow lazy. Around here they're cutting the *datilillos* for fences and taking the dead *cirios* for souvenirs. Tourism is a joke because the very people running the trailer park steal their customers' tires at night. There are no more mountain sheep because they're shot by the officials paid to protect them. The whole peninsula is corrupt. This is terrible coffee so no charge. Drive safely and have a good trip."

I had a different set of grievances but I knew the feeling.

My informal survey of the peninsula was crowned by a chance encounter just before I left. At the wedding reception after my bell caper I struck up a friendship with a lively middle-aged couple who asked, through some twist of conversation, what exotic foods I'd eaten. Had I tasted rattlesnake? I hadn't. "It's just like chicken," said she, and I repressed my "Then why not just eat chicken?" They insisted that two other wedding guests and I join them for rattler at a friend's ranch two days later.

The morning of the excursion we three guests were picked up by the couple's chauffeur; our hosts would be arriving separately. We were driven two hours on the highway, then over back roads to a modest ranch house by a citrus orchard. The ranch's caretakers had set a table under a mesquite tree and coals were smoldering. We were greeted by the couple who had invited us, another wedding guest whose family owned the ranch, and a couple I didn't know. "I had no idea he was to be here," said one of my companions, nodding toward the unfamiliar couple. The man, in his fifties, was distinguished in a generic way. After we opened beers, I sat next to him at the picnic table and we exchanged first names. "Are you from La Paz?" I asked.

"Yes. I've lived there all my life, except for eight years in Mexico City when I had the privilege of representing the state in the Chamber of Deputies."

"And what do you do now that you're back?"

"I'm governor."

How was it that from two feet away I hadn't recognized this face I'd seen on five hundred posters? I decided it was because the ubiquitous black-and-white photo made him look lightly tan whereas, in the flesh, he was bright pink. My friend who had recognized him rushed to offer me some credentials; I was a concert pianist.

"Really!" he said. "Would you play a benefit concert for our children's fund?"

"I'd be honored." I gave him my phone number.

The rattlesnake that had prompted the invitation didn't appear until dessert. It was served in coils, with the head and rattles cut off and the pale meat clinging to a delicate skeleton. The meat between the bones was difficult to dislodge and I settled for peeling off a few lateral strips. As I expected, it was not like chicken, more like a bland, slightly salty crustacean made savory by the coals. It was preceded by tasty beef fajitas wrapped in homemade tortillas. The stunner came at the beginning, when the governor asked if I wouldn't like to start with some *sopa de caguama.*

Caguama was sea turtle and I had eaten my share of it, *caguama* steaks as well as soups, during my first years on the peninsula. For Baja Californians it was almost a ritual food, served during all-day family gatherings, a symbol of hospitality. I previously ate it because it was a local specialty and had become a ritual of our visits more than because I liked it, for I found it pungent and rubbery. I had no trouble giving it up when the species was so depleted from overharvesting that it was in extreme peril and banned as food. Several years back I had reported to the interior department a restaurant I suspected of serving *caguama,* prompting a biologist friend to speculate that instead of cracking down, the officials had probably rushed over for lunch. Since its prohibition, *caguama* had been jokingly referred to as *cerdito de aleta,* or "finned pork," and I heard many stories of its continued use, particularly by public officials, on ceremonial occasions. My curiosity being such that I perversely go along with activities I don't approve of so as not to scare off whatever is coming next, I wanted to see how far things would go. If the governor was going to offer to thaw a pronghorn, I wanted to know about it. "I'll have a little," I said.

One of my companions glared at me. As soon as I dispatched my soup, she asked the governor how he, who should be setting the example, could possibly serve a creature so illegal and in so much peril. He answered calmly that she was right about the *caguama* but sometimes they got caught in fishermen's nets and drowned, and wouldn't it be a shame to waste them? On the way home my other companion remarked that if there were a sea turtle for everyone who used the old they-drown-anyway alibi, the species would be flourishing. I mentally replayed the governor's repeated reassurances as he promoted the new salt project. "The state government is the principal pro-motor of preservation and conservation of the environment. In every in-vestment our priority will be to protect the ecology."

It wasn't until I got home and picked up a newspaper that I realized the significance of this Saturday itself, elevating a casual incident into an em-blem of what was wasting the peninsula. I had celebrated the twenty-fifth an-niversary of Earth Day by eating endangered species with the governor.

RANCHO SAN FULANO

12

After years of drought that those without land took for good weather, the sky revenged itself by unleashing downpours and pommeling winds for three weeks nonstop. It was 1990, the year before I started renting houses in La Paz, and I had flown down to spend Christmas with Tim and Nora. Tim kept a rattlesnake in a glass cage in the bedstead of their waterbed, slipping it an occasional mouse, and to include it in the festivities, he fed it an extra mouse. It choked on its treat and died. The season seemed out of joint and I would have flown home after New Year's, but Tim was hatching plans. He knew of a piece of land for sale along the coast of the Sierra de la Giganta. Three men owned it in partnership and two wanted out. It was the only land for sale along an unroaded stretch of the coast and it was vulnerable to the first developer to punch a road through. Amid the setbacks and disappointments of environmental politics, here was one tangible, useful, foolproof thing we could do for the peninsula: we could rescue a piece of land. The cost for my third, I realized, was roughly what it would cost to remodel an Aspen bathroom. To inspect it we would first have to reach a fishing village over a road cut down a cliff only four years ago, negotiating switchbacks that were potentially lethal with slide mud until the weather cleared. Tim would drive me north to the land, then on to a flight home from San Diego. Meanwhile the rain pounded and I slept on Tim's office floor with my head under the desk to hide from street lights. As a houseguest I felt as rank as the Christmas snake.

One mid-January morning when the sky brightened, Tim and I loaded his truck and started north. Late afternoon we pulled onto a track gummy with rainwater and picked up an old man who wanted a ride to a ranch below the drop-off. We ascended to a brink and got out to look. Beyond us swept a coastal cliffline extending paws of vitrified ash into the gulf under fleets of rain-swollen clouds, huge and chilling. As we started the descent, the old man told us that a cousin who had driven the road many times had recently veered off to his death. Squinting through an eye like a blown fuse, he kept repeating, "*Despacito, despacito.*" Slow, slow. . . . On outer turns our wheels spanned the entire roadbed between the wall and the drop-off. The rancher crossed himself when we passed a Virgin in a niche. After he got out at the bottom, we crawled several kilometers along the gulf. The air was opaque when we pulled into an arroyo for the night.

We gathered firewood by flashlight, all of it soaked, and Tim shamelessly drenched it in diesel fuel. Someone had entrusted him with a carton of tourist brochures from Cabo San Lucas to haul to San Diego and we broke into them, balling them up and shoving them under the wood, then dealing them like cards on top. As technicolor pages curled into flame, tongues of emerald and turquoise hissed through the wood. I held a piece of kindling to the glow and read, "Enjoy the luxury of that precious uncrowded feeling. . . ." Clouds gradually thinned and a lone flight to La Paz nattered through Orion. "Kansas City prime beef, poultry and lettuce imported from the U.S.A. Mariachi and margaritas, the finest of both, nightly in our dramatic cocktail lounge. We've turned on the lights in Cabo!" I declaimed from another brochure. An owl hooted faintly up the streambed. "Every accommodation has been carefully designed to ensure discreet and undisturbed privacy." The gulf lapped invisible boulders across the road and the fire crackled with authority. "I think it's burning on its own," I remarked.

Tim unveiled his crocodile smile. "It only took three hotels."

We woke to a glistening desert under a sky of blue milk. We continued to the village and hired an elder with the grand name of Persiliano to skiff us to San Fulano. For nearly an hour we rounded a headland of pocked volcanic strata and spires crowned with osprey nests. We cleared a bend and headed straight toward a vision of Polynesia. The saturated palisade of the Sierra de la Giganta reared toward us in rain-forest greens, beneath which a grove of date palms stood fretted like an engraving. We landed at a kilometer-long crescent beach of bright pebbles and walked toward a gate. Behind it stood a *palapa,* a palm-thatched one-room building, twelve-sided, steep as a cinder-cone and topped by a thatched knob that sprouted a living date palm. The windows were hinged boards that could be propped open with palm staves or battened against the weather. Built by the two who were selling, it was potentially ours. Hidden through the palms was a small house on stilts owned by the third partner, whom we were still to meet, a Mexican engineer who spoke four languages, had lived all over the world, including the Polynesia this rain-soaked ranch evoked, and considered San Fulano the most beautiful spot he had seen. Behind the palms, in a collection of small buildings, lived a young rancher named Lico, along with his wife and children. Serving as caretaker, self-sustaining, Lico ran cows, burros and mules in the desert, fished and grew a few vegetables.

Tim, Persiliano, Lico and I spent the day walking the property. Surrounded by land belonging to an *ejido*, a communal ranch whose members all lived up top, beyond the two-thousand-foot cliff that formed the skyline, San Fulano was a tiny habitation on an isolated coast. Stretching two kilometers along the Gulf, it reached inland nearly to the cliff. We skiffed the steep-walled coast beyond the beach, then hiked up the property's farthest arroyo. Tim turned over a rock where a lizard had disappeared and pulled out a small snake instead. "Drop it!" Lico gasped. "It's deadly!" It was a night snake, with venom as lethal as a coral's but with a mouth too small to puncture the least human protrusion and harmless to us. Tim held it with the nonchalance that is his public manner with reptiles, a test of the onlooker's character. Persiliano turned to Lico and said, "That snake is no threat. Animals are dangerous only the way people are dangerous. Attack them and they strike back, leave them alone and they won't bother you. In any case, they have the same rights we do." Our own sentiments, unexpectedly expressed, and an encouraging sign for a purchase that began, we liked to say later, with a hotel fire.

Having bought two-thirds interest in San Fulano as a conservation measure, we did use it as an occasional getaway but the remoteness that hid it from the world also protected it from us. Tim and Nora had children in the La Paz schools and our visits together were limited to Christmas and spring breaks. Water in the San Fulano well was potable but salty, so we took drums of our preferred water from La Paz—along with food, books, camping equipment and supplies for Lico and his family, all of which had to be loaded into cars and pickups, driven up the highway, down the switchbacks, transferred to some fisherman's overloaded hired boat, skiffed around the headland and dispersed to our several campsites—a sequence we tediously played backward when we left. In exchange we ditched the phone, mail, clocks, commitments and all news but ranch gossip. In the palapa we cooked on a propane stove, pursued reading and Scrabble by propane light. Tim heaped palm litter into the fire ring, using delittering as a pretext for pyromania. At

Christmas we laid presents under sprays of dates affixed, unbotanically, to the base of the palm that speared the roof, then wreathed with snake skeletons, bones, feathers, shells, starfish, dried wasp nest, sea fans and a vine called *farolito,* named for its lanternlike pods. The ranchers brought us goat cheese, homemade tortillas and conversation; we supplied them with foodstuffs unavailable at the ranch or the village. When the La Paz water ran out, as it always did, we drank from the well without incident. Even bolstered by rum I never managed to stay up until midnight on New Year's Eve, though Tim and a guest, without witnesses, once claimed to have done so.

To settle in was to part a curtain in this impenetrable coast. The mountain flank that presented a tight facade to the sea actually crumbled, between shore and cliff face, into canyons, arroyos, valleys and patches of flatness like the palm grove and the ranch. The Polynesian greens were the wonder of a season and returning dryness bared the two-thousand-foot wall behind us, volcanic but stratified so as to resemble what is called, in sedimentary situations, layer-cake geology. Nor was it accidental that some of the layers resembled sandstone, for sandstone was composed of the same grains of quartz, compressed by sedimentation. But it was violence, one volcanic blowout after another, rather than patient deposition that heaped these layers pocked with anomalies from gas bubbles to bits of the former earth crust that had blown sky high and settled into a new ashen conglomerate. Spiked with cactus and desert shrubs, unsettled by subsequent shifting and faulting, the cliff was our dubiously solid backdrop. Near the top, running for the range's entire two hundred kilometers and prominent in our view, was a light-colored layer, a fast blowout that didn't have time to oxidize and darken and which we referred to as *la Zona Rosa,* or Pink Zone, after Mexico City's entertainment district. Nora, a geology major, noticed all the cross-faulting that turned the runoff canyons into mazes and theorized that they were subsidiary faults running parallel to the San Andreas Fault that had created the gulf itself. A retired geologist and Christmas guest decided that San Fulano was a graben, a stretch that sank when formations to either side parted like hands dropping a plank. Once, cross-legged on my air mattress, floating on my own breath in the coast's cupped hand, I felt a wild jostled moment—as if I were suddenly at sea—that vanished like a gasp of wind. I had suppressed the memory until, an hour later in the palapa, others were discussing their own strange moment and we realized we had experienced a small temblor. San Fulano was active, we decided, but only geologically.

We explored the arroyos around us, scrambled as far as we could up their headwalls, tried to mirror their contours in our convoluted brains. The year we read *The Secret Garden* to the children by gaslight, we found a steep arroyo that widened to a gentle valley, then pinched to a ridge that curved acrophobically to a hidden plateau, a rectangular swale like the canopy of a four-poster, a meadow one would roll in except that the greenery was needled and barbed. Lico told us more than we could retain about those plants. If you drank the boiled roots of this one you could alleviate kidney problems. That one, cooked and applied topically, sped the healing of wounds. The flesh of a certain cholla—Lico cut a pad, hacked off the spines and fed me a piece—eased the pain of thirst until water could slake it. But beware the *palo flecha*, a shrub like a shrunken oleander. If you rubbed your eyes after touching it, they would become inflamed. In spring even the blown pollen could cause eye trouble. A cousin who took a nap under a *palo flecha* had wakened blind. . . . I had heard so often of the cousin who woke blind under the *palo flecha*, in the Sierra de San Francisco as well as La Giganta, that I decided the victim was a cousin of the tree, not the teller, the eternal victim in a family drama.

I avoided the *palo flecha* and pitched my tent in a weedy clearing backed by a mesquite tree. Shouts of children playing at the palapa were muffled by the tearing of the waves, the cries of desert birds. I learned to thread my path through the weeds in the dimmest starlight. I didn't lack company, for a palm behind the mesquite served as a roost for several dozen vultures. They used other palms as staging areas but for spending the night only that palm, with its singular merit, would do. An hour before nightfall they began circling the tree, then landing near the top of the fronds' upward curve, setting the leaves rustling and bouncing portentously. Once alight they held their wings aloft for a moment, making sure of their purchase, then folded them in a sighlike motion and drew their meat-raw heads into their neck feathers like old folks settling into mufflers. Sometimes a newcomer would land on an occupied frond. With no apparent rancor the first bird would circle the tree once or twice and settle elsewhere. At last in place, a bouquet of black tulips facing the sea, they melted into the night, to be discovered at dawn in the same position. Almost reluctantly they unfolded their wings, taking the light from across the gulf, then turned to absorb heat through their feathers' dark topsides. They tucked their heads into their wings to preen, or perhaps to eat lice and maggots from yesterday's meal. As the dates at the palms' center caught the sun's first gold, the green and black medallion undid itself as one by one the vultures floated off and gyred skyward until they became gnats swarming the heavens.

It would seem simple enough to buy a small piece of land and let it remain what it was. But the family that once owned it was still living there as caretakers for the new owners, who were ourselves. Fifty years back, Lico's father and half-uncle had founded the ranch, and Lico's parents still lived there off and on. Lico's family and a younger brother, also with family, continued to inhabit the ranch, rotating and sometimes overlapping. It disconcerted me that we had so casually become the owners, but some years back the ranchers had chosen to sell to the engineer and the two partners we bought out. Along with their own cows, burros and two mules, they ran ten cows belonging to the widow of the man who had plunged off the road to the village. Tim and I wanted to see the animals reduced, beginning with the widow's cows, but it was difficult to pull off on a coastful of cousins. Our third partner, the quadrilingual engineer, who was there less than we were, thought we could dispense with caretakers altogether. We were afraid the buildings would be looted, the beach trashed, that charcoal makers would attack our ironwoods and that the *ejido* up top would herd their cattle down the switchbacks to San Fulano and further consume our desert.

But keeping ranchers, technically self sustaining, had its problems. We brought motor oil and unobtainable food but health crises in isolation were sometimes insurmountable. Lico's wife developed severe kidney problems and he worried about getting her to a hospital in an emergency. An alternative route to San Fulano did exist—a ninety-kilometer track led from the highway, through the *ejido,* to the brink of a trail that switchbacked down the cliff to the ranch. If Lico had a vehicle on top, he could at least get his wife up the switchbacks by mule and drive her out. When he threatened to leave San Fulano at a time when no other family members could replace him, Tim concocted a solution. Someone had stored a van with Baja Expeditions a year back, hadn't been seen since and the vehicle was in the way. The father of one of Tim's guides, meanwhile, was out of a job. We would drive the old man in the old van to the brink, walk down, let the old man decide whether he was interested in caretaking the ranch if Lico bailed out, and a Baja Expeditions employee would retrieve us from the fishing village the next day.

The morning we were to leave, Tim handed me the keys to the abandoned vehicle and asked me to gas it up. A battered greenish-black Dodge delivery wagon with tiny wheels, beady headlights and storage space as windowless as a coffin, it looked possessed by an evil spirit. Between the driver and passenger seats stood a strange carpeted mound. When it wouldn't start, I summoned one of Tim's employees. He lifted the carpeted lid, revealing the carburetor, opened it, poured in gas and cranked the engine. I suddenly remembered an image from childhood, the birth of the Mexican volcano Paricutín, which began as a two-foot cindercone in someone's cornfield, for just so did sparks and rumblings spray from the carpeted mound while I backed halfway across the warehouse. The employee calmly replaced the carburetor lid and mentioned to Tim that there were no license plates. Tim fetched some old plates from in back, mumbling, "All right, I'll screw in some registration." I retreated to my own car and picked up the old man across town. To make conversation, I asked his line of work. "I was working in the flour mill," he said, "but two months ago I had a heart attack and now they won't hire me back." When I returned to Baja Expeditions I asked Tim if he knew the man's medical condition. He didn't, agreed that we couldn't possibly leave him as guardian, but we had promised him the trip and it seemed unfair to cancel it now. As a solution to our problems, this was a disaster not to be missed.

We camped overnight by the highway, then started next dawn on the tortuous track to the cliff, asking at ranches about the many branching roads. Some ranches were friendly, offered us coffee and talked of relatives we knew. Others were distinctly cool. The old man rode in the passenger seat and I sat in a plastic chair in the windowless back, bouncing to the ceiling and unable to see a road I had long wondered about. We arrived at the *ejido*'s little town, a place I was also eager to know because it was the headquarters of the commonly held land around San Fulano, the unseen locus of power. There was a scattering of buildings, a grade school and a Conasupo—one of the government stores that provides staples where commerce is unprofitable. The two men and a woman running the store regarded us silently, bristling. The Conasupo offered three items: coffee beans, flour and a wall of apricot nectar. We bought coffee and flour for Lico and three apricot nectars to go. "Where are you headed?" the woman asked, breaking the silence. Normally we would have answered gregariously but their manner chilled us. "That way," muttered Tim, gesturing vaguely toward the drop-off.

"Are you guiding them?" one of the men asked our passenger.

"No," he replied, equally aloof. "I've never been here before."

The final ten kilometers from the town to the brink were the least traveled and the tiny wheels gave us so little clearance that we frequently wielded the shovel. By late afternoon we had maneuvered the van to the road's end, pulling it to the brink so that Lico would actually be able to spot it on the high horizon. We descended the switchbacks, keeping an anxious eye on our heart patient, and arrived at the palapa just as Lico returned from the fishing village by skiff. He was astonished that Tim and I had materialized from nowhere, a stranger in tow, but was more preoccupied by something he had seen from the water. There was a fire on top of the cliff!

"That was no fire," said Tim, grinning. "That was the sunset bouncing off the windshield of your new van."

Soon after we returned to La Paz, we received a call from Lico. He had hiked eagerly to his new vehicle, to find it stripped of its battery, tools, spare tire, jack, plastic chair and stereo. He lodged a complaint with the *ejido* member delegated to represent the law, then got a ride to the highway and the nearest phone. It wasn't until we returned to San Fulano a few weeks later, during spring break, that we heard the rest. We had, it seems, arrived at the little town in the most sinister looking vehicle the citizens had ever seen. Out of it came two unknown gringos and an unknown Mexican. When the silent trio at the Conasupo, full of suspicion, asked our plans, we hadn't answered. We took their questions for intrusion; they took our silence for evasion. We proceeded to the cliff and abandoned the van. The only types who would ditch a working vehicle, ugly or not, were drug runners, and obviously we had continued down the cliff on foot and made our connection by boat. So that the van couldn't be used for narcotraffic again, three *ejido* members proceeded to decommission it. Once its mobile parts were dispersed, it turned out to be a gift to cousin Lico!

Back, one by one, came the battery, the tools, the spare, the jack, the chair, even the torn-out stereo, though no one knew how to reconnect its ganglia. In the aftermath Lico showed me the legal report written at the *ejido,* two sentences scrawled on a leaf from a small notebook. "Where's the official seal?" I asked, and we laughed over the whole episode. A year later I asked Lico whether he ever got the van working. No, he said, it kept breaking down and he wound up selling it piecemeal.

"And the body itself," I asked, "was there any use for it?"

"There was for the top. They were able to cut a triangle just the right size to cover the ironwood in a charcoal pit."

On a roadless coast, without electricity or even shortwave radio, San Fulano would seem a safe refuge from civilization, yet at times the snarl of combustion was inescapable. Shrimp boats, singly or in pairs, would enter the bay and dredge it, motors revving around the clock, up to three days at a time. With hulls like tide-beaten shoes, cables that swooped from the spars to hold net-dragging poles that protruded at rakish angles, clouded by seagulls like flies around a carcass, the boats were as gamy as a drunk's line drawing. Back and forth they churned, dragging their nets in slow transects, scouring the bottom while our nerves throbbed with them. Dispatched from Guaymas, across the gulf, they were largely staffed by men from the local village, and elsewhere on the coast, who led the boats to the richest fishing. The men didn't see themselves as traitors and agents of destruction, either unaware they were decimating sealife that was unlikely to return to healthy populations during their lifetime, or resigned that the loss of lower species was a small price to pay for supporting their families on better wages than they could earn on land. Some locals understood the devastation well enough and some, like Lico, particularly resented being kept awake by the ruination of their own fishing grounds. Networks of family and neighborly loyalty, however, silenced the dissenters. The fishermen kept the species they could sell, ate what they liked and threw the rest back to the sea. When they left the bay, it was like relief from a migraine.

Once, shortly after a shrimp boat left us in peace, the largest *caguama* shell we had ever seen washed onto the beach in front of the palapa. The meat had been scooped out, doubtless consumed on the boat, and the head, entrails and carapace had been heaved overboard in one piece. That day the vultures didn't need to fan out along the coast. Drifting down from their palm tree, they turned the great shell into a pulsing mass of dark feathers. Every so often Lico's dog raced toward the tortoise in a flurry of vultures that hopped to the side. The dog circled the bulk, sniffed it bureaucratically, lifted its leg on it while staring nobly into the sky, then trotted briskly off while the vultures, relaxed from their break, waddled back and resumed their feasting. Tim had planned to keep the shell for his collection of beach detritus that was beginning to ring the palapa, but at dawn the next morning Lico's father burned it. We asked him why and he replied that it was making the cows go thirsty. Nora and I, exchanging a look, asked him to explain. The vultures gorged themselves at the *caguama,* he said, then went to drink at the waterhole and shat such a putrescence that the cows wouldn't go near enough to drink. The only way to save the cows was to burn the tortoise.

Tim and I had become co-owners of San Fulano as a small conservation measure, the defense of one piece of land. Never content with small victories, once we were established, Tim decided that as landowners we should petition the government to protect the mountain range in which our property sat. Over the years he had built up contacts with the country's leaders. Because ecologists and officials often needed to get to Baja California's natural features, which were the destinations of his trips, as outfitter he had gotten to know many of Mexico's influential politicians, makers of documentaries and newscasters, along with such well-known conservationists as Jean-Michel Cousteau. He had also become a naturalized Mexican citizen— a sentimental move, he said, because he felt more Mexican than American, but a move that demonstrated commitment when he wanted to influence policy. He particularly cultivated a rising political star named Luis Donaldo Colosio, meeting with him several times and speaking with him by phone. The interior department, he thought, would take seriously a proposal from us declaring the unroaded stretch of the Sierra de la Giganta a biosphere reserve. To give the proposal cachet, the biosphere could be dedicated specifically to the desert mountain sheep, a herd of which inhabited La Giganta farther south. The animal could serve as what publicity-minded environmentalists were calling "charismatic megafauna," and conserving the species at the top would help protect the rest of the ecosystem. What the interior department needed was a proposal that defined the area's boundaries, described its contents, assured that inhabitants could continue current activities that were doing no harm, and prohibited new roads, mining and luxury tourism. My own sense was that even if by some fluke we got the biosphere declared, we would only be adding a new shaded area to certain maps. Tim replied, correctly, that we had to start somewhere, and I duly knocked out versions in English and Spanish.

Tim took the proposal to interior officials in La Paz and reported that they were giving it consideration. Shortly afterward, on a quick visit to San Fulano to deliver motor oil to Lico, he saw a bighorn sheep bound across the property, the best of omens. Colosio, as expected, received the nomination that was tantamount to winning the presidency. If not an environmentalist per se, he was far more open to environmental concerns than his predecessors; with Bill Clinton and Al Gore in Washington and Colosio in Mexico City, the two countries might steer our battered continent toward less suicidal policies. Best of all, Colosio had committed verbally to Tim that he would declare the Sierra de la Giganta a biosphere reserve. Over Christmas in San Fulano in 1993, Tim talked eagerly of my flying with him to the mainland to meet with Colosio. Why a candidate in midcampaign would want to meet with a nonvoter without influence was beyond me, but I was certainly willing to speak my piece to the crown prince of Mexico. During the campaign three months later, Colosio came to La Paz, but only for a few hours and Tim was not on his schedule. He gave a speech by the decorative windmills of the civic theater, then flew to Tijuana, where he was shot; eerily, I learned of the assassination mere blocks from where, twenty-six years earlier, an American stranger had told me of the murder of Bobby Kennedy—a politician on whom I also once pinned the future. Colosio's replacement, the future president, was a man named Ernesto Zedillo, of whom we knew nothing. When I mentioned, some time later, how our hopes for Washington, Mexico City and La Giganta had unraveled, as environmental hopes predictably did, Tim seemed unperturbed. A valid proposal was on file at the interior department. Eventually it would fall under friendly eyes.

Tim remained committed to the big picture, looking for openings, still cultivating the powerful, promoting policy. I followed the politics of Baja California Sur with increasing despair. I had even lost my spot for contemplation, for the eagle monument had been surrounded by a barracks so bristling with soldiers and military vehicles that now I only hoped I wouldn't be detained for inspection as I sped past. Military roadblocks, at which uniformed teenagers with semiautomatics asked travelers if they were carrying arms or drugs, popped up at unexpected times and places the length of the highway. The governor who had served me endangered species on Earth Day was now saying that the state could tolerate no more natural reserves. He went so far as to claim that Mexicans who opposed the salt project in Laguna San Ignacio were traitors to their country, though he in fact favored the industrialization of the last pristine Mexican refuge for the grey whale by a company that was half-Japanese. Not to be outdone, the bishop of La Paz stated that God had created salt for man to exploit, ignoring that the same God seemed to have created an unexploited lagoon for His creatures. To maintain my roots in a land where hypocrisy was the crown species, I focused on life that persevered, despite all, close to hand. At San Fulano I particularly took heart in the fecundity of the hooded oriole. On my first visit to the peninsula, nearly three decades back, I had watched them pull fan palms into threads and weave bulbous globes that were continuous with the leaves. At San Fulano I watched them hook fibers from other plants over fronds of date palms and sling baskets from our own green plumes. Through binoculars I followed their fussy clatter through the groves as they brought brush to their homesites and food to their young. I watched them attain the powdery apricot of their mature plumage from their tentative yellow-green. It was the same deep shade that fountained in sprays of orange branches bearing orange dates like a golden source from the core of the palm itself. San Fulano, conjured from a distance, was a starburst of orange on green. Beyond false-front politicians, neglected decrees and unfunded biospheres there were certain constants in Baja California that gave me—not exactly hope, but reassurance: the clamoring bells of La Paz, the sigh of the whale, Héctor's friendship, the piano subculture, the flash of the hooded oriole, black and white markings on orange that was headed, always, toward something green.

The fate of so much that I had followed closely—the Peninsular prong-horn, the turning of ironwood to coal, the proposed salt project, the unde-veloped coast of La Giganta—frayed into a doubtful future. In the room in Aspen where I attempted to order the peninsula into words, I faced a collage Katie Lee had made for me after one of our first explorations in the late sixties. A weathered beach plank, it had been glued with an arrangement of other finds from the beach, and as I stared at it over the years, it resolved into bits of punctuation. The curving dolphin ribs were commas. Starfish were asterisks. A pair of sand dollars was a full colon. A row of shark vertebrae was an ellipsis. And snaking through all was a line of wave-beaten pieces of glass shining emerald and opal and amethyst and aquamarine and pearl and sap-phire. Minutes before sundown every year for two days in October, days when I was planning my annual return south, the setting sun through a west window caught the beach glass sideways, lighting it from within and turning it to a jeweled question mark. Just as the peninsula ended, physically, in an arch, so did a pliant question mark seem the appropriate punctuation at land's end in a refracting peninsula of words. It was not just a matter of what would happen to Baja California in the reader's lifetime or the next millen-nium. Beyond such immediate concerns, what would Baja California be like in, say, sixty million years, when the human race might have seeded itself through space but would more likely be gone and when, in the fullness of tectonic time, Baja California might become what it had always seemed—an island?

ACKNOWLEDGMENTS

Earlier versions or portions of these chapters have appeared in the following
   publications:
"Main Transpeninsular Highway" and "Vintage Brandy" in *Mountain Gazette*
"The Search for Mata Hari" in *Dark Horse*
"Black Pearl," "Guinea Pigs for Turkeys," and "Salt on Their Tales" in *American Way*
"Under the Cypress" in *Orion*
"Curse of the Adorers" and "Rancho San Fulano" in *Southwest Review*

ABOUT THE AUTHOR

ruce Berger is the author of *The Telling Distance,* which won the 1990 Western States Book Award for Creative Nonfiction, and *There Was a River,* both published by the University of Arizona Press, as well as the poetry collection *Facing the Music.* His articles and essays have appeared in *The New York Times, The Yale Review, Orion, Sierra,* and elsewhere.

He has played piano professionally in the United States and, for three years, in Spain. He first reached Baja California in 1968, before pavement made it accessible to most Americans, and has been haunting its habitats ever since.